Absolu

BED &
BREAKFAST

*Almost

TEXAS

EDITED BY CARL HANSON

SASQUATCH BOOKS
SEATTLE

Printed in the United States of America.
Distributed in Canada by Raincoast Books Ltd.
03 02 01 00 99   5 4 3 2 1

Cover design: Jane Jeszeck
Cover illustration: CORBIS/Robert Holmes
Interior design and composition: Alan Bernhard
Editor: Carl Hanson
Copy editor: Christine Clifton-Thornton

ISSN 1522-5488
ISBN 1-57061-194-7

Sasquatch Books
615 Second Avenue
Seattle, Washington 98104
(206) 467-4300
books@SasquatchBooks.com
http://www.SasquatchBooks.com

CONTENTS

ABSOLUTELY EVERY BED & BREAKFAST SERIES

Welcome to *Absolutely Every° Bed & Breakfast: Texas (°Almost)*, a comprehensive guide to virtually every bed and breakfast establishment in Texas. We've done the work for you: Everything you need to know in choosing a bed and breakfast is included on these pages, from architectural style to atmosphere, from price range to breakfast variety. Listings are in alphabetical order by town, so locating the perfect stay at your destination is a snap, and the simple format makes comparing accommodations as easy as turning the page. So whether you're looking for an elegant Victorian inn, a stunning ranch house in the heart of cattle country, or a cozy seaside cottage, *Absolutely Every° Bed & Breakfast: Texas (°Almost)* will help you find it.

In addition to Texas, the *Absolutely Every* series covers Arizona, Colorado, New Mexico, Northern California, Southern California, Oregon, and Washington; look for the latest edition of each in your local bookstore. The guides list small- and medium-sized inns, hotels, and host homes that include breakfast in the price of the room. The lists of B&B establishments are compiled from a variety of sources, including directories, chambers of commerce, tourism bureaus, and the World Wide Web. After gathering a complete list, the editors send each innkeeper a survey, asking for basic lodging information and for those special details that set them apart. The completed surveys are then examined and fact-checked for accuracy before inclusion in the book. The °*Almost* in the series title reflects the fact that a small number of innkeepers may choose not to be listed, may neglect to respond to the survey and follow-up phone calls, or are not listed because of negative reports received by the editors.

The editors rely on the honesty of the innkeepers in completing the surveys and on feedback from readers to keep the *Absolutely Every Bed & Breakfast* series accurate and up-to-date. (*Note:* While innkeepers are responsible for providing survey information, none are financially connected to the series, nor do they pay any fees to be included in the book.) Please write to us about your experience at any of the bed and breakfasts listed in the series; we'd love to hear from you.

Enjoy your bed and breakfast experience!

—The editors, *Absolutely Every Bed & Breakfast*

HOW TO USE THIS BOOK

Absolutely Every Bed & Breakfast: Texas is organized alphabetically by town and by establishment name, and includes a comprehensive index. The concise, at-a-glance format of the complete bed and breakfast listings covers fifteen categories of information to help you select just the right bed and breakfast accommodation for your needs. This edition offers you a choice of establishments in cities, towns, and outlying areas.

THE BED & BREAKFAST LISTINGS

Note that although specifics of each establishment have been confirmed by the editors, details such as amenities, decor, and breakfast menus have been provided by the innkeepers. Listings in this guide are subject to change; call to confirm all aspects of your stay, including price, availability, and restrictions, before you go. Some bed and breakfast listings offer only selected information due to lack of response or by request of the innkeeper; complete listings include the following information.

Establishment name
Address: Note that street addresses often vary from actual mailing addresses; confirm the mailing address before sending a reservation payment.
Telephone numbers: Includes any toll-free or fax numbers.
Innkeeper's languages: Languages spoken other than English.
Location: Directions from the nearest town, highway, or landmark.
Open: Notice of any seasonal or other closures.
Description: Overview of architecture, furnishings, landscaping, etc.
Rooms: Number of rooms with private bathrooms vs. shared baths; availability of suites and/or additional guesthouses; and the innkeeper's favorite room.
Rates: Range of room prices, which vary based on private or shared bathroom, season, and individual room amenities. Also noted here are any minimum stay requirements and cancellation policies (usually two weeks' notice is required for a full refund).

Breakfast: Description of breakfast served (full, continental, continental plus, or stocked kitchen).

Credit cards: Indicates which, if any, credit cards are accepted. Note that credit cards may be listed for reservation confirmation purposes only; be prepared to pay by check or cash.

Amenities: Details any special amenities that are included.

Restrictions: Lists any restrictions regarding smoking, children, and pets. Also listed here are any resident pets or livestock.

Awards: Any significant hospitality or historic preservation awards received.

Reviewed: Publications in which the B&B has been reviewed.

Rated: Indicates whether the B&B has been rated by institutions such as the American Automobile Association (AAA), American Bed & Breakfast Association (ABBA), or the Mobil Travel Association.

Member: Indicates membership in any professional hospitality associations or organizations.

Kudos/Comments: Comments from guests who have stayed in the establishment.

ABILENE

About 150 miles west of Fort Worth on I-20, Abilene is a vintage west Texas cattle and farming town and home to three universities and the Abilene Zoological Gardens. Get a glimpse of frontier life at Buffalo Gap Historic Village and check out the old warbirds at Linear Air Park. In May, the Western Heritage Classic kicks up its heels. September brings the West Texas Fair.

BJ'S BED & BREAKFAST

508 Mulberry Street, Abalone, TX 79601   915-675-5855
BJ, Innkeeper   800-673-5855
EMAIL bfender@earthlink.net   FAX 915-677-4694

LOCATION	From Business Highway 20 (South 1st Street) near downtown, turn north onto Grape. Go 5 blocks to North 5th Street and turn right. Go one block, turn left onto Mulberry.
OPEN	All year
DESCRIPTION	A 1902 two-story host home, remodeled in 1920 to prairie style, with a stucco exterior and a wraparound porch, situated in the historic district of Abilene. The interior has high ceilings, oak floors, and an extensive collection of blue and white china and other artifacts collected from around the world.
NO. OF ROOMS	Two rooms with private bathrooms and two rooms share one bathroom.
RATES	Year-round rate for a single or double with a private bathroom is $75, and a single or double with a shared bathroom is $65. There is no minimum stay and cancellation requires 48 hours' notice.
CREDIT CARDS	American Express, Discover, MasterCard, Visa
BREAKFAST	Continental breakfast is served and includes fruit bowl, juices, cereals, toast, breakfast rolls.
AMENITIES	Ceiling fans, refrigerator, air conditioning, and swing on front porch.
RESTRICTIONS	No smoking, no pets, children over 12 are welcome.
REVIEWED	*Recommended Country Inns—The Southwest; The Complete Guide to Bed & Breakfasts, Inns & Guesthouses in the United States, Canada and Worldwide*
MEMBER	Historic Hotel Association of Texas, Texas Hotel & Motel Association, Abilene Hotel and Motel Association
KUDOS/COMMENTS	"Everything was very clean and breakfast was delicious." "Clean, orderly, good breakfasts."

Blue Willow Bed & Breakfast

435 College Drive, Abilene, TX 79601   915-677-8420

Alba

About 40 miles northwest of Tyler on Highway 182, Alba's main attraction is Lake Fork. Local and nearby happenings include Eagle Fest, the Sweet Potato Festival, and Canton's First Monday Trades Days, the largest flea market in the world.

Lake Fork Lodge—Bass & Breakfast

Intersection of Highways 515 and 17, Alba, TX 75410   903-473-7236
Kyle Jones, Innkeeper   FAX 903-473-7236
EMAIL *lakefork@koyote.com*   WEBSITE *www.lakeforklodge.com*

LOCATION	Twenty-nine miles northeast of Canton. From Canton, take Highway 19 north 20 miles to Emory, and head south on Highway 69 for 1.5 miles. Turn left (east) onto Highway 515. The lodge is 7 miles on the left.
OPEN	All year
DESCRIPTION	A 1986 brick ranch-style lodge situated on 5 waterfront acres overlooking Lake Fork.
NO. OF ROOMS	Seven rooms with private bathrooms. Try the Caney Creek Room.
RATES	March through May, rates are $85-160 for a single or double. June through February, rates are $75-135 for a single or double. Ask about a cancellation policy.
CREDIT CARDS	American Express, MasterCard, Visa
BREAKFAST	Full, hearty breakfast is served buffet style in the dining room and features unique recipes including wild game, locally grown fresh fruit, and homemade pastries. Catering is also available.
AMENITIES	Two hot tubs, billiard room, barbecue grills overlooking the lake, meeting facilities, remote controlled gates for privacy, boat launch, fishing pier, boat stalls, two fireplaces. air conditioning, dog kennels, fishing guide coordination.
RESTRICTIONS	No smoking, children over 10 are welcome. Woody is the resident Lab. "He usually remains in one of the kennels."
REVIEWED	*Sports Afield* magazine, featured on ESPN's Jimmy Houston's Outdoors and Suzuki's Great Outdoors, featured on Fox Sports Southwest's Outdoor Trails

ALBANY

Nearby Fort Griffin State Park is home to Texas' official herd of longhorns.
Witness reenactments of historical battles and take in the Fort Griffin Fandangle,
an historical musical drama performed every Thursday, Friday, and Saturday
during the last two weekends of June. Albany is 30 miles northeast of Abilene at
the junctions of Highways 180, 6, and 283.

THE FOREMAN'S COTTAGE
ON THE MUSSELMAN RANCH

Ibex Road, Albany, TX 76430   915-762-3576
John & Carolyn Musselman, Innkeepers   FAX 915-762-3576

LOCATION	At the stoplight at Courthouse Square, head south on Highway 6 for 1 mile to FM 601 (Ibex Road); turn left and drive 7 miles to the entrance, on the right.
OPEN	All year
DESCRIPTION	A 1952 simple wood cottage furnished with antiques and western decor. The home was originally the foreman's cottage on a working horse and cattle ranch.
NO. OF ROOMS	One room with a private bathroom and two rooms share one bathroom. Try the Pioneer's Room.
RATES	Year-round rates are $69 for a single or double with a private bathroom and $49-55 for a single or double with a shared bathroom. The entire cottage rents for $180 for six ($20 more for eight guests). There is no minimum stay and cancellation requires three days' notice.
CREDIT CARDS	No
BREAKFAST	Continental breakfast is stocked in the full kitchen and includes sweet rolls, orange juice, cereals, milk, preserves, various coffees, teas, sometimes sausage rolls or little sausages, cheese, crackers, and fresh fruits.
AMENITIES	Cheese tray served upon arrival, barbecue, 5,000 acres to explore, tanks to fish, creeks to wade, air conditioning and heat.
RESTRICTIONS	No pets in the cottage. There are cattle on the property.

THE OLE NAIL HOUSE INN

329 South 3rd, Albany, TX 76430
Joie Parsons, Resident Owner

915-762-2928
800-245-5163

VIRGINIA'S BED & BREAKFAST

349 Breckenridge Road, Albany, TX 76430
Virginia Baker, Resident Owner

915-762-2013

ALLEN

BLEE COTTAGE BED & BREAKFAST

103 West Belmont Drive, Allen, TX 75013
WEBSITE *www.bbonline.com/tx/blee*

972-390-1884

ALPINE

North of Big Bend National Park and southeast of El Paso, Alpine has much to offer: the Cowboy Poetry Gathering in March, the Gem and Mineral Show in April, the Cinco de Mayo Celebration and Cabrito Cook-off in May, the July Fourth Parade and Outdoor Summer Theatre in July and August.

HOLLAND HOTEL

209 West Holland Avenue, Alpine, TX 79830

915-837-3844
800-535-8040

THE WHITE HOUSE INN

2003 Fort Davis Highway, Alpine, TX 79830   915-837-1401
Anita & Dick Sheffield, Resident Owners   FAX 915-837-2197
EMAIL *dsheff@unidial.com*

LOCATION	About 1 mile north from Highway 90 on Highway 118 (Ft. Davis Highway).
OPEN	All year
DESCRIPTION	A 1930 two-story inn.
NO. OF ROOMS	Three rooms with private bathrooms.
RATES	Year-round rates for a single or double are $80-105. There is no minimum stay and cancellation requires five days' notice.
CREDIT CARDS	MasterCard, Visa
BREAKFAST	Full gourmet breakfast varies daily and is served in the dining room.
AMENITIES	Robes, coffee delivered to rooms, TV in rooms, individual thermostats in each room.
RESTRICTIONS	No smoking, no pets, children over 12 are welcome.

AMARILLO

Amarillo is in the center of the Texas Panhandle, due north of Lubbock, at the intersection of I-40 and I-27. Visit Palo Duro Canyon; sit beneath the cliffs and take in the outdoor summer musical "Texas." The American Quarter Horse Museum is another area must-see. Lake Meridith and the Alibates Flint Quarries National Monument are about 30 minutes north.

ADABERRY INN

6818 Plum Creek Drive, Amarillo, TX 79124   806-352-0022

Auntie's House B&B

1712 South Polk Street, Amarillo, TX 79102   806-371-8054
Corliss & Skip Burroughs, Resident Owners   888-661-8054
WEBSITE www.auntieshouse.com

LOCATION	A quarter mile from the intersection of I-40 and I-27 in Amarillo's downtown historic district. Take the Washington exit off I-40, remain on the eastbound access road, and turn left (north) on Tyler. Turn right (east) on 17th and right (south) on Polk. The B&B is the fourth house on the right.
OPEN	All year
DESCRIPTION	A 1912 two-story Craftsman (prairie) host home furnished in "electric vintage Auntie style" and listed on the National Historic Register.
NO. OF ROOMS	Four rooms with private bathrooms.
RATES	Year-round rate for a single or double is $85 and a suite is $125. The private cottage is $225 during the weekends and $175 during midweek. There is no minimum stay and cancellation requires 72 hours' notice.
CREDIT CARDS	American Express, Discover, MasterCard, Visa
BREAKFAST	Full breakfast is served in the dining room and includes breads, meat, eggs, fruit, juice, and coffee.
AMENITIES	Hot tub, fresh flowers, central heat and air conditioning, sitting porch, lemonade and hot chocolate available.
RESTRICTIONS	No smoking, no pets, children over 12 are welcome. Mr. Mo, also known as Kitty Boy, is the resident cat.
MEMBER	Texas Hotel & Motel Association

Galbraith House Bed & Breakfast Inn

1710 South Polk Street, Amarillo, TX 79102   806-374-0237
Dr. Panpit Klug, Innkeeper
WEBSITE www.galbraith-house.com

LOCATION	At the center of town, exit Interstate 40 at Washington Street. Take Washington Street north to 17th and turn right (east). Take 17th east to South Polk and turn right (south). You are there.
OPEN	All year

DESCRIPTION	A 1912 two-story Craftsman/prairie-style inn with lavish hardwoods. It is listed on both the National and State Historic Registers.
NO. OF ROOMS	Four rooms with private bathrooms.
RATES	Year-round rates are $85-100 for a single or double. There is no minimum stay, and cancellation requires 24 hours' notice.
CREDIT CARDS	American Express, Discover, MasterCard, Visa
BREAKFAST	Full breakfast is served in the dining room.
AMENITIES	Air conditioning, Jacuzzi, gazebo, and frog pond.
RESTRICTIONS	Smoking on porches only, no pets, children over 12 are welcome.
KUDOS/COMMENTS	"Lovely facility; clean, well done. No on-site manager but breakfast service was pleasant and hospitable." "An unhosted B&B full of antiques. Food prepared according to guests' wishes. Conveniently located in quiet neighborhood near shopping."

MARTHA'S MIDTOWN B&B

2005 South Jackson Street, Amarillo, TX 79109   806-374-2689

PARKVIEW HOUSE BED & BREAKFAST

1311 South Jefferson Street, Amarillo, TX 79101   806-373-9464
Carol & Nabil Dia, Innkeepers   FAX 806-373-3166
Arabic spoken
EMAIL Parkviewbb@aol.com
WEBSITE members.aol.com/Parkviewbb

LOCATION	At the edge of Amarillo's historic district. From I-40, take the Washington Street exit, travel just 6 blocks, turn right (east) on West 14th Street, and go 1 block; the inn is on the corner of West 14th and South Jefferson Streets. From I-27 (also known as the Canyon E-way), take the Washington Street exit and go approximately 1 mile to West 14th Street, turn right (east) and travel 1 block.
OPEN	All year
DESCRIPTION	A 1908 two-story prairie-style Victorian inn with Old World ambiance, abundant antiques and collectibles, and homey Victorian decor, situated in a parklike environment with tranquil gardens and a shaded seating area with statuary and birdbaths.

NO. OF ROOMS	Four rooms with private bathrooms and three rooms share three bathrooms.
RATES	Year-round rates are $75-135 for a single or double with a private bathroom, $65-75 for a single or double with a shared bathroom, and $85 for a suite. There is no minimum stay and cancellation requires seven days' notice from May 15th through August, three days during the remainder of the year.
CREDIT CARDS	American Express, MasterCard, Visa
BREAKFAST	Full breakfast is served in the kitchen and may include any of the following: seasonal fresh fruit, French toast, muffins with cinnamon butter, quiche, fresh herb and vegetable omelets, pancakes, coffeecakes, fruit breads, homemade granola, breakfast casseroles, various juices and teas, and a special blend of American-Turkish coffee.
AMENITIES	Refreshments upon arrival, air conditioning, clock radios, glass of wine, bedside chocolates, hot tub under the stars, robes, fresh fruits and cold drinks, fabric-draped queen-size beds, private reading areas.
RESTRICTIONS	No smoking, children over seven are welcome by prior arrangement only.
REVIEWED	*The Official Guide to American Historic Inns, Recommended Country Inns—The Southwest, Frommer's, Bed & Breakfast USA*
MEMBER	Professional Association of Innkeepers International, Historic Accommodations of Texas

ARGYLE

ROADRUNNER FARM BED & BREAKFAST

10501 Fincher Road, Argyle, TX 76226   817-455-2942

ARLINGTON

SANFORD HOUSE

506 North Center Street, Arlington, TX 76011   817-861-2129
WEBSITE *www.thesanfordhouse.com/*

ATHENS

An Athens must-see is the Texas Freshwater Fisheries Center, a two-million-gallon aquarium with replicated habitats that hosts all manner of Texas' freshwater fish. May gets cookin' with the Uncle Fletch Hamburger Cook-off and American Music Festival/Chili Cook-off. Celebrate the Black-eyed-pea Fall Harvest the second weekend in October. Nearby events and happenings include First Monday Trades Days in Canton (the world's largest flea market), the Palestine/Rusk open-air train, and Tyler's Rose Center and annual rose festival.

AVONLEA BED & BREAKFAST

410 East Corsicana Street, Athens, TX 75751   903-675-5770

DUNSAVAGE FARMS B&B

FM 804, Athens, TX 75751   903-675-2281
Lyn Dunsavage, Resident Owner

OAK MEADOW BED & BREAKFAST

2781 FM 2495, Athens, TX 75751   903-675-3407
Gwen & Joe Mills, Innkeepers   877-675-3407
EMAIL jlmills@flash.net   FAX 903-675-6316
WEBSITE www.bbonline.con/tx/oakmeadow

LOCATION	From the square, take Highway 31 east for 2 miles to the Wal-Mart. At the light, turn right onto FM 2495 and drive 1.3 miles.
OPEN	All year
DESCRIPTION	A 1983 two-story traditional country inn with exquisite paneling and hardwood accents.
NO. OF ROOMS	Three rooms with private bathrooms. The Mills recommend the Nest over the carriage house.
RATES	Year-round rates are $85 for a double and $95 for a suite. There is no minimum stay and cancellation requires 10 days' notice for a full refund.
CREDIT CARDS	No

Oak Meadow Bed & Breakfast, Athens

BREAKFAST	Full country breakfast is served and includes eggs, bacon, sausage, sausage gravy, fruit, grits or hashbrowns, juice, and coffee.
AMENITIES	Evening dessert and drinks served upon arrival or after dinner; rooms have queen-size beds, ceiling fans, air conditioning controls; reading loft; the Nest above the carriage house features a sitting room with a TV and bar.
RESTRICTIONS	No smoking, no pets, no children.
MEMBER	East Texas Bed & Breakfast Association

PINE CONE COUNTRY INN BED & BREAKFAST

Route 4, Box 4321, Athens, TX 75751   903-479-3807
Pat & Jim Hayes, Innkeepers   800-449-7463
EMAIL *patjim@flash.net*   FAX 903-479-3352
WEBSITE *www.bbchannel.com*

LOCATION	Twelve miles north of Athens on Highway 19, on the west side of the highway. Ninety miles east of Dallas.
OPEN	All year
DESCRIPTION	A 1960s-era country inn with country decor and antique furnishings, located on a wooded hillside and 60 acres.
NO. OF ROOMS	Four rooms with private bathrooms.
RATES	Year-round rates are $85-95 for a single or double. There is no minimum stay, and cancellation requires seven days' notice.
CREDIT CARDS	American Express, Discover, MasterCard, Visa

Pine Cone Country Inn Bed & Breakfast, Athens

BREAKFAST	Full breakfast is served in the dining room and includes juices, fruit, biscuits, muffins, meat, an egg dish, jams, and jellies.
AMENITIES	Sun room with fireplace, TV/VCR and video library, covered patio and deck, bird-watching, air conditioning, meeting room, robes in some rooms, soft drinks, dessert, hors d'oeuvres, wine, boardgames.
RESTRICTIONS	No smoking, no pets, children over 10 are welcome. Chrissy is the resident German shepherd, Up and Down are the mutts, and Drifter is the calico cat.
MEMBER	Professional Association of Innkeepers International
KUDOS/COMMENTS	"Beautiful country home and grounds. True country with a touch of class. Great food and hospitality."

AUBREY

THE GUEST HOUSE

Route 1, Box 203, Aubrey, TX 76227   817-440-2076
Lynn Weil & Jeanne Shelton, Resident Owners

AUSTIN

Northwest of San Antonio, Austin is the Texas state capital and home of the
University of Texas. The Austin area abounds with attractions, activities, and
events, including the LBJ Presidential Library and Museum, Zilker Park Hike
and Bike Trails, Lady Bird Johnson National Wildflower Research Center, and the
South by Southwest Music Festival, which features over 600 bands. Don't forget
Barton Springs, the Pecan Street Festival, and the Governor's Mansion. A bit of
Austin esoterica: The Congress Avenue bridge is home to the largest free-tail bat
colony in North America.

ADAMS HOUSE

4300 Avenue G, Austin, TX 78751   512-453-7696
Minimal Spanish spoken   FAX 512-453-2616
EMAIL *reservations@theadamshouse.com*
WEBSITE *www.theadamshouse.com/*

LOCATION
From I-35, turn west onto Airport, then left onto 45th Street, then
left again onto Avenue G. The house is at the intersection with 43rd
Street.

OPEN
All year

DESCRIPTION
A 1911 two-story colonial revival decorated with antiques and art
and featuring original pine and slate floors and 12-foot ceilings. The
home was totally restored in 1996 by historic architect Gregory
Free.

Adams House, Austin

NO. OF ROOMS	Three rooms with private bathrooms and one room shares one bathroom.
RATES	Year-round rates are $75 for a single or double with a private bathroom and $125 for a suite. There is a two-night minimum stay during weekends and cancellation requires 48 hours' notice.
CREDIT CARDS	American Express, Diners Club, Discover, MasterCard, Visa
BREAKFAST	On weekends, full breakfast is served in the dining room and includes waffles, omelets, quiche, homemade breads, fresh fruits, fresh-squeezed juice, fresh-ground coffee. Continental is served on weekdays. Dietary needs can be accommodated.
AMENITIES	Fresh flowers downstairs and in rooms, 1 block to museum and park, very close to restaurants and coffee houses.
RESTRICTIONS	No smoking, no pets, children over 12 are welcome. Dulce is the resident cocker spaniel.
REVIEWED	*Frommer's*
MEMBER	Historic Accommodations of Texas, Greater Austin Bed & Breakfast Association, Texas Hotel & Motel Association
RATED	1997, Historic Preservation Award, by the Heritage Society of Austin

Aunt Dolly's Attic

12023 Rotherham Drive, Austin, TX 78753   *512-837-5320*

Austin's Wildflower Inn

1200 West 22 1/2 Street, Austin, TX 78705   *512-477-9639*
Kay Jackson, Innkeeper   *FAX 512-474-4188*
EMAIL kjackson@io.com

LOCATION	Less than 1.5 miles west of the state capitol. Head west on 15th Street to Rio Grande. Turn right on Rio Grande and go to M. L. King Boulevard. Take a left, go to San Gabriel, and turn right. Go to 22nd Street (at the first stop sign), turn left, go to Longview (second street to the right), turn right, and drive 1 block. As you approach the first corner on Longview, the inn will be facing you on the left.
OPEN	All year

Austin's Wildflower Inn, Austin

DESCRIPTION	A 1933 two-story colonial inn with elegant country decor, a spacious front porch, and beautiful gardens.
NO. OF ROOMS	Two rooms with private bathrooms and two rooms share one bathroom. Try the Carolyn Pearl Walker Room or the Texas Country Room.
RATES	Year-round rates are $89-94 for a single or double with a private bathroom and $79 for a single or double with a shared bathroom. There is a minimum stay on weekends and cancellation requires 72 hours' notice.
CREDIT CARDS	American Express, MasterCard, Visa
BREAKFAST	Full breakfast is served in the dining room or in the garden and includes fresh-brewed coffee, muffins, a wildflower specialty, fresh fruit, and orange juice.
AMENITIES	Central air conditioning and heat, each room has a ceiling fan and telephone, fax.
RESTRICTIONS	No smoking. Daisy and Barney are the resident mini-dachshunds; Tootsie is the cat. "Our pets are well behaved. Many of our guests have never known that there were pets on the premises. However, there are many guests who come for dachshund therapy. No one has ever had an allergic reaction to any of our pets."
MEMBER	Historic & Hospitality Accommodations of Texas, Texas Hotel & Motel Association, Austin Area Bed & Breakfast Association
KUDOS/COMMENTS	"Decor and host both charming; conveniently located; full and delicious breakfast." "Great breakfasts."

BAD GRIESBACH BED & BREAKFAST

1006 East 50th Street, Austin, TX 78751   512-452-1004

THE BROOK HOUSE

609 West 33rd Street, Austin, TX 78705   512-459-0534
Barbara Love, Resident Owner
WEBSITE *www.citysearch.com/aus/brookhouse*

CARRINGTON'S BLUFF

1900 David Street, Austin, TX 78705   513-479-0638
Lisa Monroe, Innkeeper   800-871-8908
EMAIL *governorsinn@earthlink.net*   FAX 512-476-4769
WEBSITE *www.citysearch.com/aus/carringtonbluff*

LOCATION	Ten blocks west of downtown Austin and the state capital building, 1.5 miles west of I-35 and the Martin Luther King exit.
OPEN	All year
DESCRIPTION	An 1877 English country inn decorated with English and American antiques, accented with English country fabrics, situated on a bluff on a tree-covered acre in the heart of Austin. The house was part of an original homestead of the Republic of Texas and is listed on the State Historic Register.
NO. OF ROOMS	Eight rooms with private bathrooms. Try the Evelyn Carrington Room.
RATES	Year-round rates are $59-109 for a single or double and $109 for a suite. There is no minimum stay and cancellation requires 72 hours' notice.
CREDIT CARDS	American Express, Carte Blanche, Diners Club, Discover, MasterCard, Visa
BREAKFAST	Full breakfast is served on fine china in the dining room and includes fresh fruit, homemade granola, choice of yogurts, bakery items, and a house specialty entrée.
AMENITIES	Each room features cable TV, private phones, data port, coffee and tea facilities, iron and ironing boards, robes, hair dryers, Caswell Massey toiletries.

RESTRICTIONS	No smoking inside
REVIEWED	*Texas Monthly, Elle Decor, American Airlines* magazine, *The Great Stays of Texas, Women's Sport and Fitness*
MEMBER	Historic Accommodations of Texas, Professional Association of Innkeepers International, Texas Hotel & Motel Association
KUDOS/COMMENTS	"Wonderful location and lovely decor. Hostess makes you feel at home. I visit there every time I'm in Austin."

THE CHEQUERED SHADE

2530 Pearce Road, Austin, TX 78730　　　　　　　　　512-346-8318
Millie Scott, Resident Owner
WEBSITE *www.chequeredshade.citysearch.com*

KUDOS/COMMENTS "Across from a lake. Very peaceful. Very nice lady."

FAIRVIEW—
A BED & BREAKFAST ESTABLISHMENT

1304 Newning Avenue, Austin, TX 78704　　　　　　　*512-444-4746*
Duke & Nancy Waggoner, Innkeepers　　　　　　　　*800-310-4746*
EMAIL *fairview@io.com*　　　　　　　　　　　　*FAX 512-444-3494*
WEBSITE *www.fairview-bnb.com*

LOCATION	From I-35, take the Riverside Drive exit (233) and go west approximately 1 mile to Congress Avenue. Turn left (south) on Congress, and turn left at the next stoplight, onto Academy. Go 0.3 mile to Newning Avenue and turn right. The inn is the sixth house on the right.
OPEN	All year
DESCRIPTION	A 1910 two-story colonial revival host home decorated with turn-of-the-century Victorian furnishings and surrounded by an acre of grounds with large live oak trees and award-winning gardens. Designated an Austin Historic Landmark.
NO. OF ROOMS	Six rooms with private bathrooms. Try the Governor's Suite.
RATES	Year-round rates for a single or double are $109-169. There is a minimum stay required on selected weekends and holidays, and cancellation requires three days' notice.
CREDIT CARDS	American Express, Diners Club, Discover, MasterCard, Visa

BREAKFAST	Full breakfast is served in the great room and begins with the "designer juice of the day," coffee, tea, fresh fruit, an egg dish or a bread entrée such as Belgian waffles or fresh spinach frittata, with bacon, sausage, or ham on the side.
AMENITIES	Phones and cable TV in rooms, air conditioning, lemonade or hot tea and cookies in the afternoon, refrigerators for guest use.
RESTRICTIONS	No smoking (except outside), no pets, children over 12 are welcome. Rosie is the garden cat; Teysha is the inn cat.
REVIEWED	*Texas Monthly* magazine, *Dallas Morning News, Professional Inn Guide, Recommended Country Inns—The Southwest, Texas Bed & Breakfast Cookbook, The National Trust Guide to Historic Bed & Breakfasts, Bed & Breakfasts and Country Inns, Elle Decor*
MEMBER	Professional Association of Innkeepers International, Texas Hotel & Motel Association, Historic and Hospitality Accommodations of Texas
RATED	AAA 3 Diamonds, Mobil 3 Stars
AWARDS	1993 Austin Heritage Society Award for Preservation
KUDOS/COMMENTS	"Unusual egg creation for breakfast and kudos for assisting me during an ice storm."

GOVERNORS' INN

611 West 22nd Street, Austin, TX 78705
Lisa Monroe, Innkeeper
EMAIL governorsinn@earthlink.net
WEBSITE www.citysearch.com/aus/carringtonbluff

513-477-0711
800-871-8908
FAX 512-476-4769

LOCATION	Five blocks west of downtown Austin and the state capital building, 1 mile west of I-35 and Rio Grande Drive.
OPEN	All year
DESCRIPTION	A restored 1877 two-story neoclassical Victorian inn furnished with antiques. Listed on the State Historic Register.
NO. OF ROOMS	Ten rooms with private bathrooms. Try the Governor Connaly Room.
RATES	Year-round rates are $59-109 for a single or double and $109 for a suite. There is no minimum stay and cancellation requires 72 hours' notice.
CREDIT CARDS	American Express, Carte Blanche, Diners Club, Discover, MasterCard, Visa

BREAKFAST	Full breakfast is served on fine china in the dining room and includes gourmet coffee, fresh fruit, homemade granola, a choice of yogurts, bakery items, and a house speciality entrée.
AMENITIES	Each room features cable TV, private phones, data port, coffee and tea facilities, iron and ironing boards, robes, hair dryers, Caswell Massey toiletries.
RESTRICTIONS	No smoking
REVIEWED	*USA, Texas Monthly, Elle Decor, The Great Stays of Texas, Women's Sport and Fitness*
MEMBER	Historic Accommodations of Texas, Professional Association of Innkeepers International, Texas Hotel & Motel Association

GREGG HOUSE AND GARDENS

4201 Gregg Lane, Austin, TX 78744   *512-448-0402*
Nelda B. Haynes, Innkeeper   *FAX 512-462-0512*
EMAIL jhaynes@qsigroup.com

LOCATION	From downtown Austin, take I-35 south, cross Oltorf, then turn left onto Woodward (the next exit). Continue on Woodward across Highway 71 until Woodward ends at St. Elmo Road. Turn left onto St. Elmo Road. After the stop sign, turn left at the next street, Gregg Lane. From Austin Bergstrom International Airport, take Highway 71 west and turn left onto Woodward. Follow the above directions.
OPEN	All year
DESCRIPTION	A 1950s-era prairie-style guesthouse with hardwood floors throughout, a large patio and covered deck, located on 2 wooded acres with large gardens and a fish pond.
NO. OF ROOMS	Two rooms with private bathrooms and two rooms share one bathroom. Try the Elm Suite.
RATES	Year-round rates are $60-65 for a single or double with a private bathroom and $40-45 for a single or double with a shared bathroom. There is no minimum stay and cancellation requires 24 hours' notice.
CREDIT CARDS	No
BREAKFAST	Continental breakfast is made to order and served in the dining room or country kitchen. Lunch, dinner, and special meals (such as diabetic) are also available.
AMENITIES	Hot tub, swimming pool, fish pond, huge patio with stone barbecue pit, covered wooden deck, city bus service, washer/dryer, kitchen available for guests, cable TV.

RESTRICTIONS	No smoking, no pets, no children. The resident goat is named Boyfriend.
REVIEWED	*The Texas Monthly—Texas Bed & Breakfasts*
MEMBER	Bed & Breakfast Texas Style

HEALTHY QUARTERS

1215 Parkway, Austin, TX 78703   *512-476-7484*
Marilyn Grooms, Innkeeper   *800-392-6566*
EMAIL HealthyQuarters@webtv.net   *FAX 512-480-9356*
WEBSITE WWW.HealthyQuarters.com

LOCATION	Exit I-35 at Martin Luther King Boulevard (19th Street) and go west on MLK until it dead-ends at Lamar Boulevard. Turn left onto Lamar, then right at the first light onto Parkway. Healthy Quarters is the fourth house on the right on Parkway.
OPEN	All year
DESCRIPTION	A 1930 cottage with casual decor. The B&B shares the property with an alternative healing center.
NO. OF ROOMS	Two rooms with private bathrooms.
RATES	Year-round weekend rate is $85 for a single or double. Midweek rates are less. There is no minimum stay and cancellation requires 72 hours' notice.
CREDIT CARDS	American Express, Discover, MasterCard, Visa
BREAKFAST	Continental plus is served in the guestrooms and includes organic milk, eggs, yogurt, English muffins, cold cereal, organic fruits, herbal teas, organic coffee, a wide choice of juices, and bottled water.
AMENITIES	Private entrances, phones, cable TV/VCR, refrigerator, microwave, toaster, coffee-maker, iron and ironing board, washer/dryer available; Jacuzzi tub in the Ivy Room.
RESTRICTIONS	No smoking, no pets, children are welcome. Mr. Woo is the resident Shar-Pei. "Mr. Woo loves people and loves to wag his tail."
REVIEWED	*Texas Bed & Breakfast Guide, A Lady's Day Out in Austin and Surrounding Areas*
MEMBER	Texas Hotel & Motel Association

HOUSTON HOUSE

815 East 31st Street, Austin, TX 78705   512-479-0375

INN AT PEARL STREET

809 Martin Luther King Jr. Boulevard, Austin, TX 78710   512-477-2233
Gina Starr, Resident Owner
WEBSITE *www.innpearl.com*

INN AT RIVER OAKS FARM

2105 Scenic Drive, Austin, TX 78703   512-474-2288

LAKE TRAVIS BED & BREAKFAST

4446 Eck Lane, Austin, TX 78734   512-266-3386
Judy & Vic Dwyer, Innkeepers   888-764-LTBB
EMAIL *LTBINNB@aol.com*   FAX 512-266-9490
WEBSITE *www.laketravisbb.com*

LOCATION	West of downtown Austin, Eck Lane intersects Ranch Road 620, 1 mile south of Mansfield Dam and 1 block south of the signal light for Hudson Bend Road. Turn onto Eck and proceed 1 mile to a blue gate.
OPEN	All year
DESCRIPTION	A 1979 three-story Texas Hill Country inn situated high on a cliff with a panoramic view of the lake, hills, and shoreline of Lake Travis.
NO. OF ROOMS	Four rooms with private bathrooms. Try the Heart's Delight Suite.
RATES	Year-round rates are $145-225 for a single or double. There is a two-night minimum stay and cancellation requires seven to 14 days' notice.
CREDIT CARDS	American Express, MasterCard, Visa
BREAKFAST	Full breakfast is delivered to guestrooms and includes coffee, tea, juice, fruit, breads, and a hot entrée.

AMENITIES	Pool, spa, fitness deck, private boat dock with kitchen and bar, sun deck, boat tie-up facilities, pool table, game room, library with large-screen theater, videos, 13 decks on property, hammocks, refrigerators, microwave, coffee and tea service, massages available, boat tours, sailing and fishing trips, walking distance to winery.
RESTRICTIONS	No smoking, no pets, no children.
REVIEWED	*Frommer's San Antonio & Austin, The Texas Monthly: Texas Bed & Breakfast*
MEMBER	Texas Hotel & Motel Association, Greater Austin Bed & Breakfast Association
KUDOS/COMMENTS	"Beautiful, big deck with swimming pool, each room with balcony, easy steps down to boat dock."

LAZY OAK BED & BREAKFAST

211 West Live Oak Street, Austin, TX 78704   *512-447-8873*
Renee & Kevin Buck, Innkeepers   *FAX 512-912-1484*
WEBSITE *www.sleepeatfun.com*

LOCATION	From downtown, take Congress Avenue south 1.5 miles past the river, and turn right onto Live Oak.
OPEN	All year
DESCRIPTION	A 1911 two-story plantation-style farmhouse decorated with a mix of antiques and eclectic furnishings. Local artists' work are shown in rooms.
NO. OF ROOMS	Five rooms with private bathrooms.
RATES	Year-round rates are $95-105 for a single or double. There is a minimum stay during football weekends and special events. Cancellation requires 72 hours' notice.
CREDIT CARDS	American Express, Diners Club, Discover, MasterCard, Visa
BREAKFAST	Full breakfast is served in the dining room and includes vegetarian egg soufflé, homemade pastries and muffins, large fruit platter, cereals, breads, yogurt, coffee, teas, and juices. Vegetarian and vegan diets can be accommodated.
AMENITIES	Central air conditioning and heat, robes, cable TVs, private phone lines, shampoos and conditioners, hair dryers, hot tub on back deck, barbecue grill, *The New York Times* every Sunday, frog serenade every night in the summer from the fishpond out back.
RESTRICTIONS	No smoking, no pets, children over 15 are welcome. Molly Brown is the resident dog and George is the cat.
REVIEWED	*A Lady's Day Out in Austin*

MEMBER	Greater Austin Bed & Breakfast Association
AWARDS	1997, Best Hosts, Austin Chronicle
KUDOS/COMMENTS	"Friendly hosts, relaxed atmosphere."

Mary's Bed & Breakfast

4400 Burnet Road, Austin, TX 78756   512-452-2684

The McCallum House

613 West 32nd Street, Austin, TX 78705   512-451-6744
Roger & Nancy Danley, Resident Owners   FAX 512-451-4752
EMAIL *mccallum@austintx.net*   WEBSITE *mccallumhouse.com*

LOCATION	From I-35, take the 38 1/2 Street exit, go 1.25 miles west to Guadalupe, turn south to 32nd Street, and turn right. The house is the third on the left.
OPEN	All year
DESCRIPTION	A 1907 three-story Princess Anne Victorian inn with Victorian decor and an Arts & Crafts influence. Listed on the National and State Historic Registers.
NO. OF ROOMS	Five rooms with private bathrooms. Try the Garden Apartment.
RATES	Weekends, holidays, and special events, rates are $104-139 for a single or double. Midweek rates are $80-119 for a single or double. There is a two-night minimum stay during weekends, three nights during holidays. Cancellation requires 48 hours' notice.
CREDIT CARDS	Discover, MasterCard, Visa
BREAKFAST	Full breakfast is served in the dining room or guestrooms by request and includes a fresh fruit cup; crepes, quiche, or a baked egg dish; homemade muffins or coffeecake.
AMENITIES	Air conditioning, private kitchens and porches, private phones with answering machines, TVs and some VCRs, desks, sitting areas, cookies, mints, pretzels, coffee and tea anytime, magnifying mirrors.
RESTRICTIONS	No smoking inside, no pets, children over 12 are welcome.
REVIEWED	*Recommended Country Inns—The Southwest, Texas Bed & Breakfast*

The McCallum House, Austin

MEMBER	Historic Accommodations of Texas, Professional Association of Innkeepers International, Texas Hotel & Motel Association
RATED	AAA 3 Diamonds, Mobil 2 Stars
AWARDS	1987, Preservation Award, Heritage Society of Austin

MILLER–CROCKETT HOUSE

112 Academy Drive, Austin, TX 78704   512-441-1600
Pat Klesick, Owner
WEBSITE www.millercrockett.com

PARK LANE GUEST HOUSE

221 Park Lane, Austin, TX 78704   512-447-7460
Shakti & Dev Kirn Khalsa, Innkeepers 800-492-8827
WEBSITE www.eden.com/~cheryl/BB.html FAX 512-442-7591

LOCATION	Take exit 232 (Town Lake/Riverside Drive) off I-35 and head west on Riverside Drive to the second light, then turn left on Congress Avenue. Go through the first light, at Academy Street, and make the next left.

OPEN	All year
DESCRIPTION	A 1940 traditional Texas-style limestone and yellow pine home decorated with handcrafted and antique furnishings, Persian carpets, stained glass, and French doors, and located on half an acre.
NO. OF ROOMS	Two rooms with private bathrooms. Try the Garden Cottage.
RATES	Year-round rates are $79-89 for a single or double and $129 for a suite. There is no minimum stay and cancellation requires five days' notice.
CREDIT CARDS	American Express, MasterCard, Visa
BREAKFAST	Continental breakfast includes orange juice, fresh fruit salad, fresh-baked bread or muffins, organic coffee, and tea.
AMENITIES	Robes in rooms, flowers from the gardens, coffee and tea always available, central air conditioning. The cottage is handicapped accessible and has a large living room for groups and meetings.
RESTRICTIONS	No smoking. Ask about the policy regarding dogs. Sophie, Sadie, and Devi are the resident Keeshonds.
REVIEWED	*Inn Places, Damron Accommodations, Ferrari's International Guide to Gay and Lesbian Bed & Breakfasts*

SERENITY AT LAKE TRAVIS

15401 Watumba Road, Austin, TX 78734   512-266-0159
Peggy Dowlearn, Innkeeper   FAX 512-266-0160
EMAIL *pdowlearn@msn.com*   WEBSITE *www.serenitybnb.com/*

LOCATION	From I-35, turn west onto FM 620 and drive 20 miles. Pass the Mansfield Dam and turn right at the next light onto Hudson Bend Road. Drive 1 mile and take a right onto Watumba. Drive one-and-a-half blocks to the B&B.
OPEN	All year
DESCRIPTION	A 1993 two-story stone host home situated on a quiet hilltop overlooking Lake Travis and the hills.
NO. OF ROOMS	Two rooms share one bathroom.
RATES	Year-round rates are $75 for a single or double. There is no minimum stay and cancellation requires 24 hours' notice.
CREDIT CARDS	No
BREAKFAST	Full breakfast is served in the dining room and includes coffee or tea, juice, fresh fruit, eggs, bacon or sausage, biscuits and jelly or honey. Dietary needs are accommodated. Lunch, dinner, and special meals are available with advance notice.

| AMENITIES | Fresh flowers, robes, cable TV/VCRs, phones in rooms; videos, computer, and fax available; fresh ice water and beverages; full kitchen; stereo; upstairs deck with panoramic views. |
| RESTRICTIONS | Smoking on decks only |

SOUTHARD HOUSE BED & BREAKFAST

908 Blanco Street, Austin, TX 78703   512-474-4731
WEBSITE accommodations.austin360.com/southardhouse/

STRICKLAND ARMS BED & BREAKFAST

604 East 47th Street, Austin, TX 78751   512-454-4426
WEBSITE www.prismnet.com/~arms/

SUMMIT HOUSE BED & BREAKFAST

1204 Summit Street, Austin, TX 78741   512-445-5304
WEBSITE summit.home.texas.net/

TRIPLE CREEK RANCH

16301 Fitzhugh Road, Austin, TX 78751   512-264-1371
Nola & David Fowler, Resident Owners

WOODBURN HOUSE BED & BREAKFAST

4401 Avenue D, Austin, TX 78751   512-458-4335
Herb Dickson & Sandra Villalaz-Dickson, Resident Owners
WEBSITE woodburnhouse.com

KUDOS/COMMENTS "Charming and restful. Nice restoration with modern amenities. Guests receive great attention." "Beautiful and professionally run bed & breakfast. Great owners."

AVINGER

MCKENZIE MANOR

Route 1, Box 404A, Avinger, TX 75630   903-755-2240
Paul & Carol Harrell, Resident Owners

BACLIFF

REDI HOUSE AND SPA

227 Grand Avenue, Bacliff, TX 77518   281-559-1118
WEBSITE www.myplanet.net/redihouse

BAIRD

CORNER HOUSE BED & BREAKFAST

340 Vine Street, Baird, TX 79504   915-854-1890

BANDERA

On Highway 16, northwest of San Antonio in the Texas Hill Country, Bandera is known as the Cowboy Capital of Texas and boasts rodeos twice a week in the summer. The world-famous two-steppin' honky-tonks are open year-round. Bandera also has one of the oldest Polish communities in the United States. Tube or canoe the spring-fed Medina River and check out Lost Maples and Hill Country State Natural Areas.

BANDERA CREEK GUEST COTTAGE

148 West Robindale Road, Bandera, TX 78003   830-460-3517
Gay Guilott, Innkeeper   FAX 830-796-3526
EMAIL *gayg@txdirect.net*   WEBSITE *www.ggrealty.com*

LOCATION	Half a mile south of Bandera at the intersection of Highway 16 and Robindale.
OPEN	All year
DESCRIPTION	A 1940 country hideaway decorated with antique furnishings, Pergo flooring throughout, and artwork from a local artist.
NO. OF ROOMS	One room with a private bathroom.
RATES	Year-round rate is $85 for a single or double. There is no minimum stay.
CREDIT CARDS	No
BREAKFAST	Continental plus is stocked in the kitchen and includes eggs, bacon, bread, cereal, coffee, yogurt, milk, fruit, and juices. Cooking utensils are also provided.
AMENITIES	Air conditioning and heat, phone, TV, stereo with CD player, two large tree-shaded patios, large firepit barbecue, several acres on Bandera Creek, private entrance through a fenced courtyard, fully stocked kitchen.
RESTRICTIONS	No pets, no children. Foxy and Ralph are the resident pooches; Piggly is the potbellied pig. There are also cows, emus, a pygmy goat, and four cats roaming the property.

DIAMOND H RANCH BED & BREAKFAST

5322 State Highway 16 North, Bandera, TX 78003   830-796-4820

DIXIE DUDE RANCH

PO Box 2121, Bandera, TX 78003

800-375-9255
FAX 210-796-3067

HACKBERRY LODGE

1005 Hackberry, Bandera, TX 78003
Herb & Janice Kuykendall, Innkeepers
Spanish spoken
EMAIL hkbryldg@htfm.ne
WEBSITE welcome.to/hackberrylodge

830-460-7134

LOCATION	Take Highway 16 (Bandera Road) out of San Antonio at Loop 410 or Loop 1604. Main Street in Bandera is approximately 36 miles north of Loop 410. Go right at Main Street, left onto Hackberry, then right onto 11th Street. The driveway is the first on the left.
OPEN	All year
DESCRIPTION	An 1856 two-story stone Victorian country inn with Victorian decor.
NO. OF ROOMS	Seven rooms with private bathrooms.
RATES	Year-round rates are $68-135 for a single or double. There is no minimum stay.
CREDIT CARDS	No
BREAKFAST	Continental plus is served in the dining room and features home-baked Tex-Mex goods.
AMENITIES	Beer, snacks, and chili; stocked summer kitchen; refrigerator, range, microwave available to guests at all times; outdoor barbecue pit; air conditioning; handicapped accessible; private weddings made special.
RESTRICTIONS	No smoking. Bonnie is the resident poodle; Maggie is the dalmation; Buffie is the Himalayan cat.
REVIEWED	*Okay* magazine, London

RICOCHET RANCH

PO Box 1745, Bandera, TX 78003

830-796-7475

Running R Ranch

Route 1, Box 590, Bandera, TX 78003
EMAIL rrranch@texas.net
WEBSITE www.rrranch.com

830-796-3984
FAX 830-796-8189

Bastrop

The Colony Bed & Breakfast

703 Main Street, Bastrop, TX 78602
Carla Dickson, Resident Owner

512-303-1234

Pecan Street Inn

1010 Pecan Street, Bastrop, TX 78602

512-321-3315

Bay City

Bailey House

1704 3rd Street, Bay City, TX 77414

409-245-5613

BEAUMONT

Ninety miles east of Houston and 25 miles west of the Louisiana border, Beaumont features a nice Old Towne district with museums, restaurants, and shops.

CALDER HOUSE

1905 Calder Street, Beaumont, TX 77701   *409-832-1955*

GRAND DUERR MANOR

2298 McFaddin Street, Beaumont, TX 77701   *409-833-9600*
Karl Duerr, Innkeeper
German spoken

LOCATION	From Houston, take the 7th Street exit and turn right on 7th Street; drive to McFaddin; the inn is on the corner of 7th Street and McFaddin. From Louisiana, take the 11th Street exit and loop under I-10; take the feeder road and turn right on 7th Street; go to McFaddin; the inn is on the corner of 7th Street and McFaddin.
OPEN	All year
DESCRIPTION	A 1937 two-story inn.
NO. OF ROOMS	Four rooms with private bathrooms. The Duerrs recommend the Master Suite.
RATES	Year-round rates are $119-159 for a single or double with a private bathroom. There is no minimum stay and reservation requires a 50 percent deposit.
CREDIT CARDS	None
BREAKFAST	Full breakfast is served in the dining room.
AMENITIES	Complimentary wine or champagne; tray with coffee, tea, and hot chocolate; flowers and candles in rooms; cable TV, radio, alarm clock; photographs taken and mailed to guests.
RESTRICTIONS	No smoking, no pets, children are welcome in the cottage only.

BEEVILLE

NUECES INN BED & BREAKFAST

201 East Houston, Beeville, TX 78104   512-362-0868
Wayne & Ida Dirks, Resident Owners

BELLVILLE

HIGH COTTON INN

214 South Live Oak, Bellville, TX 77418   409-865-9796
George & Anna Horton, Resident Owners   800-321-9796
WEBSITE www.highcottonbakery.com   FAX 409-865-5588

BEN WHEELER

Well situated halfway between Canton and Tyler on Highway 64, Ben Wheeler
allows easy access to the Tyler Rose Festival in October and the Canton First
Monday Trades Days.

ALEXANDER'S B&B

Route 1, Box 56, Ben Wheeler, TX 75754   903-852-5299
Nat F. & Peggy Alexander, Resident Owners   800-568-7120

LOCATION	From the red light in Canton, go 15.5 miles east on Highway 64, or from Tyler, go 20 miles west on Highway 64.
OPEN	During Canton Trade Days only
DESCRIPTION	A 1979 two-story barn-style host home with comfortable furnishings; located on 3 acres with a beautiful yard.
NO. OF ROOMS	One room with a private bathroom and three rooms share two bathrooms.

RATES	Rates are $85 for a double with a private bathroom and $75 for a double with a shared bathroom. There is a discount for multiple-night stays.
CREDIT CARDS	No
BREAKFAST	Full country breakfast is served in the dining room.
AMENITIES	Swings and chairs in the yard.
RESTRICTIONS	No smoking, no pets

STANGER SPRINGS BED & BREAKFAST

Route 1, Box 38, Ben Wheeler, TX 75754   *800-947-0390*
Bessie Stanger, Resident Owner

KUDOS/COMMENTS   "Beautiful place to stay."

TUMBLE-ON-IN BED & BREAKFAST

RR 1, Ben Wheeler, TX 75754   *903-963-7669*
EMAIL tumbleoninn@aol.com   *WEBSITE members.aol.com/tumbleoninn*

BIG SANDY

Halfway between Dallas and Shreveport, 23 miles east of Longview on Highway 80, this rural community was the first settlement (circa 1830s) in the northeast Pine Belt. Big Sandy is handy to the Sabine River and several lakes.

ANNIE POTTER'S VICTORIAN VILLAGE BED & BREAKFAST

106 North Tyler Street, Big Sandy, TX 75755   *903-636-4355*
                                                FAX 903-636-4037

LOCATION	Fifteen miles north of Tyler on Highway 155.
OPEN	All year

DESCRIPTION	A 1901 three-story Victorian country inn, listed on the State Historic Register.
NO. OF ROOMS	Ten rooms with private bathrooms and four rooms share three bathrooms.
RATES	Year-round rates for a single or double with a private bathroom are $75-120; a single or double with a shared bathroom is $55; and a suite rents for $100. There is no minimum stay and cancellation requires 72 hours' notice.
CREDIT CARDS	American Express, Discover, MasterCard, Visa
BREAKFAST	Full breakfast is served Victorian style in the Tea Room. Lunch is also available.
AMENITIES	Fresh hot coffee and tea, pastries baked daily, antique bathtubs, TVs, refrigerators in rooms, and balconies in suites.
RESTRICTIONS	No smoking, no pets
REVIEWED	*Texas Highways, Southern Living*
MEMBER	East Texas Bed & Breakfast Association, Bed & Breakfast Texas Style

BLANCO

In the Texas Hill Country, Blanco boasts the historic home of LBJ's mother. Market Days are hopping during the third Saturday of each month from April through November, and check out the Weekend Jamboree during the second weekend in June. For recreation, don't miss Blanco State Park.

GREEN ACRES BED & BREAKFAST

HC4 Box 375, Blanco, TX 78606   830-833-5551
Mary Jane Green, Resident Owner

BOERNE

German immigrants settled this little community on Cibolo Creek about 150 years ago. About 30 miles northwest of San Antonio on I-10, Boerne (Burn-knee) features antique shops, art galleries, crafts, specialty shops, and the Cascade Caverns. Events and activities include the Texas Trade Fair, Old Time Fiddlers Contests, Fall Antique Show, and the Follow the Star Christmas Drive-Through.

BORGMAN'S SUNDAY HOUSE BED & BREAKFAST

911 South Main Street, Boerne, TX 78006　　　　　　　830-249-9563

GUADALUPE RIVER RANCH

605 FM 474, Boerne, TX 78006　　　　　　　830-537-4837
Elisa McClure, Resident Owner
WEBSITE *www.guadaluperiverranch.com*

HILL COUNTRY ISLAND

Route 2, Box 6851, Pipe Creek, TX 78063　　　　　　　830-535-4050
Mary Autry, Resident Owner

OBERLAKKEN

111 Staffel, Boerne, TX 78006　　　　　　　830-816-2184
Ed & Virginia Davis, Resident Owners　　　FAX 830-816-2184 (press *51)

LOCATION	From San Antonio, go west on I-10. Take Business Highway 87 into town. Cross over the bridge and turn left on West Theissen Street at the Landmark Antique Store. Turn left on Staffel.
OPEN	All year
DESCRIPTION	A 1994 two-story host home on Cibolo Creek, decorated in Old World style.
NO. OF ROOMS	Three rooms with private bathrooms. The main house has two suites and the guesthouse has one room with a private bathroom.

RATES	Year-round rates for a single or double are $70-79. There is no minimum stay.
CREDIT CARDS	No
BREAKFAST	Full breakfast is served in the dining room and includes fresh juice and fruit, sweet breads, coffee, teas, sausage, bacon, hashbrowns, egg dishes, and stuffed French toast.
AMENITIES	Fireplace; book, music, and video libraries; cable TV in rooms; air conditioning.
RESTRICTIONS	No smoking, no pets, ask about children.

OLD FATHER INN

120 Old San Antonio Road, Boerne, TX 78006   830-249-8908
WEBSITE www.texassleepaways.com

YE KENDALL INN

128 West Blanco Road, Boerne, TX 78006   830-249-8548
WEBSITE www.yekendallinn.com

BONHAM

West of Paris on Highway 82, Bonham celebrates the Bois d'Arc Festival in May, the County Fair in October, and Old Fashioned Saturday on the Square in November. Explore Fort Inglish Park and the historic Sam Rayburn House and Library. Trade Days are the first Saturday after the first Monday of each month. For outdoor recreation, visit Bonham State Park and Lake Bonham.

THE CARLETON HOUSE BED & BREAKFAST

803 North Main Street, Bonham, TX 75418   903-583-2779
Karen & Steve Halbrook, Innkeepers
WEBSITE www.carletonhouse.com

LOCATION	Sixty miles northeast of Dallas, 30 miles east of Sherman. Take Highway 121 north into Bonham. Highway 82/56 will bring you to the courthouse square. At the red light, turn north (left) onto Main Street and go 4 blocks to the corner of 8th and Main Streets.

OPEN	All year
DESCRIPTION	An 1888 three-story Eastlake Victorian host home featuring three balconies, two porches, fishscale shingles, and ornate gingerbread woodwork, and decorated with antiques.
NO. OF ROOMS	Four rooms with private bathrooms. Try the Carleton Suite.
RATES	Year-round rates are $70-85 for a single or double and $100 for a suite. There is no minimum stay and cancellation requires 48 hours' notice.
CREDIT CARDS	American Express, Diners Club, Discover, MasterCard, Visa
BREAKFAST	Full breakfast is served in the dining room and includes fruit, juices, coffee, an egg dish, muffins, and homemade jams. Dinner and special meals are also available.
AMENITIES	Jacuzzis, fireplaces, central heat and air conditioning, meeting facilities, TV/VCR, videos, games, alarm clocks, antique car rides, bath luxuries, chocolates, strolling musician, piano, pump organ and other musical instruments, swings, outdoor benches, antique gardens, ice, bottled water, bike storage, stationery, radio, writing and reading materials, old books.
RESTRICTIONS	No smoking, no pets, children over 12 are welcome. Sampson and Samantha are the resident cocker spaniels. "Sampson can chase a spot of light longer than the Energizer bunny can last."
MEMBER	Red River Valley Bed & Breakfast Association

GRANNY LOU'S BED & BREAKFAST

317 West Sam Rayburn Drive, Bonham, TX 75418   903-583-7912
Wayne & Brenda Moore, Innkeepers   800-997-7912
EMAIL *bmoore@grannylou.com*   FAX 903-583-3317
WEBSITE *www.grannylou.com*

LOCATION	Take I-75 or Highway 121 north from Dallas to McKinney. Take exit 45 (Highway 121) north 35 miles to Bonham. As you enter the city limits, Highway 121 merges with Highway 56 east. Granny Lou's is on the south side of Highway 56 (West Sam Rayburn Drive), 2 blocks west of downtown Bonham.
OPEN	All year
DESCRIPTION	A restored 1880s-era Queen Anne Victorian home decorated with antiques, blended with the comfort of modern amenities; situated on 3 acres, just 2 blocks from downtown Bonham. The guest cottage, located next door to the main house, has two bedrooms and one bath.
NO. OF ROOMS	Four rooms with private bathrooms.

RATES	Year-round rates are $75 for a single or double, $105 for a suite, and $125 for the cottage. There is no minimum stay and cancellation requires three days' notice.
CREDIT CARDS	American Express, MasterCard, Visa
BREAKFAST	Full breakfast is served buffet style in the dining room and includes an egg dish or entrée, baked goods, and fruit. Cereal is always available.
AMENITIES	Each guestroom is comfortably furnished with antiques and includes cable TV, telephone, alarm clock; toiletries and irons are available as needed; hot tub out back off the large deck; guest refrigerator on second floor includes variety of complimentary beverages. The guest cottage is handicapped accessible and includes two bedrooms, one bathroom, a kitchen, and laundry room.
RESTRICTIONS	No pets, children over 12 are welcome. Families with young children are encouraged to stay in the guest cottage. There are six outdoor cats on the property.

BOWIE

An old cotton-buying town, Bowie features many historic buildings and antique shops. It is the home of Amon Carter and Johnson's Chicken Ranch.

OLD TUCKER HOMEPLACE

Highway 59 South, Bowie, TX 76230　　　　　　　940-872-2484
Robert & Martha Fuller, Innkeepers

LOCATION	From the intersection of Highways 59 and 287, the B&B is 8.2 miles south on Highway 59.
OPEN	All year
DESCRIPTION	A 1983 two-story Texas ranch house built in the style of dwellings constructed on the land in the 1880s with furnishings appropriate to the period.
NO. OF ROOMS	Three rooms with private bathrooms and two rooms share one-and-a-half bathrooms.
RATES	Year-round rates are $75-95 for a single or double with a private bathroom and $25-35 for a single or double with a shared bathroom. There is no minimum stay. Ask about a cancellation policy.
CREDIT CARDS	No

BREAKFAST	Full hearty breakfast is served in the dining room, guestrooms, on the porch, or in the gazebo and may include sausage, eggs, biscuits and gravy. Lunch, dinner, and special meals are available with advance notice.
AMENITIES	Fishing in stocked pond, wildlife observation blinds, rocking chairs on porch, central air conditioning, meeting areas, hiking, cattle feeding.
RESTRICTIONS	None. Well-behaved pets and children are welcome. There are several outdoor cats, two bird dogs, a Border collie, a number of horses, and 50 cattle on the property.
REVIEWED	*Texas Bed & Breakfast*

BRADY

Brady Lake is great for bass fishing. Check out the PRCA rodeos at White Complex. If your tastes run to the more esoteric, try the World Championship Barbecue Goat Cook-off.

BRADY HOUSE

704 South Bridge Street, Brady, TX 76825　　　　915-597-5265
Kelly & Bobbie Hancock, Innkeepers　　　　888-272-3901
French spoken　　　　FAX 915-597-9699
EMAIL *bradyhs@centex.net*　　　WEBSITE *www.bradyhouse.com*

LOCATION	Six blocks south of Courthouse Square on Highway 87/Bridge Street, in the center of Texas where the Hill Country meets West Texas, 126 miles northwest of San Antonio.
OPEN	All year
DESCRIPTION	A 1908 two-story Richardson-style, Craftsman-influenced host home with a wide porch, decorated with art and antiques, and situated on an acre of landscaped grounds.
NO. OF ROOMS	Three rooms with private bathrooms.
RATES	Year-round rates are $85 for a single or double and $95 for a suite. There is a minimum stay over Labor Day weekend. Please inquire about a cancellation policy.
CREDIT CARDS	Discover, MasterCard, Visa
BREAKFAST	Full gourmet country breakfast is served in the dining room and includes an egg entrée, meats, fruit, juice, potatoes, homemade pastries. Continental breakfast is available for those who prefer a lighter meal. Special meals are available with advance notice.

AMENITIES	Robes, satellite TV, air conditioning, parklike grounds, small in-room refrigerators with complimentary beverages.
RESTRICTIONS	No smoking, no pets, children over 12 are welcome.
REVIEWED	*National Trust for Historic Preservation, The Texas Monthly: Hill Country Guide*
MEMBER	Professional Association of Innkeepers International

BRAZORIA

From Brazoria, Varner-Hogg State Park is due north; the beaches, including undeveloped Bryan Beach State Recreation Area, are to the south. Nearby Clute is home to the Great Mosquito Festival.

ROSES AND THE RIVER BED & BREAKFAST

7074 County Road 506, Brazoria, TX 77422   *409-798-1070*
Dick & Mary Jo Hosack, Innkeepers   *800-610-1070*
Some Spanish spoken   *FAX 409-798-1070*
EMAIL *nosack@tgn.net*   WEBSITE *www.zetamgmt.com/rosesriver.htm*

LOCATION	Take Highway 288 south from Houston to the Highway 523 exit, which dead-ends at Highway 521. Turn left and follow Highway 521 west for approximately 45 minutes, turning left when it "dead-ends" in downtown Brazoria. Stay on Highway 521 west over the San Bernard River and take the next right.
OPEN	All year
DESCRIPTION	A 1980 two-story Texas farmhouse with elegant and comfortable decor, situated on the San Bernard River with landscaped grounds that include 260 rose bushes.
NO. OF ROOMS	Three rooms with private bathrooms.
RATES	Year-round rate is $125 for a single or double. There is no minimum stay and cancellation requires 72 hours' notice.
CREDIT CARDS	American Express, Discover, MasterCard, Visa
BREAKFAST	Full gourmet breakfast is served in the dining room and includes juice, muffins or rolls, an entrée such as strata, egg soufflé omelet, Northwest salmon scramble, and side dishes.
AMENITIES	Fresh flowers in each room, robes, hair dryers, old-time tub converted into whirlpool, individual temperature controls in rooms, boat rides after breakfast, bird-watching.

RESTRICTIONS	No smoking inside, no pets, children over 12 are welcome. Hilde is the resident schnauzer and there are six cats on the grounds.
REVIEWED	*Romantic Texas*
MEMBER	Professional Association of Innkeepers International, Historic & Hospitality Accommodations of Texas
RATED	AAA 3 Diamonds

BREMOND

CEDERWILDE BED & BREAKFAST

RR 1, Box 186, Bremond, TX 76629   254-746-7035

BRENHAM

Seventy-five miles northwest of Houston on Highway 290, Brenham is home to Blue Bell Creameries, the Antique Rose Emporium, Washington on the Brazos Park and Museum, and the Pleasant Hill Winery.

ANT STREET INN

107 West Commerce Street, Brenham, TX 77833   409-836-7393
Tommy & Pam Traylor, Innkeepers   800-481-1951
EMAIL stay@antstreetinn.com   FAX 409-836-7595
WEBSITE www.antstreetinn.com

LOCATION	Between Austin and Houston on Highway 290, 1 block south of the courthouse in the center of historic downtown.
OPEN	All year
DESCRIPTION	An 1899 brick Romanesque inn decorated with elegant antiques. Listed on the State Historic Register.
NO. OF ROOMS	Thirteen rooms with private bathrooms. Try the Galveston Room.
RATES	Year-round rates are $85-165 for a single or double. There is no minimum stay and cancellation requires 72 hours' notice.
CREDIT CARDS	American Express, Discover, MasterCard, Visa

BREAKFAST	Full, artfully arranged breakfast is served in the dining room and includes chilled juices, fruit of the season, egg casseroles, fresh muffins, pastries, and other favorites discovered by innkeeper Pam Traylor while she was working with *Southern Living* magazine's Cooking School. Catering is also available.
AMENITIES	Free Blue Bell ice cream, hardwood floors, antique rugs, ceiling fans, cable TV, phones, computer data ports, rocking chairs on porch, early coffee and tea, individual climate control, 12-foot ceilings, excellent lighting, ballroom for weddings and receptions, meeting rooms for conferences and retreats.
RESTRICTIONS	No smoking, no pets, children over 12 are welcome.
MEMBER	Historic Accommodations of Texas, Professional Association of Innkeepers International
RATED	AAA 3 Diamonds, Mobil 3 Stars
KUDOS/COMMENTS	"Superb collection of antique beds and furnishings. Accommodating for business or pleasure." "Beautiful rooms and renovation. Lovely antiques. Great innkeepers." "Unique, comfortable, and elegantly furnished inn with wedding facilities and excellent food." "The most elegant and friendly facility imaginable. Excellent breakfasts, wonderful Victorian antiques, beautiful fabrics, high quality and fantastic comfort throughout." "Best collection of antiques outside of a museum. Hosts are friendly and helpful." "Wonderful B&B and hosts."

THE BRENHAM HOUSE

705 Clinton Street, Brenham, TX 77833   *409-830-0477*

CAPTAIN CLAY HOME BED & BREAKFAST

Route 5 (FM 390), Box 149, Brenham, TX 77833   *409-836-1916*
Thelma Zwiener, Resident Owner
Spanish spoken

LOCATION	From Brenham, take Highway 105 east for about 2 miles. Turn left on Highway 50, then right on FM 390. Go up the hill and the gate is just past the two stone buildings on the right.
OPEN	All year
DESCRIPTION	An 1852 one-and-a-half-story early Greek revival inn with Victorian furnishings, two porches, and a view.

NO. OF ROOMS	Three rooms with private bathrooms and one room with a shared bathroom.
RATES	Year-round rates are $45-85 for a single or double.
CREDIT CARDS	MasterCard, Visa
BREAKFAST	Full country-style breakfast is served in the dining room and includes coffee or tea, fruit juice, fresh seasonal fruit, eggs, potatoes, or French toast, sausage, bacon or ham, sweetbreads, and biscuits.
AMENITIES	Six-person hot tub enclosed in a gazebo, garden, and a pond for fishing.
RESTRICTIONS	Smoking on porches only, no pets, and well-supervised children are welcome. Owners raise miniature horses.
REVIEWED	*Texas Highways, Houston Life* magazine, *The Texas Monthly: Guide to Bed & Breakfasts*
KUDOS/COMMENTS	"Rooms furnished nicely. Located on miniature horse farm."

COTTONTAIL INN

Route 4, Box 367, Brenham, TX 77833   *409-836-9485*

FAR VIEW

1804 South Park Street, Brenham, TX 77833   *409-836-1672*
David & Tonya Meyer, Resident Owners
WEBSITE www.bbhost.com/farview

KUDOS/COMMENTS	"Well-run, excellent hosts, perfect location for business travelers wanting nice surroundings."

HEARTLAND COUNTRY INN

Route 2, Box 446, Brenham, TX 77833   *409-836-1864*

INGLESIDE BED & BREAKFAST

409 East Main, Brenham, TX 77833   409-251-7707
Connie Hall, Innkeeper   888-643-7707
EMAIL connie@inglesidebb.com   FAX 409-251-7717
WEBSITE www.inglesidebb.com

OPEN	All year
DESCRIPTION	A 1924 two-story brick inn with Queen Anne and Victorian furnishings, decorated with antiques and collectibles, with an expansive front porch. The entire property is shaded by old oak trees.
NO. OF ROOMS	Three rooms with private bathrooms and two rooms share one bathroom.
RATES	Year-round rates are $100-120 for a single or double with a private bathroom and $85 for a single or double with a shared bathroom. There is no minimum stay and cancellation requires seven days' notice.
CREDIT CARDS	Discover, MasterCard, Visa
BREAKFAST	Full country-gourmet breakfast is served in the dining room and may include caramelized banana omelets, baked blueberry pecan French toast, lemon pancakes with strawberry butter; all breakfasts include fresh fruit, juice, coffee, and fresh-baked bread or pastry.
AMENITIES	Wine and cheese in the late afternoon; terry cloth bathrobes in the rooms with shared baths; to help celebrate a special event, the innkeeper will make arrangements for flowers, wine, or other special items; air conditioning; the B&B is a short walk to the historic downtown area.
RESTRICTIONS	No smoking, no pets, children over 12 are welcome.
MEMBER	Texas Hotel & Motel Association

JAMES WALKER HOMESTEAD BED & BREAKFAST

Route 7, Box 7176, Brenham, TX 77833   409-836-6717
John & Jane Barnhill, Resident Owners

Mariposa Ranch Bed & Breakfast, Brenham

MARIPOSA RANCH BED & BREAKFAST

8904 Mariposa Lane, Brenham, TX 77833   *409-836-4737*
Johnna & Charles Chamberlain, Innkeepers
Spanish spoken
EMAIL *mariposainn@earthlink.net*
WEBSITE *mariposranch.net*

LOCATION	Ten miles north of Brenham, 30 miles southwest of College Station. From Brenham, follow Highway 36 north for 8 miles to FM 390. Turn right (east) and drive 0.5 mile to the ranch entrance, on the left.
OPEN	All year
DESCRIPTION	Five country inns, four of which are historical, on a 100-acre working ranch. Architectural styles include a Texas plantation farmhouse, a Greek revival country inn, and a log cabin. Listed on the State Historic Register.
NO. OF ROOMS	Seven rooms with private bathrooms and two rooms share one bathroom. Try the Texas Ranger Log Cabin.
RATES	Year-round rates are $90-100 for a single or double with a private bathroom, $80 for a single or double with a shared bathroom, $140 for a suite, and $250 for the cabin. There is no minimum stay and cancellation requires seven days' notice with a $15 charge.

CREDIT CARDS	MasterCard, Visa
BREAKFAST	Full country breakfast is served in the dining room and includes fruit, homemade bread, an egg dish, and meat. A special package ("An Enchanted Evening") that includes candlelight, champagne, fresh flowers, and candy is available.
AMENITIES	Miles of hills and valleys, total peace and quiet, rockers, hammocks; all accommodations are furnished with fine period antiques and include refrigerators, TVs, robes, and air conditioning; most have fireplaces and clawfoot tubs; facilities for retreats, weddings, and parties; croquet and horseshoes.
RESTRICTIONS	Smoking outside only, no pets. Maggie is the resident Lab, Belle and Winston are the cocker spaniels. "All our dogs are very well behaved and guests love visiting with them. They each usually pick out a cabin or house and spend the night there with our guests—on the porch, of course."
REVIEWED	*A Lady's Day Out, Romantic Texas, Bed & Breakfasts and Country Inns, The Official Guide to American Historic Inns*
MEMBER	Historical Accommodations of Texas, Professional Association of Innkeepers International, Texas Hotel & Motel Association
KUDOS/COMMENTS	"Ultimate in comfort and hospitality. Very relaxing. Wonderful host and good cook."

THE MILL HOUSE

Route 3, Box 365, Brenham, TX 77833   *409-830-1360*
Mike & Jerry McLennan, Resident Owners

MOCKINGBIRD HILL FARM

6503 Baranowski Road, Brenham, TX 77833   *409-836-5329*

NUECES CANYON BED & BREAKFAST

9501 US Highway 290 West, Brenham, TX 77833   *409-289-5600*
Beverley & George Caloudas, Resident Owners   *800-925-5058*
Spanish and Greek spoken   *FAX 409-289-2411*

LOCATION	Eight miles west of Brenham on US Highway 290 West.
OPEN	All year
DESCRIPTION	A one-story 1985/1995 traditional-style country inn furnished with antiques. "Our guests immediately feel comfortable and at home."
NO. OF ROOMS	Twelve rooms with private bathrooms.
RATES	Year-round rates for a single or double are $79-125. There is a minimum stay during some weekends. Ask about a cancellation policy.
CREDIT CARDS	American Express, MasterCard, Visa
BREAKFAST	Continental plus breakfast is served in the guestrooms and includes cold cereals, fresh fruits, fresh-baked rolls, yogurt, special breads, juices, and teas.
AMENITIES	Air conditioning, horse boarding, meeting facilities, handicapped accessible, robes.
RESTRICTIONS	No smoking in rooms, no pets
MEMBER	Washington County Bed & Breakfast Association, Texas Hotel & Motel Association

SCHUERENBERG HOUSE

503 West Alamo Street, Brenham, TX 77833   *409-830-7054*

SECRETS

405 Pecan Street, Brenham, TX 77833   *409-836-4117*
Charles, Natalie, & Allison Andreas, Resident Owners

VERNON'S BED & BREAKFAST

Route 7, Box 7630, Brenham, TX 77833   *409-836-6408*
Glenwood & Martha Vernon, Resident Owners

BROADDUS

About 45 minutes east of Lufkin in East Texas, Broaddus is handy to Sam Rayburn Lake.

SAM RAYBURN LAKE BED & BREAKFAST— THE COLE HOUSE

Route 1, Box 258, Broaddus, TX 75929   *409-872-3666*
Gene & Jean Cole, Innkeepers

LOCATION	Take Highway 69 southeast from Lufkin to Zavalla. Go left on Highway 147 toward Broaddus and left on FM 3185.
OPEN	All year
DESCRIPTION	A 1963 frame cottage with contemporary decor, overlooking the lake.
NO. OF ROOMS	Two rooms share one bathroom.
RATES	Year-round rates are $37.50-55 for a single or double. There is a two-night minimum stay from March through October. Cancellation requires 48 hours' notice.
CREDIT CARDS	No
BREAKFAST	Continental breakfast is stocked in the guesthouse the night before and includes coffee, tea, breads, fruit, and juice.
AMENITIES	House overlooks the largest lake in Texas, gazebo on a bluff overlooking the lake, microwave, TV, central air conditioning and heat, screened summer room with picnic table, fruit bowl, fresh flowers in season.

Sam Rayburn Lake Bed & Breakfast — The Cole House, Broaddus

RESTRICTIONS	No smoking, no pets, well-behaved children are welcome. Mr. Squeaker is the resident cat.
REVIEWED	*Texas Bed & Breakfast, Country Inns of Texas*

BRYAN

About 100 miles northwest of Houston via Highways 290 and 6, Bryan is on the doorstep of Texas A&M University and College Station.

ANGELSGATE BED & BREAKFAST

615 East 29th Street, Bryan, TX 77803   *409-779-1231*

BONNIE GAMBREL BED & BREAKFAST

600 East 27th Street, Bryan, Texas 77803   *409-779-1022*
Dorothy & Blocker Trant, Innkeepers   *888-271-7985*
Sign language "spoken"   *FAX 409-779-1040*
EMAIL *btrant@myriad.net*
WEBSITE *www.texassleepaways.com/bonniegambrel*

LOCATION	Exit Highway 6 at William J. Bryan, head west to Preston, then go south to the corner of Preston and East 27th Street.
OPEN	All year
DESCRIPTION	A 1913 two-story Dutch colonial host home with a gambrel roof and wraparound porches, decorated with comfortable antiques and tasteful reproductions. Listed on the National Historic Register.
NO. OF ROOMS	Three rooms with private bathrooms and two rooms share two bathrooms. Try the Gregorian Suite or the Carriage House.
RATES	Year-round rates are $100-125 for a single or double with a private bathroom and $50-90 for a single or double with a shared bathroom. There is no minimum stay and cancellation requires one month's notice during high season (April, May, and September through December), two weeks the rest of the year.
CREDIT CARDS	Discover, MasterCard, Visa
BREAKFAST	Full breakfast is served in the dining room and includes home-baked breads, muffins, seasonal fruit, meats, eggs, cheese dishes, coffee, and tea. Special meals are available with advance notice.

Bonnie Gambrel Bed & Breakfast, Bryan

AMENITIES	Pool, exercise room, hot tub, concert grand piano, TVs in rooms, homemade cookies and coffee for early risers, central heat and air conditioning, reading materials, gazebo, fax and copy machines, typewriters, washer/dryer, picnic area in backyard.
RESTRICTIONS	No smoking, no pets. "We love babies and are set up to accommodate them. Children must be potty trained if not in a crib, and controlled by parents."
MEMBER	Bed & Breakfast Association of the Brazos Valley
RATED	1996, Christmas Lighting Award, Historical Home Division, City of Bryan

COUNTRY ROADS BED & BREAKFAST

4965 Rabbit Lane, Bryan, TX 77808   409-778-6695

THE DANSBY GUESTHOUSE

611 East 29th Street, Bryan, TX 77803   409-779-1997
WEBSITE www.texassleepaways.com/dansby   888-422-1997

REVEILLE INN

4400 Old College Road, Bryan, TX 77803
409-846-0858
EMAIL *howdy@reveilleinn.com*
WEBSITE *www.reveilleinn.com*

THE RITCHEY RANCH B&B

5025 Wallis Road, Bryan, TX 77808
409-778-7566
Kay Ritchey, Innkeeper
FAX 409-778-7567
EMAIL *stay@ritcheyranch.com*
WEBSITE *www.ritcheyranch.com*

LOCATION	From Bryan/College Station, go north on Highway 6. Take the Highway 21 (US 290) exit, turn right onto Highway 21, and go 2 miles. Turn right onto Wallis Road, go 0.9 mile, and turn left. Go 0.5 mile and look for the Texas flag flying on a flagpole in the front yard.
OPEN	All year
DESCRIPTION	A 1921 country farmhouse with Texas country decor, situated on a 160-acre working cattle ranch with a 6-acre lake.
NO. OF ROOMS	Two rooms with private bathrooms. Try the Lakeside Suite.
RATES	Year-round rates are $85-125 for a single or double. There is a minimum stay during Texas A&M events and cancellation requires two weeks' notice.
BREAKFAST	Full breakfast is served in the guestrooms and includes homemade muffins and breads, hot and cold cereals, milk, juices, tea, cocoa, cider, and fruit.
AMENITIES	Fresh flowers, one suite with clawfoot tub for soaking and a fireplace in the living room, spacious decks for lounging, porch swings on verandas, fishing and hiking, arched wooden bridges over lake, snack at check-in, both suites climate controlled.
RESTRICTIONS	No smoking, no pets. Honea is the resident collie; Blackie is the cat; and there are numerous Brangus cattle on the property. "Honea will sometimes sleep at your door, providing that extra sense of security. The cat, Blackie, is very independent and prefers to stroll from our house, through the barns, to the guesthouse."
REVIEWED	*The Texas Monthly: Texas Bed & Breakfast*
MEMBER	Bed & Breakfast Association of the Brazos Valley

THE VILLA AT MESSINA HOF

4545 Old Reliance Road, Bryan, TX 77808   409-778-9463
The Bonarrigos, Innkeepers   800-736-9463
EMAIL villa@messinahof.com   FAX 409-778-1729
WEBSITE www.messinahof.com/vintor.htm

LOCATION	Two miles east of Highway 6 on the north side of Old Reliance Road, 5 miles east of the center of Bryan.
OPEN	All year
DESCRIPTION	A 1999 two-story European-style country inn decorated with European antiques, overlooking a beautiful 40-acre vineyard.
NO. OF ROOMS	Ten rooms with private bathrooms.
RATES	Year-round rates are $140-250 for a single or double. There is a minimum stay during special local events and cancellation requires seven days' notice.
CREDIT CARDS	American Express, MasterCard, Visa
BREAKFAST	Continental plus is served in the dining room or guestrooms and includes fine meats, imported cheeses, breads, pastries, Messina Hof jellies and chocolate sauces, fruits, a signature blend of coffee, juices, and tea. Lunch and dinner are also available.
AMENITIES	Wine and cheese served each evening, fresh flowers, pillow chocolates, coffee-makers in rooms, refrigerator, telephone, TV, hair dryers, iron and ironing board, extra-large towels, terry-cloth robes, daily newspaper, private lake with bass and catfish, winery tours and tastings, off-street parking, air conditioning and heat, handicapped accessible, rose garden, marble baths.
RESTRICTIONS	No smoking, no pets. There are Muscovy ducks on the lake and property.

WILDERNESS BED & BREAKFAST

3200 Wilderness Road, Bryan, TX 77807   409-779-0675
James W. Carter, Innkeeper   800-899-4538
Spanish spoken   FAX 520-441-8475
EMAIL JWCARTER@mail.tca.net
WEBSITE PersonalWebs.myriad.net/JWCARTER/index.html

LOCATION	On the west side of College Station, off the West Bypass, FM 2818. Follow signs to the George Bush Presidential Library. From the north, turn right at the Bryan–College Station city limits sign onto Gabbard. From the south, pass George Bush Drive, go 2 miles, and turn left onto Gabbard Road at the city limit signs. Wilderness Road is the second street on the right.

OPEN	All year
DESCRIPTION	A 1981 two-story Spanish stucco host home with red tile. The hosts are retired after 35 years in the Foreign Service. The decor reflects their world travels and includes many oriental antiques.
NO. OF ROOMS	One room with a private bathroom and two rooms share one bathroom.
RATES	Year-round rates are $75 for a single or double with a private bathroom and $60 for a single or double with a shared bathroom. Rates during special Texas A&M events are slightly more. There is no minimum stay and cancellation requires seven days' notice.
CREDIT CARDS	American Express, Discover, MasterCard, Visa
BREAKFAST	Full Texas- or Canadian-style breakfast is cooked to order and includes eggs, bacon or sausage, toast, buckwheat cakes, fresh-baked rolls, a choice of cereals, juice, coffee, milk, and tea.
AMENITIES	Guests are welcome to full use of the house, including a special guest lounge with TV and library; deck in back, swing in the grove; robes in all rooms; complimentary beverages and snacks in the evenings.
RESTRICTIONS	No smoking, no pets, children over 12 are welcome. The house is not handicapped accessible. Beauregard, Shelly, and Jazz are the resident pooches. "They enjoy guests, but are not pests. They bark the first time someone comes to the door."
MEMBER	Bed & Breakfast Texas Style

BUCHANAN DAM

On the southern shore of Lake Buchanan in the Texas Hill Country, Buchanan Dam is about 70 miles northwest of Austin on Highway 29. Explore Longhorn Caverns, an old hideout for Texas bandits, and Inks State Park. Further to the southwest, Enchanted Rock State Park is also well worth a visit.

MYSTIC COVE

Route 1, Box 309B, Buchanan Dam, TX 78609　　　　512-793-6642
Bill & Sue Roming & Shirley Lingerfelt, Innkeepers　　FAX 512-793-6659

LOCATION	About 4.5 miles north of Highway 29 on Highway 261.
OPEN	All year
DESCRIPTION	A 1987 two-story rock and cedar ranch house with western decor and views of Lake Buchanan.

NO. OF ROOMS	Two rooms in the main house with private bathrooms and two guesthouses with private bathrooms.
RATES	Year-round rates are $65-105 for a single or double. There is a minimum stay required on weekends and holidays, and cancellation requires seven days' notice.
CREDIT CARDS	No
BREAKFAST	Continental breakfast is served in the main house dining room.
AMENITIES	Lake front, air conditioning, porches and decks, hot tub, sandy beach, room in the main house has a sun porch, wood-burning stove, flotation tank, boathouse with dock.
RESTRICTIONS	No smoking, no pets, children over 12 are welcome.

BUFFALO GAP

BUFFALO GAP BED & BREAKFAST

Highway 89, Buffalo Gap, TX 79508   915-572-3145

BULVERDE

HOMESTEAD BED & BREAKFAST

1324 Bulverde Road, Bulverde, TX 78163   830-980-2571
WEBSITE *www.bnbtexasstyle.com*   800-899-4538

BURNET

In the Highland Lakes area of the Texas Hill Country, Burnet is 62 miles northwest of Austin via I-35 and Highway 29. In April, Burnet hosts the annual Bluebonnet Festival. A restored vintage steam train makes two excursions from Austin to Burnet each weekend. Other area attractions include Longhorn Caverns, Inks State Park, Old Fort Crogan, and Lake Buchanan.

AIRY MOUNT INN

PO Box 351, Burnet, TX 78611   *512-756-4149*
Charles & Rosanne Hayman, Innkeepers   *FAX 512-756-5135*
Limited Spanish and French spoken
EMAIL arimount@tstar.net
WEBSITE www.b&bgetaways.com

LOCATION	One mile east of Burnet on Highway 29.
OPEN	All year
DESCRIPTION	An 1878 rustic two-story Texas limestone inn with a wraparound porch, constructed by a Confederate general, situated on a hilly pasture in the Texas Hill Country. Listed on the National Historic Register.
NO. OF ROOMS	Three rooms with private bathrooms.
RATES	Year-round rates are $95-120 for a single or double. Cancellation requires four days' notice.
CREDIT CARDS	MasterCard, Visa

Airy Mount Inn, Burnet

BREAKFAST	Full gourmet breakfast is served by candlelight in the dining room and includes fresh fruit, homemade breads, muffins, cinnamon rolls, and assorted entrées, with bacon, potatoes, orange juice, and coffee.
AMENITIES	TV/VCRs in rooms, video library, washer/dryer, porch with barbecue, space for large parties in main house.
RESTRICTIONS	No smoking, no pets, children over five are welcome. Jake, Pepper, and Queenie are the resident pooches.
REVIEWED	A *Lady's Day Out; Texas Bed & Breakfast; The Complete Guide to Bed & Breakfasts, Inns and Guesthouses in the United States, Canada & Worldwide*
MEMBER	Texas Register of Historic Landmarks
KUDOS/COMMENTS	"Hostess is charming."

POST OAK FARM

1019 Hoover Valley Road, Burnet, TX 78611   512-756-4647
Helen Candler Miller, Innkeeper
Spanish (poquito) spoken
EMAIL *hcm@postoakfarm.com*
WEBSITE *www.postoakfarm.com*

LOCATION	From the intersection of Highways 29 and 281 in Burnet, take Highway 29 west 2 miles to County Road 116. Turn left, go 0.8 mile, turn left, and drive about 0.3 mile to the main house.
OPEN	All year
DESCRIPTION	A 1908 country farmhouse decorated with country antiques and situated on a 450-acre working ranch/farm.
NO. OF ROOMS	Three rooms with private bathrooms.
RATES	Year-round rate is $85 for a single or double. There is no minimum stay. No deposit is required.
BREAKFAST	Full country breakfast is served in the dining room and includes fresh fruit and juice, biscuits, French toast, scrambled eggs, bacon, and sausage. Coffee is served from 6 a.m. Guests have full use of the kitchen.
AMENITIES	Large screened-in swimming pool, horseback riding and lessons, air conditioning, fireplace in the living room, ceiling fans, large screened-in porch.
RESTRICTIONS	No smoking. Emma, Riley, and Josie are the resident pooches. The property is populated by five riding horses, one stallion, and brood mares.
MEMBER	Texas Hotel & Motel Association

ROCKY REST BED & BREAKFAST

404 South Water Street, Burnet, TX 78611   512-756-2600
Epifania Sheppard, Resident Owner

KUDOS/COMMENTS   "Nice old rock home, historic, hostess Fannie Sheppard was
                 gracious and friendly."

WILLIAMS POINT

1326 Lakeside Drive, Burnet, TX 78611   512-756-2074
Art & Pauline Williams, Innkeepers

LOCATION   From Highway 281 between Burnet and Marble Falls, take Park
                 Road 4 west to Rural Road 2342. Turn left and go 1 mile and watch
                 for the Williams Point sign at County Road 135. Turn right and
                 follow the sign.

OPEN   All year

DESCRIPTION   A 1979 one-and-a-half-story country home on the shores of Lake
                 LBJ, situated at the point where Williams Creek enters the
                 Colorado River and Lake LBJ.

NO. OF ROOMS   Two rooms with private bathrooms.

RATES   March through November, the rate is $55 for a single or double.
                 December through February, the rate is $45 for a single or double.
                 There is no minimum stay. Ask about a cancellation policy.

CREDIT CARDS   No

BREAKFAST   Choice of continental or full breakfast is served in the dining room.
                 Continental includes juice, fresh fruit, toast, rolls, banana bread.
                 Add eggs with ham or sausage for a full breakfast.

AMENITIES   Barbecue pit, boathouse with rooftop deck for sunning and
                 stargazing, fishing and boat docks.

RESTRICTIONS   No smoking, no pets. Baby is the resident rat terrier.

BURTON

Halfway between Houston and Austin on Highway 290, Burton has a wonderful historic district that features the Burton Cotton Gin Museum. The Cotton Gin Festival is the third weekend in April. Satisfy your sweet tooth at Blue Bell creamery and hunt for treasure at the Antique Rose Emporium.

THE COTTAGE AT CEDAR CREEK

6005 Lorena Lane, Burton, TX 77835   *409-278-3770*
Lorena Ricks, Resident Owner
EMAIL lmricks@phoenix.net

LOCATION	Take Highway 290 (2 miles west of Burton) to Highway 237 and head toward Round Top and LaGrange. Go 2 miles west to Hinze Road. Take a right onto the second gravel road.
OPEN	All year
DESCRIPTION	A restored 1900 Victorian cottage on 160 acres, furnished with locally made antiques.
NO. OF ROOMS	A private two-room cottage with a private bathroom.
RATES	The entire cottage rents for $90-150. There is a three-night minimum stay required during the spring and fall antique fairs.
CREDIT CARDS	No
BREAKFAST	Full breakfast is served either in the dining room or the guestrooms and includes juice, fruit, homemade breads, sausage or bacon, eggs, and French toast.
AMENITIES	Central heat and air conditioning, flowers, gardens, creeks, and ponds.
RESTRICTIONS	No smoking, no pets, no children

KNITTEL HOMESTEAD INN

520 North Main Street, Burton, TX 77835   *409-289-5102*
Steve & Cindy Miller, Innkeepers   *FAX 409-289-5102*

LOCATION	Located in the center of town at the corner of Main and Washington, across from Burton State Bank. Burton is halfway between Houston and Austin on Highway 290.
OPEN	All year

Knittel Homestead Inn, Burton

DESCRIPTION	An 1870 two-story Queen Anne Victorian inn that resembles a Mississippi steamboat with wraparound porches, decorated with antiques and country furnishings. Listed on the National Historic Register.
NO. OF ROOMS	Three rooms with private bathrooms. Try the Rose Room.
RATES	Year-round rates are $80-90 for a single or double. There is a minimum stay during certain festival weekends in the spring and cancellation requires two weeks' notice.
CREDIT CARDS	No
BREAKFAST	All-you-can-eat country breakfast is served on Sunday mornings in the dining room, and at Burton Cafe (owned by the innkeepers) on Monday through Saturday. Breakfast features fresh fruit, egg dishes, pancakes, deluxe French toast, bacon or sausage, biscuits and gravy.
AMENITIES	Central heat and air conditioning; home-baked treats; coffee, tea, sodas, and juices; access to TV/VCR, movies; games; books; magazines; fragranced soaps and bubble baths, cordless telephone.
RESTRICTIONS	No smoking, no pets, children over the age of 12 are welcome.
REVIEWED	*The Texas Monthly: Texas Bed & Breakfast, Recommended Country Inns—The Southwest*
MEMBER	Texas Hotel & Motel Association, Washington County Bed & Breakfast Association

Long Point Inn

Route 1, Box 86-A, Burton, TX 77835   *409-289-3171*

Calvert

The home of Belle Star, Calvert boasts a large and beautiful historic district, with yearly home tours during the first weeks of December and May. Check out the citywide antiques sale during mid-August. The George Bush Presidential Library and Museum at Texas A&M University is about 30 miles south of town on Highway 6. Calvert is 90 miles northeast of Austin on Highway 14.

Calvert Inn Gourmet Bed & Breakfast and Restaurant

400 East Texas Street, Calvert, TX 77837   *409-364-2868*
Frank & Sandy Hudson, Innkeepers   *800-290-1213*
EMAIL *stay@calvertinn*   *FAX 409-364-2667*
WEBSITE *www.calvertinn.com*

LOCATION	From Highway 6, turn east onto Gregg Street, cross the railroad tracks, go 3 blocks, and at the little church turn right onto Elm.
OPEN	All year
DESCRIPTION	A grand 1905 two-story Victorian plantation inn, built with cypress wood, with two wraparound porches, chandeliers, natural woodwork, wainscoting, a magnificent staircase, and decorated with antiques and Victorian furnishings.
NO. OF ROOMS	Three rooms with private bathrooms. Try the Honeymoon Room.
RATES	Year-round rate is $105 for a single or double. There is a minimum stay during university events and cancellation requires seven days' notice, three weeks during major university events. There is no charge if the room can be rebooked.
CREDIT CARDS	American Express, Discover, MasterCard, Visa
BREAKFAST	Full gourmet breakfast is served in the dining room and might include Hawaiian-baked banana with mango and kiwi, German apple pancake with warm butterscotch sauce, and eggs sardou with warm muffins. Three-course luncheons and five-course dinners are available with a reservation.

THE PINK HOUSE

808 Pin Oak, Calvert, TX 77837   409-364-2868
WEBSITE www.calvertinn.com

THE PROCTOR HOUSE

508 East Gregg, Calvert, TX 77837   409-364-3702

CANADIAN

THE THICKET

Route 3, Box 15A, Canadian, TX 79014   806-323-8118

CANTON

The big event here is Canton's First Monday Trades Days, a gigantic monthly swap meet, flea market, and antique sale held the weekend before the first Monday of each month. The event is billed as the largest of its kind in the world. Nearby attractions include Purtis Creek State Park, Cedar Creek Lake, and Tyler Rose Gardens and Azalea Trails. Keep an ear out for frequent bluegrass festivals. Canton is about one hour east of Dallas, via I-20.

ANTIQUE ARABIANS B&B

FM 3227, Canton, TX 75103   903-848-9425
R.L. & Edie Booth, Resident Owners
A little German, a little Spanish spoken
EMAIL desertbred@usa.net

LOCATION	In Canton, from the intersection of Highways 243 and 198, take Highway 198 south for 3.5 miles. Turn right on FM 3227 and go 1.5 miles to the entrance on the left.
OPEN	All year
DESCRIPTION	A 1975 southern ranch-style guesthouse on a 134-acre horse farm.
NO. OF ROOMS	Guesthouse has two rooms and two bathrooms.
RATES	March through June and September through December, the rate for a single or a double is $75. During the low season, January, February, July, and August, the rate is $60. There is no minimum stay and cancellation requires seven days' notice less a 10 percent fee.
CREDIT CARDS	No
BREAKFAST	Continental breakfast is served and includes pastries, fresh fruit, toast, jam, juice, and coffee.
AMENITIES	Fully equipped kitchen, fireplace, central heat and air conditioning, washer/dryer, TV, fishing in several stock-tanks, bird-watching, and walks around the property.
RESTRICTIONS	Smoking on porches only, no pets. Resident animals include 21 horses, a roving peacock, assorted fowl, four cats, and five hounds.

BUFFALO COTTAGE

991 Buffalo Street, Canton, TX 75103   903-567-6633
Judy Tillinghast, Innkeeper

LOCATION	From I-20, take Highway 64 for 5 miles into Canton and to the town square. Turn right onto Buffalo Street.
OPEN	All year
DESCRIPTION	A 1938 cottage with a covered brick patio, beveled French doors, and furnished with antiques and country French decor.
NO. OF ROOMS	Three rooms share two bathrooms.
RATES	Year-round rate is $65 for a single or double. There is no minimum stay.
CREDIT CARDS	No
BREAKFAST	Full breakfast is served in the dining room and includes juice, fruit, French toast, egg casserole or other egg dishes, and rolls.
RESTRICTIONS	No smoking, no pets, children over 15 are welcome. There are two dogs and two cats in residence.

BUNNY HOLLOW INN

901 West Dallas, Canton, TX 75103   903-567-4854
Treva Burns, Resident Owner   800-246-5313

COUNTRY LIVING BED & BREAKFAST

Route 1, Box 147B, Canton, TX 75103   903-848-1027
Ida Mae McCain, Resident Owner   800-460-9027

GENESIS RANCH

Route 4, Box 376, Canton, TX 75103   903-479-3695
Connie & Bob Reese, Resident Owners

HEAVENLY ACRES GUEST RANCH

Route 3, Box 470, Mabank, TX 75147   903-887-3016
Diana & Bruce Avellanet, Innkeepers   800-283-0341
WEBSITE www.heavenlyacres.com   FAX 903-887-1573

LOCATION	Twelve miles southwest of Canton off of Highway 198.
OPEN	All year
DESCRIPTION	Four cabins, each with their own distinct decor, located on a 100-acre ranch.
NO. OF ROOMS	Four cabins with full kitchens and private bathrooms.
RATES	Cabins are $104 for a single or double. Cancellation requires seven days' notice, 60 days for large groups.
CREDIT CARDS	American Express, Discover, MasterCard, Visa
BREAKFAST	Full country breakfast baskets are delivered to the cabins.
AMENITIES	Two private fishing lakes; small motorized boats and paddleboats; a "petting zoo" with potbellied pigs, acrobatic goats, and chickens; meeting and dining hall available for groups. Cabins are equipped with TV/VCRs and video library, gourmet coffee and teas, homemade cinnamon rolls upon request.
RESTRICTIONS	No smoking, no pets. Children are welcome. The potbellied pigs are named Peaches and Elvira.
REVIEWED	*Texas Bed & Breakfast*
MEMBER	Bed & Breakfast Texas Style, Canton's Bed & Breakfast Association
KUDOS/COMMENTS	"A great get-away from the city."

REED'S BED & BATH

1450 South Buffalo, Canton, TX 75103   903-567-4733
Patrice Reed, Resident Owner

SALINE CREEK FARM B&B

182 Van Zandt County Road 1316, Canton, TX 75140   *903-829-2709*
Karen Franks, Innkeeper   *800-308-2242*
EMAIL kfranks@vzinet.com   *FAX 903-829-2086*
WEBSITE www.bbhost.com/salinecreekfarm

LOCATION
: Approximately 1 hour from Dallas, via I-20 east. Continue on I-20, 2 exits past Canton to FM 1255. At the stop sign, turn left, and continue north on FM 1255 for approximately 5.5 miles. Watch for County Road 1316, which will come in from the right. Turn right at the first drive on the right.

OPEN
: All year

DESCRIPTION
: A 1988 two-story traditional country inn and cabins with country and Victorian decor.

NO. OF ROOMS
: Five rooms with private bathrooms and two rooms share one bathroom.

RATES
: Year-round rates are $85-125 for a single or double with a private bathroom and $75-125 for a single or double with a shared bathroom. There is a minimum stay during some Canton Trades Days weekends and cancellation requires seven days' notice.

CREDIT CARDS
: American Express, Discover, MasterCard, Visa

BREAKFAST
: Full breakfast is served in the dining hall. A typical breakfast includes an egg dish, breakfast meat, homemade muffins, breads, or sweet rolls, fresh fruit, coffee, tea, hot chocolate, and juices. Special dietary needs (low-fat and diabetic) can be accommodated with advance notice.

AMENITIES
: Each cabin includes a refreshment center with teas, hot chocolate, microwave, popcorn, and soft drinks; private lake stocked with large bass and catfish (please bring your own fishing equipment); separate dining hall, which seats up to 20, available for meetings, wedding receptions, and special occasions; the cowboy cabin overlooks the private fishing lake and has TV/VCR, full-size refrigerator, and coffee-maker.

RESTRICTIONS
: No smoking, no pets, no children. Gizzie is the resident Pekingese. "Gizzie is an old dog, partially blind and deaf. She is outside most of the time and appreciates not being startled as she sleeps a lot. Sometimes cantankerous, best not to pet her."

MEMBER
: Texas Hotel & Motel Association, East Texas Bed & Breakfast Association

THE WIND SOCK INN

Route 3, Box 60B, Canton, TX 75103   *903-848-0618*
Hugh & Ann Thornton, Resident Owners   *800-476-2038*
EMAIL *windsock@gte.net*   *FAX 903-848-7013*

LOCATION	From Canton's Courthouse Square, turn right on Highway 198 and drive 7 miles to FM 1651. Turn left and go 2 miles to the inn on the left.
OPEN	All year
DESCRIPTION	A 1994 ranch-style country inn situated on 33 acres.
NO. OF ROOMS	Six rooms with private bathrooms and one room with a shared bathroom. Plus two, two-bedroom cottages.
RATES	Year-round rate for a single or double with a private bathroom is $85 plus $20 per additional person. There is a two-night minimum stay and cancellation requires seven days' notice.
CREDIT CARDS	American Express, Discover, MasterCard, Visa
BREAKFAST	Full breakfast is served in the dining room and includes a breakfast casserole, three kinds of cereal, fresh fruit, yogurt, fresh-baked muffins, sweet rolls, bagels, two kind of juice, coffee, tea, and cocoa.
AMENITIES	Fresh flowers in every room, gift basket of toiletries in each bathroom, special requests for birthdays and anniversaries, evening dessert and coffee.
RESTRICTIONS	No smoking, no pets, well-behaved children are welcome. Cribs and high chairs are available.
MEMBER	Bed & Breakfast Texas Style, Texas Hotel & Motel Association

WINDMILL

Route 6, Box 449, Canton, TX 75103   *903-567-2769*
George & Naoma Turner, Resident Owners

CANYON

Fifteen miles south of Amarillo, via I-27 and Highway 87, Canyon is 10 miles west of Palo Duro Canyon. Sit beneath the canyon walls and enjoy the musical drama "Texas." Other local points of interest include the Panhandle Plains Historical Museum and the Creekwood Ranch Wild West Show. The Fair on the Square is held the first weekend in October.

COUNTRY HOME BED & BREAKFAST

Route 1, Box 447, Canyon, TX 79015   806-655-7636
Tammy Money-Brooks, Innkeeper   800-664-7636
EMAIL countryhome@amaonline.com
WEBSITE www.us.worldpages.com/

LOCATION	Located 15 miles south of Amarillo. Take I-27 south to Canyon, turn right on 4th Avenue, then turn left on 8th Street. Go 1.3 miles and the B&B is on the right.
OPEN	All year
DESCRIPTION	A 1990 one-and-a-half-story country Victorian host home with a 60-foot front porch and elegant country decor, situated on a 200-acre ranch.
NO. OF ROOMS	Two rooms share one-and-a-half bathrooms.
RATES	Year-round rate is $95 for a single or double. There is no minimum stay. Ask about a cancellation policy.
CREDIT CARDS	American Express, Discover, MasterCard, Visa
BREAKFAST	Full breakfast is served in the dining room and includes sausage quiche, puffed peach pancakes, baked apples, coffee, and juice. Special meals can be prepared for banquets or receptions.

Country Home Bed & Breakfast, Canyon

AMENITIES	Wedding specialists (wedding packages, gazebo, 200 white chairs, tables, linens, centerpieces, cakes, catering, live music, DJs, dances, photographers, horse and carriage, honeymoon suite with hot tub), horse barn, horse boarding, sun room, front porch with rockers and swing.
RESTRICTIONS	No smoking, no pets, no children. The resident animals include four Himalayan cats (Hansel, Gretel, Jack, and Jill) and 24 chickens.
REVIEWED	*Recommended Country Inns—The Southwest*
MEMBER	Texas Hotel & Motel Association
RATED	Mobil 3 Stars
KUDOS/COMMENTS	"Wonderful hospitality! Great food."

HUDSPETH HOUSE BED & BREAKFAST

1905 4th Avenue, Canyon, TX 79015   806-655-9800
Mark & Mary, Resident Owners   800-655-9809
WEBSITE *www.hudspethinn.com*   FAX 806-655-7457

LOCATION	In greater downtown Canyon
OPEN	All year
DESCRIPTION	A 1909 three-story prairie-style inn, listed on the State Historic Register. This 8,200-square-foot boarding house was once used as faculty housing for the university.
NO. OF ROOMS	Eight rooms with private bathrooms. Georgia O'Keefe took meals in the house with Miss Hudspeth.
RATES	Summer rates are $65-110. The remainder of the year rates are $55-95. There is no minimum stay and cancellation requires seven days' notice for weekend reservations, 24 hours for weekdays.
CREDIT CARDS	American Express, Diners Club, Discover, MasterCard, Visa
BREAKFAST	Full breakfast is served in the dining room and includes pancakes or French toast, bacon, coffee, teas, orange juice, and fruit.
AMENITIES	Hot tub, all rooms have air conditioning and cable TVs.
RESTRICTIONS	No smoking, no pets
MEMBER	Texas Hotel & Motel Association

THE RANCH HOUSE BED & BREAKFAST

Route 1, Box 436, Canyon, TX 79015   806-655-0339
Janice & Laddie Cluck, Resident Owners

CARMINE

Don't miss Shakespeare at Winedale, Festival Hill Concerts at Round Top, and antique shows during the first weekends of April and October. Carmine is about 20 miles west of Brenham on Highway 290.

SUGAR HILL RETREAT

1 Sugar Hill Lane, Carmine, TX 78932   409-278-3039
Reuben & Diana Wunderlich, Resident Owners

LOCATION	Between the towns of Giddings and Brenham on Highway 290.
OPEN	All year
DESCRIPTION	A renovated 1910 two-story farmhouse.
NO. OF ROOMS	Four rooms share three bathrooms.
RATES	Please inquire about current rates and cancellation information.
CREDIT CARDS	No
BREAKFAST	Full country breakfast is served in the dining room. Special meals are available on request.
AMENITIES	Fresh flowers, picnic area, walking trail in the woods, pond fishing, clawfoot bathtubs, coffee and cold drinks, fireplace.
RESTRICTIONS	No smoking, no pets
MEMBER	Texas Hotel & Motel Association

CAT SPRING

A picture-perfect hamlet 60 miles west of Houston via I-10 and FM 949, Cat Spring allegedly was named by a very literal German settler who saw a wildcat drinking from a spring. Sounds plausible enough. The Salt-Grass Trail Ride begins here and ends many miles later at the Houston Rodeo.

SOUTHWIND BED & BREAKFAST

14022 Sycamore Road, Cat Spring, TX 78933   *409-992-3270*
Sunny & John Snyder, Resident Owners   *FAX 409-992-3270*
Spanish spoken
EMAIL snyder@c-com.net
WEBSITE www.c-com.net/~snyder

LOCATION	Head north on Highway 36 through Sealy for 1.3 miles to FM 1094 (at the fourth traffic light). Turn left on FM 1094 and drive 11.1 miles to Hall Road (just past the intersection of FM 1094 and FM 949). Turn right on Hall Road and drive 0.5 mile, turn right again onto Sycamore, and go 0.4 mile to Southwind.
OPEN	All year
DESCRIPTION	A converted Dutch barn host home and a restored early Texas cabin decorated with antiques and rustic country furnishings. The B&B is also a horse farm and has facilities to accommodate those traveling with horses.
NO. OF ROOMS	Two rooms with private bathrooms. Try the cabin.
RATES	Year-round rates are $75 for a single or double and $65-125 for the cabin. There is no minimum stay and cancellation requires seven days' notice.
CREDIT CARDS	MasterCard, Visa
BREAKFAST	Full breakfast is served in the dining room and includes two main entrées (eggs, meat, fresh blueberry French toast, waffles, hotcakes), homemade biscuits, homemade jams and toppings, fresh fruit, juice, coffee, tea and milk. Diabetic or low-fat meals are available with advance notice.
AMENITIES	Fresh flowers; wine, beer, or soft drinks, and cheese upon arrival; central air conditioning and heat; ceiling fans; each unit has its own refrigerator and private entrance; walking trails; handicapped accessible.
RESTRICTIONS	No smoking, no pets. There is a stable for boarding horses. There are horses and Texas longhorn cattle on the property.
REVIEWED	*Day Trips from Houston*

CENTER POINT

About an hour northeast of San Antonio via I-10 and Highway 27, Center Point is just 10 miles south of Kerrville and close to Fredericksburg. Take in the Cowboy Artist Museum; go on Mooney Aircraft Tours or the Kerrville Camera Safari. Lost Maples State Park and Kerrville State Recreation Area are close at hand.

MARIANNE'S BED & BREAKFAST

Route 1, Box 527, Center Point, TX 78010   830-634-7489
Marianne Zuercher, Resident Owner
German spoken

LOCATION	Nine miles east of Kerrville.
OPEN	All year
DESCRIPTION	A 1965 brick ranch house surrounded by 18 acres. Also a 1994 one-bedroom cottage.
NO. OF ROOMS	Two rooms and a cottage with private bathrooms.
RATES	April through September, a single or double is $70-90. October through March, rates are $65-80.
CREDIT CARDS	No
BREAKFAST	Full breakfast is served in the dining room and includes homemade cinnamon rolls or breads, omelets, Belgian waffles, crepes, brown-sugar bacon, sausage, casseroles, homemade jams and jellies.
AMENITIES	Hot tub, patio, sheep and baby lambs wander the ranch. Observe wild birds and deer, fish for catfish in the pond, share recipes with Marianne.
RESTRICTIONS	No smoking except in patio area. Pets and children are welcome.
REVIEWED	*Texas Bed & Breakfast*
MEMBER	Texas Hotel & Motel Association

CHAPPELL HILL

More than 25 homes in this quiet rural town bear Texas Historical Markers.
Check out the Scarecrow Festival in October and the Blue Bonnet Festival in
April. Chappell Hill is about a dozen miles east of Brenham off Highway 290.

THE BROWNING PLANTATION

9050 Browning Street, Chappell Hill, TX 77426   *409-836-6144*
Waddy & Marilyn Wadkins, Innkeepers   *888-912-6144*
EMAIL *plantation1@email.msn.com*   *FAX 409-251-9609*
WEBSITE *www.browningplantation.com*

LOCATION	On Highway 290 between Brenham and Hempstead. Take FM 1155 to Chappell Hill. At the stop sign, turn left, go 100 feet, and turn right. The plantation is 0.5 mile down the lane.
OPEN	All year
DESCRIPTION	A large, three-story pre-civil war Greek revival plantation home, meticulously restored and furnished with 19th century antiques, resting on 200 acres with lawns and gardens. Listed on both the National and State Historic Registers.
NO. OF ROOMS	Five rooms with private bathrooms in the main house. There are two rooms with private bathrooms in the cabin.
RATES	Year-round weekend rate for a single or double is $110. Rooms in the cabin are $85 on weekends. Midweek rates are 10 percent less.
CREDIT CARDS	American Express, Discover, MasterCard, Visa
BREAKFAST	Full southern breakfast is served in the formal dining room and includes homemade biscuits and jelly, fresh fruit, meats, eggs and grits. Special meals are available.
AMENITIES	Swimming pool, air conditioning, hammock, swing, piano, drinks in the library, stargazing on top of the house, spa, fishing, flower gardens.
RESTRICTIONS	No smoking, no pets, children are welcome.
REVIEWED	*Best Places to Stay in the Southwest, The National Trust Guide to Historic Bed & Breakfast Inns & Small Hotels, Recommended Romantic Inns of America, Texas Bed & Breakfast, Day Trips from Houston, Recommended Country Inns—The Southwest*

CHRISTOVAL

QUAIL CREEK BED & BREAKFAST

HC 63 Box 3, Christoval, TX 76935   915-255-2207

CISCO

A tiny town with a true old-time Texas feel, right down to its courthouse square and "real" corner drugstore. Take in the Folklife Festival in May. Nearby Eastland features the Old Rip Festival in spring and Polo on the Prairie. Cisco is about 50 miles east of Abilene just north of I-20 on Highway 183.

THE GRAY BULL GUEST HOUSE

8826 Highway 6, Cisco, TX 76437   254-442-1046
Carol Stuard, Innkeeper   FAX 254 442-3782
EMAIL clstuard@eastland.net

LOCATION	Halfway between Cisco and Eastland on Highway 6.
OPEN	All year
DESCRIPTION	A 1985 western ranch-style rough cedar guesthouse located on a working Brahman cattle ranch.
NO. OF ROOMS	One room with a private bathroom.
RATES	Year-round rate is $55. There is no minimum stay. Please call by 5 p.m. if canceling.
CREDIT CARDS	No
BREAKFAST	Continental plus is left in the refrigerator and includes coffee, juice, homemade muffins and jelly, and an occasional egg dish.
AMENITIES	Steinway piano in the living room, VCR and videos available upon request, down comforter, complete kitchen (microwave, stove, refrigerator, coffee-maker), handicapped accessible, horse boarding, owner will take guests to see the gray Brahman cattle upon request.
RESTRICTIONS	No smoking, no pets. There are Brahman cattle on the property. "If you are lucky there will be babies during your visit, but there are always a few gentle calves who love to be petted and fed by hand."

CLEBURNE

CLEBURNE HOUSE BED & BREAKFAST

201 North Anglin Street, Cleburne, TX 76031   817-641-0085
Drew & Steve Griffin, Resident Owners

CLEBURNE'S 1896 RAILROAD HOUSE

421 East Henderson Street, Cleburne, TX 76031   817-517-5529

CLIFTON

The Texas state legislature designated Clifton the Norwegian Capital of Texas. Don't miss the county-wide garage sale on the third Saturday in April, FreedomFest on the last Saturday in June, and the Norwegian Country Home Tour on the first Saturday in December. Clifton is about 30 miles northwest of Waco on Highway 6.

COURTNEY HOUSE BED & BREAKFAST

1514 West 5th Street, Clifton, TX 76634   254-675-3061
     800-300-3061

GOODNIGHT STATION

Clifton, TX   254-675-2337

HEART COTTAGE BED & BREAKFAST

Route 1, Box 217, Clifton, TX 76634   254-675-3189
Vivian Ender, Innkeeper   FAX 254-675-3186
EMAIL HeartCottageBNB@htcomp.net
WEBSITE www.htcomp.net/HeartCottageBNB

LOCATION	Five miles east of Clifton on FM 219. Turn left onto Country Road 3242 and drive 0.4 mile to the peach-colored house with green trim, on the right.
OPEN	All year
DESCRIPTION	A 1909 private Victorian guesthouse with contemporary country decor and some antiques, with panoramic views of the rolling hills.
NO. OF ROOMS	One room with a private bathroom.
RATES	Year-round weekend rate is $125 for a single or double. The midweek rate is $85. There is no minimum stay and cancellation requires seven days' notice.
CREDIT CARDS	No
BREAKFAST	Continental breakfast is left in the guesthouse refrigerator and includes juice, fruit, bagels and muffins, cream cheese and butter, milk, coffee, and tea.
AMENITIES	Snacks, cookies or brownies, soft drinks and bottled water, Adirondack chairs on porch, satellite TV/VCR.
RESTRICTIONS	No smoking
REVIEWED	The Texas Monthly: Texas Bed & Breakfast

RIVER'S BEND BED & BREAKFAST

Route 1, Clifton, TX 76634   254-675-4936
Helen Hubler, Innkeeper

LOCATION	About 4 miles from Clifton and 35 miles north of Waco.
OPEN	All year
DESCRIPTION	A 1986 one-story country inn with contemporary decor, situated on a riverbank on a 240-acre farm.
NO. OF ROOMS	One room with a private bathroom and two rooms share one bathroom. Try the River Room.
RATES	Year-round rates are $95-175. There is no minimum stay and cancellation requires two weeks' notice.

CREDIT CARDS	No
BREAKFAST	Full breakfast is stocked in the kitchen and includes homemade breads and muffins, eggs, meat, fruit, juice, cereal, coffee, tea, and hot chocolate.
AMENITIES	Air conditioning, river access, barbecue pits, over 85 species of birds recorded on the 240-acre property by a wildlife photographer.
RESTRICTIONS	No smoking inside. "Can accommodate any animals."
MEMBER	Bed & Breakfast Texas Style

COLLEGE STATION

FLIPPEN PLACE BED & BREAKFAST

1199 Haywood Drive, College Station, TX 77845   *409-696-7930*

TWIN OAKS BED & BREAKFAST

3905 F And B Road, College Station, TX 77845   *409-846-3694*

COLUMBUS

Dating back to 1823, Columbus is the oldest Anglo-American settlement in Texas. The town features four historic house museums, the restored Stafford Opera House and dinner theater, and the world's only Santa Claus museum. The Confederate Museum is in a restored water tower. Enjoy the Springtime Festival in May and the Colorado County Fair in September. From Houston, go 55 miles west on I-10.

MAGNOLIA OAKS AND LITTLE RED HOUSE

630/634 Spring Street, Columbus, TX 78934	*409-732-2726*
Bob & Nancy Stiles, Innkeepers	*FAX 409-733-0872*
EMAIL rmstiles@aol.com	*WEBSITE magnoliaoaks.com*
LOCATION	Take I-10 to exit 696 and drive 8 miles north to the courthouse square. Turn west onto Spring Street and go 2 blocks. Approximately one hour west of Houston.

OPEN	All year
DESCRIPTION	An 1890 Eastlake Victorian inn and an 1865 German saltbox inn decorated with Victorian, Texana, and Americana furnishings, situated on 0.75 acre with magnificent magnolia and oak trees and gardens. Listed on the State Historic Register.
NO. OF ROOMS	Seven rooms with private bathrooms.
RATES	Year-round rates are $80-125 for a single or double and $150 for a suite. There is a minimum stay during the springtime festival and cancellation requires 14 days' notice.
CREDIT CARDS	MasterCard, Visa
BREAKFAST	Full Texas breakfast is served in the dining room and includes an egg dish, breakfast meat, fresh fruit, homemade sweetbreads and biscuits, juices, coffee. The host plays guitar and sings on weekends. Dinner parties and brunch are also available with advance notice.
AMENITIES	Magnolia Oaks bath amenities, robes, flowers, chipping/putting green, croquet, bikes, hundreds of books, Jacuzzi tub in one bath, homemade cookies and drinks in the afternoon, central heat and air conditioning, meeting place available at Hometown Hall on the square for seminars and retreats, garden arbor, fountain, swing, many bird-feeding areas.
RESTRICTIONS	No smoking, no pets. Children are welcome in the Little Red House. Berkley is the resident Maine coon cat.
REVIEWED	*The Great Stays of Texas, Recommended Country Inns—The Southwest, Non-Smokers Guide to Bed & Breakfasts*
MEMBER	Historic Accommodations of Texas

COMANCHE

THE GUEST HOUSE AT HERITAGE HILL

Route 3, Box 221, Comanche, TX 76442   915-356-3397
Harold & Sherry Perkins, Resident Owners   FAX 915-356-5435

COMFORT

Forty-five miles northwest of San Antonio via I-10, Comfort is an unincorporated, rural community located in the heart of the German-pioneered Texas Hill Country, with over 100 pre-1900 buildings on the National Register of Historic Places and 45 antique dealers. The Treue der Union Monument is the only monument to the Union located in the South and one of only six sites in the United States where the flag flies at perpetual half-mast. Cabin Fever Days Antique Sale takes place the first weekend in February. The Comfort Village Antique Show runs the third weekend in October.

BRINKMANN HOUSE BED & BREAKFAST

714 Main Street, Comfort, TX 78013   830-995-3141

CARRINGTON HOUSE BED & BREAKFAST

13 US Highway 87, Comfort, TX 78013   830-995-2220

THE COMFORT COMMON

717 High Street, Comfort, TX 78013   830-995-3030
Jim Lord & Bobby Dent, Innkeepers   FAX 830-995-3455
EMAIL *comfortcommon@hctc.net*
WEBSITE *www.bbhost.com/comfortcommon*

LOCATION	From I-10 east or west, take exit 524 (Highway 27) and drive 1 mile to Comfort. Turn left onto 7th Street, drive 1 block to the four-way stop sign, and turn left onto High Street.
OPEN	All year
DESCRIPTION	An 1880 two-story limestone Victorian country inn with double porches and numerous period dependency buildings including two log cabins. Each room has a different theme, from country to cowboy, garden to Victorian. Listed on the National and State Historic Registers.
NO. OF ROOMS	Nine rooms with private bathrooms. Try the Ingenhuett Suite.
RATES	Year-round rates are $65-75 for a single or double, $80-85 for a suite, and $95-110 for a guesthouse. There is a two-night minimum stay during holidays or special-event weekends, and cancellation requires seven days' notice.

The Comfort Common, Comfort

CREDIT CARDS	American Express, Discover, MasterCard, Visa
BREAKFAST	Full hot breakfast is served in addition to a buffet of fresh fruits, cereals, juices, breads, and muffins.
AMENITIES	Tree-shaded courtyard, gazebo.
RESTRICTIONS	No smoking, no pets, children over 12 are welcome.
REVIEWED	*Fodor's, America's Wonderful Little Hotels and Inns, Travel and Leisure* magazine, *Southern Living, Texas Highways, Texas Bed & Breakfast*
MEMBER	Texas Hotel & Motel Association
KUDOS/COMMENTS	"Old railroad hotel with breakfast buffet at the adjacent cafe. Individualized Victorian rooms, large garden and antique shops."

HAVEN RIVER INN

105 Highway 473, Comfort, TX 78013   830-995-3834
WEBSITE *www.innsite.com/inns/A002179.html*

IDLEWILDE BED & BREAKFAST

115 Highway 473, Comfort, TX 78013   830-995-3844
Connie & Hank Engel, Innkeepers

LOCATION	Forty-five minutes west of San Antonio. Take exit 523 off of I-10 and go south on Highway 87 toward Comfort. At the blinking yellow light, turn left (east) onto Highway 473 and go 1.3 miles.
OPEN	All year
DESCRIPTION	A renovated 1902 ranch house and two private cottages situated on 13 acres. The main house was originally built as a girls' summer camp.
NO. OF ROOMS	Two rooms with private bathrooms. Try the Lighthouse Cottage.
RATES	Year-round rates are $77-93 for a single or double. There is no minimum stay and cancellation requires seven days' notice.
CREDIT CARDS	No
BREAKFAST	Full gourmet breakfast is served by candlelight on fine china with chamber music in the dining room, guestrooms, or on the patio. All dishes are homemade using fresh ingredients. Lunch, dinner, and special meals are also available.
AMENITIES	Large swimming pool, two lighted tennis courts, large pavilion with barbecue pit, horseshoes, children's playground, fresh-cut flowers in rooms, complimentary wine for birthdays and anniversaries.
RESTRICTIONS	No smoking in rooms. Turbo, Sunflower, and Jasmine are the roving potbellied pigs; Pippin is the resident beagle/basset mix; Jordon is the cat; and there are horses and a miniature burro on the property.

Idlewilde Bed & Breakfast, Comfort

REVIEWED   *Great Texas Getaways, Bed & Breakfasts and Country Inns, The Official Guide to American Historic Inns, The Austin Chronicle Day Trips, Texas Bed & Breakfast*

LOVETT'S LANDING BED & BREAKFAST

PO Box 391, Comfort, TX 78013   830-995-2836
WEBSITE *www.lovettslanding.com*

THE MEYER BED & BREAKFAST

845 High Street, Comfort, TX 78013   830-995-2304
Joe Dobbs, Resident Owner
WEBSITE *www.innsite.com/inns/A002322.html*

COMMERCE

BOIS D' ARC BED & BREAKFAST

2212 Charity Road, Commerce, TX 75428   903-886-7705

CHAPIN HOUSE

1405 Monroe Street, Commerce, TX 75428   903-886-6713
WEBSITE *www.webvalley.com/chapinhous/index.html*

CONCAN

REAGAN WELLS RANCH

HCR 32 Box 118A, Concan, TX 78801
EMAIL sc1@flash.net

800-277-6265
WEBSITE www.reaganwells.com

CONROE

Forty miles north of Houston off I-45, Conroe kicks up its heels for several local festivals, including Boogie on the Black Top, Old Frontier Days, and the Crawfish Festival. Outdoor recreation is a stone's throw away at Lake Conroe.

HEATHER'S GLEN—
A BED & BREAKFAST AND MORE

200 East Phillips, Conroe, TX 77301
Ed & Jamie George, Resident Owners
Some Spanish spoken

409-441-6611
800-665-2643
FAX 409-441-6603

LOCATION	Two blocks from downtown Conroe.
OPEN	All year
DESCRIPTION	A 1900 three-story Victorian mansion furnished with antiques.
NO. OF ROOMS	Five rooms with private bathrooms.
RATES	Year-round rates for a single or a double are $65-95. There is no minimum stay, and cancellation requires five days' notice.
CREDIT CARDS	American Express, Discover, MasterCard, Visa
BREAKFAST	Continental plus is served in the dining room or on the veranda and may include Belgian waffles with fresh strawberries and whipped cream, meat selection, fresh fruit and breads. Special meals may be available upon request.
AMENITIES	Jacuzzi bathtubs for two in individual bathrooms, air conditioning, TV and telephones in each room, fresh-baked goods, fruits, soft drinks and juices continuously available.
RESTRICTIONS	No smoking, children over the age of 12 are welcome. A golden retriever, Morgan, and several birds share the premises, including a talking cockatiel named Peaches who visits with the guests.

MEMBER	Texas Hotel & Motel Association
RATED	AAA 2 Diamonds
KUDOS/COMMENTS	"Beautiful decor with a warm, friendly operator." "Beautifully restored Victorian. Jamie is outgoing and bubbly."

CORPUS CHRISTI

At the tip of Padre Island National Seashore, Corpus Christi is home to the recrafted Columbus ships and the USS Lexington aircraft carrier. Explore Mustang Island State Park, where bird-watching and windsurfing are top notch.

BAY BREEZE BED & BREAKFAST

201 Louisiana Parkway, Corpus Christi, TX 78404   *512-882-4123*

THE COLLEY HOUSE

211 Indiana, Corpus Christi, TX 78404   *512-887-7514*
WEBSITE www.austinite.com/colleyhouse

KUDOS/COMMENTS "Older home tastefully decorated with antiques. Very gracious hosts."

GINGER ROSE

7030 Dunsford, Corpus Christi, TX 78413   *361-992-0115*
Peg & Pete Braswell, Innkeepers   *877-894-8109*
French spoken
EMAIL ginrose@flash.net
WEBSITE www.GingerRose.com

LOCATION	A map and detailed directions will accompany a letter confirming reservation.
OPEN	All year
DESCRIPTION	A 1994 brick host home decorated with pastel colors, antiques, stained-glass and arched windows, and artwork.

Ginger Rose, Corpus Christi

NO. OF ROOMS	Two rooms with private bathrooms. Try the Tapestry Room.
RATES	April through September, rates are $70-75 for a single or double. October through March, rates are $60-65 for a single or double. There is no minimum stay and cancellation requires three days' notice.
CREDIT CARDS	No
BREAKFAST	Full gourmet breakfast is served in the dining room and might include blackberry pancakes with Grand Marnier syrup or quiche Lorraine in puff pastry.
AMENITIES	Special treats upon arrival and in the afternoons and evenings; discount coupons to some of the best local restaurants, tourist attractions, and merchants; cable TV; fresh flowers; private pool and patio; access to tennis court.
RESTRICTIONS	No smoking, no pets, children over 12 are welcome. Cocoa is the resident tabby. Cocoa is outside most of the time.

OCEAN HOUSE

3275 Ocean Drive, Corpus Christi, TX 78404   361-882-9500
Dr. E. Stanton Shoemaker, Innkeeper
WEBSITE www.oceansuites.com

SAND DOLLAR BED & BREAKFAST

3605 Mendenhall Drive, Corpus Christi, TX 78415   512-853-1222

CORSICANA

Fifty miles south of Dallas on I-45, Corsicana is close to Lakes Richland and Cedar. Check out the Cook Center for the Arts, Science, and Technology; Pioneer Village; Warehouse Living Arts Center; and Temple Beth-el. Shop antique stores and factory outlet malls.

THE WICKLOW INN, INC.

220 North 14th Street, Corsicana, TX 75110   903-872-7311
Robert & Donna O'Toole, Innkeepers   FAX 903-872-4173
EMAIL Info@wicklowinn.com   WEBSITE www.wicklowinn.com

LOCATION	Take Highway 31 (West 7th Avenue) to North 15th Street. Turn north, go 4 blocks to West 4th Avenue, and turn east. The inn is on the next corner, at West 4th Avenue and North 14th Street.
OPEN	All year
DESCRIPTION	An 1890 three-story Victorian inn built with California redwood, with a curved staircase from France, leaded glass windows, and a large front porch with swing; listed on the State Historic Register.
NO. OF ROOMS	Four rooms with private bathrooms and two rooms share one bathroom.
RATES	Year-round rates are $90 for a single or double with a private bathroom, $60-75 for a single or double with a shared bathroom, and $110-125 for a suite. There is no minimum stay and cancellation requires 72 hours' notice.
CREDIT CARDS	MasterCard, Visa
BREAKFAST	Full hearty Irish breakfast is served in the dining room and prepared by the resident chef. Lunch and dinner are also available.
AMENITIES	Central heat and air conditioning, player piano, antique pump organ, large selection of CDs and cassette tapes, cable TV, well-stocked library, special packages for anniversary or honeymoon couples, afternoon tea.
RESTRICTIONS	No smoking, no pets, children are welcome in the carriage house.
MEMBER	Bed & Breakfast Texas Style

CROCKETT

About 150 miles southeast of Dallas and 100 miles north of Houston, Crockett sits on the western edge of Davy Crockett National Forest. Mission Tejas State Historic Park and Ratcliff Lake are just to the northeast.

WARFIELD HOUSE

712 East Houston Avenue, Crockett, TX 75835   *409-544-4037*
Judy & James Ostler, Innkeepers   *888-988-8800*
EMAIL jcostler@sat.net

LOCATION	From the downtown square, head east on Highway 21 for two-and-a-half blocks. The B&B is on the left directly across from the First Presbyterian Church.
OPEN	All year
DESCRIPTION	An 1897 three-story Victorian inn and guesthouse with luxurious wall coverings and window treatments.
NO. OF ROOMS	Six rooms with private bathrooms. Try Alma's Room.
RATES	Year-round rates are $75-100 for a single or double. There is no minimum stay and cancellation requires seven days' notice.
CREDIT CARDS	American Express, Discover, MasterCard, Visa
BREAKFAST	Full breakfast is served in the formal dining room on china with silver and crystal. Teas, brunches, luncheons, and dinners are available by reservation.
AMENITIES	Central air conditioning, swimming pool and deck, enclosed hot tub.
RESTRICTIONS	No smoking, no pets, children over 11 are welcome. Jingles is the resident poodle.
MEMBER	Historic Accommodations of Texas, Professional Association of Innkeepers International

CROCKETT   85

CROSBYTON

Thirty miles east of Lubbock on Highway 82, Crosbyton boasts two excellent museums: Pioneer Memorial Museum and the Mt. Blanco Fossil Museum. Silver Falls Park is also worth a visit.

SMITH HOUSE

306 West Aspen, Crosbyton, TX 79322   *806-675-2178*
Terry & Karen Ellison, Innkeepers

OPEN	All year
DESCRIPTION	A restored 1921 two-story bungalow decorated with Victorian furnishings.
NO. OF ROOMS	Six rooms with private bathrooms and four rooms share two bathrooms. Try the Anniversary Suite.
RATES	Year-round rates are $60-65 for a single or double with a private bathroom, $50-55 for a single or double with a shared bathroom, and $75-85 for a suite. There is no minimum stay and cancellation requires notice.
CREDIT CARDS	MasterCard, Visa
BREAKFAST	Full country breakfast is served in the dining room and includes bacon and eggs, biscuits and gravy, with fruit, juice, and coffee. Special meals are available for groups.
AMENITIES	Meeting room with large-screen TV, parlor with player piano.
RESTRICTIONS	No smoking, no pets
MEMBER	Historic Hotel Association

DALLAS

The nation's ninth largest city, and Texas' premier city, Dallas is known the world over. Check out the refurbished West End for shopping and dining, and don't miss the Kennedy Memorial just around the block. The Texas State Fair is held here during September and October at Fair Park, which has achieved historical monument status due to its art deco architecture. Six Flags Over Texas is close by, as is Whiterock Lake.

AMELIA'S PLACE:
A DOWNTOWN DALLAS BED & BREAKFAST

1775 Young Street, Dallas, TX 75201   214-651-1775
Amelia Core Jenkins, Innkeeper   888-651-1775
"Schoolgirl" Spanish spoken   FAX 214-761-9475
EMAIL *ameliaj@flash.net*   WEBSITE *www.flash.net/~ameliaj*

LOCATION	In downtown Dallas at the northwest corner of Young and St. Paul Streets, a block from the city hall and the main library, 2 blocks from the convention center.
DESCRIPTION	A 1924 three-story loft-style host home in an old warehouse.
NO. OF ROOMS	Four rooms with private bathrooms and two rooms share two bathrooms. Amelia recommends the Vivian or Anita Rooms.
RATES	Year-round rates are $115 for a single or double with a private bathroom and $95 for a single or double with a shared bathroom. There is no minimum stay and cancellation requires one week's notice, 30 days for multinight or multiroom stays.
CREDIT CARDS	American Express, Diners Club, Discover, MasterCard, Visa
BREAKFAST	Full breakfast is served in the dining room and includes fresh fruit and juice, coffee or tea. A sample breakfast might include homemade buttermilk biscuits and gravy, fried eggs, bacon, and grits. Dinner is also available.
AMENITIES	Complimentary red wine and light snack in the evenings, bicycle and tandem bike, fresh flowers, laundry facilities, Amelia offers information on where to eat and what to see or do. "Kindest treatment of guests."
RESTRICTIONS	No pets, children over 12 are welcome.

THE AMERICAN DREAM B&B

PO Box 760275, Dallas, TX 75367
Pat Biczynski, Resident Owner

214-357-1106
800-373-2690
FAX 214-357-9034

ART BUFF MACCA

4224 West Red Bird Lane, Dallas, TX 75237

972-298-8586

B&G'S B&B

15869 Nedra Way, Dallas, TX 75248
Betty & George Hyde, Innkeepers
EMAIL bgbandb@airmail.net
WEBSITE www.bg-bed-and-breakfast.com

972-386-4323
FAX 972-386-9010

LOCATION	From the center of downtown Dallas, take the north Tollway to the Belt Line/Arapaho exit. Go east on Arapaho to Nedra Way and take a left.
OPEN	All year
DESCRIPTION	A modern Texas-style brick host home with eclectic decor that includes antiques.
NO. OF ROOMS	Two rooms with private bathrooms.
RATES	Year-round rates are $55-60 for a single or double. There is no minimum stay and cancellation requires seven days' notice less a $10 fee.
CREDIT CARDS	No
BREAKFAST	Full breakfast is served in the dining room and includes fruit, juice, a main dish, sweet and nonsweet breakfast breads, and meat.
AMENITIES	Kitchen privileges, TV, fax, telephones.
RESTRICTIONS	No pets. Not easily accessible to guests in wheelchairs.

Country Rose Bed & Breakfast, Lancaster

COUNTRY ROSE BED & BREAKFAST

616 East Belt Line Road, Lancaster, TX 75146   *972-218-5017*
Jim & Charlotte Burns, Innkeepers
Some Spanish spoken
EMAIL cmsb@aol.com
WEBSITE members.aol.com/cmsb

LOCATION	Fifteen minutes south of Dallas. From I-20, take the Lancaster Road exit south and continue 4.5 miles through town to the four-way stop sign at Belt Line Road. Turn left (east) onto Belt Line Road and go about 0.25 mile.
OPEN	All year
DESCRIPTION	A 1901 two-story Victorian country farmhouse with eclectic decor that includes antiques and comfortable furniture, situated on 2.5 acres.
NO. OF ROOMS	Two rooms with private bathrooms. Try the Lancaster Room.
RATES	Year-round weekend rates are $80-90 for a single or double. Midweek rates are $64-72. There is no minimum stay and cancellation requires seven days' notice.
CREDIT CARDS	Discover
BREAKFAST	Full breakfast is served in the dining room or on the porches and includes eggs Benedict, bacon and eggs, oven-baked French toast, biscuits and gravy, seasonal fruits, potatoes or grits, pork chops, and ham. Coffee, tea, and muffins are served early in the morning.

AMENITIES	Upper and lower front porches shaded by an old pecan tree, individual air conditioning in the Lancaster Room, picnic area by the (usually) dry creek.
RESTRICTIONS	No smoking, no pets, children over 14 are welcome. Samantha is the resident German shepherd. There are outdoor cats, about a dozen head of cattle grazing the fields, and lots of wild visitors.

COURTYARD ON THE TRAIL

8045 Forest Trail, Dallas, TX 75238   214-553-9700
Alan Kagan, Innkeeper   800-484-6260 (Pin# 0465)
EMAIL akrubs4u@aol.com   FAX 214-553-9700
WEBSITE www.bbonline.com/tx/courtyard

LOCATION	Six miles from downtown. Take I-75 north to Mockingbird Lane. Exit to the right and continue past Abrams until you get to the White Rock Lake exit. Drive down to the stop sign and turn left. Go past Northwest Highway and follow the road around to the second stop sign (White Rock Trail). Turn left, go to the second street (Forest Trail), and turn right. Park in front on the gravel drive.
OPEN	All year
DESCRIPTION	A 1979 two-story Spanish-style home with eclectic decor tucked away in the woods beside White Rock Lake.
NO. OF ROOMS	Three rooms with private bathrooms.
RATES	Year-round rates are $105-165 for a single or double. There is no minimum stay and cancellation requires one week's notice, two weeks during holidays.
CREDIT CARDS	American Express, MasterCard, Visa
BREAKFAST	Full breakfast is served in the dining room and includes scrambled eggs, omelets, French toast (plain or with a fruit compote sauce), breads, orange or cranberry juice, coffee, or tea.
AMENITIES	Evening wine served, swimming pool, garden, robes in each room, cable TV/VCR, video library, mints at night.
RESTRICTIONS	No smoking, no pets, no children. Skipper is the resident schnauzer.
MEMBER	Bed & Breakfast Texas Style

GASTON HOUSE

5610 Gaston, Dallas, TX 75214	*214-821-4437*
Marsha Bruton, Innkeeper	*FAX 214-821-3561*
"Southern" spoken	
EMAIL gastonh@swbell.net	
WEBSITE www.gastonhouse.com	

LOCATION — From Dallas, take I-30 to the Carroll exit and go north 1 mile. At the light (Gaston Avenue), turn right and go 1.1 miles. Pass through the light at Beacon; the B&B is the third house on the right. Park in the circular drive at the front.

OPEN — All year

DESCRIPTION — A fully restored 1900 two-story Georgian inn with homey decor. The home was one of many built by the "robber barrons" of Dallas. Mr. Munger was the initial owner of this estate, which subsequently subdivided into other lots for homeowners. The house has been fully restored. "We are not fancy, but comfortable."

NO. OF ROOMS — Two rooms with private bathrooms and two rooms share two bathrooms.

RATES — Year-round rates are $95-115 for a single or double. There is no minimum stay and cancellation requires 72 hours' notice.

CREDIT CARDS — American Express, MasterCard, Visa

BREAKFAST — Full breakfast is served in the dining room and typically includes an egg and sausage casserole or French toast, coffee, juice, and fruit.

AMENITIES — Outside dining patio, gazebo, fishpond, afternoon wine and cheese service, and bedtime snack.

RESTRICTIONS — No smoking, no pets, no children. Sugar is the resident cocker spaniel.

GINGERBREAD HOUSE

210 South Broad Street, Cedar Hill, TX 75104	*972-291-2066*
Shirley Hendricks, Innkeeper	*800-778-3241*
EMAIL gingerbreadhouse@juno.com	*FAX 972-291-2066*
WEBSITE www.quickstart.com/gingerbread	

LOCATION — Six miles southwest of Dallas. Take Highway 67 south to Belt Line Road. Go right (west) 6 blocks to Broad Street. Turn left and go one-and-a-half blocks.

OPEN — All year

DESCRIPTION	An 1884 ornate two-story Victorian inn with gingerbread trim, a front porch, bay windows on both floors, and painted in five colors; decorated with antiques and eclectic furnishings. The inn is listed on the National and State Historic Registers.
NO. OF ROOMS	Two rooms with private bathrooms.
RATES	Year-round rate is $94 for a single or double. There is a minimum stay during holiday weekends, and cancellation requires 10 days' notice and may be subject to a 15 percent charge.
CREDIT CARDS	American Express, Discover, MasterCard, Visa
BREAKFAST	Full breakfast is served in the dining room and includes fresh fruit bowl, mini-muffins, orange juice, coffee, plus a hot dish of bacon and eggs, biscuits and gravy. Lunch and dinner are also available.
AMENITIES	Clawfoot tubs, sofa or love seat in rooms, TV, phone, central heat and air conditioning, restaurant downstairs.
RESTRICTIONS	No smoking, no pets, children over 10 are welcome.
MEMBER	Bed & Breakfast Texas Style

THE HOTEL ST. GERMAIN

2516 Maple Avenue, Dallas, TX 75201   214-871-2516
WEBSITE *www.hotelstgermain.com*

THE MANSION ON TURTLE CREEK

2821 Turtle Creek Boulevard, Dallas, TX 75219   214-559-2100
WEBSITE *www.mansiononturtlecreek.com*   FAX 214-528-4187

THE SOUTHERN HOUSE BED & BREAKFAST

2625 Thomas Avenue, Dallas, TX 75204   214-720-0845
WEBSITE *www.southernhouse.com*   FAX 214-720-4447

Terra Cotta Inn, Dallas

TERRA COTTA INN

6101 LBJ Freeway, Dallas, TX 75240
Tracy McCutchin, Innkeeper
Spanish spoken
WEBSITE *www.terracottainn.com*

972-387-2525
800-533-3591
FAX 972-387-3784

LOCATION	Fifteen minutes from downtown Dallas.
OPEN	All year
DESCRIPTION	A 1978 three-story Mexican-style inn with Southwest decor, featuring central Mexican antiques.
NO. OF ROOMS	Ninety-eight rooms with private bathrooms.
RATES	Year-round rates are $61-85 for a single or double and $125 for a suite. There is no minimum stay. Cancellations require notice by 6 p.m. the day of the reservation.
CREDIT CARDS	American Express, Diners Club, Discover, JBC, MasterCard, Visa
BREAKFAST	Continental plus breakfast is served in the library and includes kolaches, tea, juice, fruit, cereal, burritos, pastries, milk, coffee, bagels, and muffins.
AMENITIES	All rooms come with full amenities, complimentary national newspapers, outdoor garden, pool, free parking, computer data ports, fax and copy service, meeting facilities with audio/visual equipment, deluxe rooms available.
RESTRICTIONS	No pets, children under 12 stay free.
RATED	AAA 3 Diamonds

Decatur

Weekend entertainment in Decatur runs from polo and golf to auto races at the North Texas Motor Speedway. Christmas is celebrated with an evening parade. Decatur is about 45 miles northwest of Fort Worth on Highway 380.

Abbercromby Penthouse Suites

103 West Main Street, Decatur, TX 76234　　　　　940-627-7005
Margaret Atkinson, Innkeepers　　　　　　　FAX 940-627-2221
Spanish spoken
EMAIL *Txabby@aol.com*
WEBSITE *members.aol.com/txabby/home.htm*

OPEN	All year
DESCRIPTION	An 1889 two-story Victorian inn with hardwood floors, situated on Courthouse Square in a tiny, turn-of-the-century Texas town. The building houses a bookstore on the first floor and is listed on the State Historic Register.
NO. OF ROOMS	Three rooms with private bathrooms.
RATES	Year-round rates are $99-135 for a single or double. There is no minimum stay and cancellation requires 48 hours' notice with a $10 fee.
CREDIT CARDS	American Express, Diners Club, Discover, MasterCard, Visa
BREAKFAST	Continental plus of quiche, fruit, and muffins is delivered to guestrooms, or a full breakfast is available at Mattie's Restaurant.
AMENITIES	Massage therapy available; romantic wedding packages; Jacuzzi for two in the Summersby Suite; robes, candy, cookies, popcorn, courtesy bar, cable TV/VCR, CD player, games, and candles in each suite.
RESTRICTIONS	No smoking, no pets

DEL RIO

Along the Rio Grande, just across from the Mexican border, and 140 miles west of San Antonio on Highway 90, Del Rio is the final resting place of Judge Roy Bean. Take a dip in Amistad Lake or San Felipe Springs, and sip vino at Val Verde Winery, Texas' oldest vintner.

1890 HOUSE

609 Griner Street, Del Rio, TX 78840   830-775-8061
WEBSITE *www.1890house.com*

VILLA DEL RIO

123 Hudson Drive, Del Rio, TX 78840   830-768-1100
Jay, Barbara, &   800-995-1887
Elizabeth (Kitty) Johnson, Resident Innkeepers   FAX 830-775-2691
Spanish, Albanian, and some Italian spoken
EMAIL *host@villadelrio.com*
WEBSITE *www.villadelrio.com*

LOCATION	Go past the old courthouse downtown. Take Pecan Street until it turns into Hudson Drive.
OPEN	All year
DESCRIPTION	An 1887 two-story combination Italian villa and Mexican hacienda listed on the State Historic Register and situated on 2 acres next to Texas' oldest winery.
NO. OF ROOMS	One room has a private bathroom and two rooms share one bathroom. The Johnsons recommend the Peacock Suite.
RATES	Year-round rates are $135 for a single or double with a private bathroom and $85-95 for a single or double with a shared bathroom. There is no minimum stay; call about the cancellation policy.
CREDIT CARDS	American Express, MasterCard, Visa
BREAKFAST	Full breakfast is served in the dining room and includes fresh fruit and breakfast meats.
AMENITIES	Evening tea, assistance with visiting Mexico.
RESTRICTIONS	No smoking, no pets, children over 12 are welcome. There are a few resident goldfish as well as some visiting neighborhood cats and birds.

REVIEWED   *The Great Stays of Texas, Romantic Texas*

MEMBER   Historic Accommodations of Texas

DENISON

The birthplace of President Dwight D. Eisenhower, Denison sits 5 miles south of the Oklahoma border on I-75. Nearby Lake Texoma is well known for striper fishing and other water activities. Check out Denison's Christmas tour of homes.

IVY BLUE, A BED & BREAKFAST INN

1100 West Sears, Denison, TX 75020   903-463-2479
Lane & Tammy Segerstrom, Resident Owners   888-489-2583

KUDOS/COMMENTS "Wonderful food, gracious hosts." "Beautiful, gourmet food, many amenities, pool, excellent service."

THE MOLLY CHERRY BED & BREAKFAST

200 Molly Cherry Lane, Denison, TX 75020   903-465-0575
Dan & Dede Dase, Innkeepers   800-926-0559

LOCATION   From Dallas, take US 75 north to Sherman-Denison exit 66. Take Spur 503 to the right and go 3 miles to the first light, turn left on Coffin, and then take an immediate right onto a service road. Go 0.25 mile on the service road to Molly Cherry Lane and turn left.

OPEN   All year

DESCRIPTION   An 1890 three-story Queen Anne Victorian host home with a wraparound porch and Victorian decor, situated on 6 wooded acres.

NO. OF ROOMS   Two rooms with private bathrooms and two cottages, each with two private bathrooms.

RATES   Year-round rates for a single or double are $89-179. There is no minimum stay and cancellation requires 72 hours' notice, 14 days during holidays or special events.

CREDIT CARDS   American Express, MasterCard, Visa

BREAKFAST   Full breakfast is served in the dining room on weekends. Gourmet breakfast baskets are delivered to guestrooms on weekday mornings.

AMENITIES	Flowers, robes, swimming pool, homemade snacks in rooms, coffee, tea, hot chocolate, central heat and air conditioning.
RESTRICTIONS	No smoking, no pets, no candles, children over 12 are welcome.

DENTON

About 40 miles north of Dallas, at the point where I-35 splits in two—with one route heading for Fort Worth, the other for Dallas—Denton is worth exploring, particularly the historic downtown square. The Texas Storytellers Festival in March and Halloween Storytellers on the Square are certainly don't-miss events. Other events and activities include the Arts and Jazz Festival in May, the North Texas State Fair in August, and the Lewisville Lake Hydrofest. Denton is home to both the University of North Texas and Texas Women's University.

MAGNOLIA INN

821 North Locust Street, Denton, TX 76201   940-381-3001
WEBSITE www.bbhost.com/redbudbb

THE REDBUD INN

815 North Locust Street, Denton, TX 76201   940-565-6414
John & Donna Morris, Resident Owners   888-565-6414
Spanish spoken   FAX 940-565-6515
EMAIL redbb@gte.net   *WEBSITE www.bbhost.com/redbud.bb*

LOCATION	Seven blocks north of the town square.
OPEN	All year
DESCRIPTION	A 1912 two-story Jacobean revival inn with Victorian decor, a large Victorian back porch with a porch swing, Victorian gardens, and a gazebo.
NO. OF ROOMS	Seven rooms with private bathrooms. Donna recommends the Magnolia South Suite.
RATES	Year-round rates for a single or double are $56-75 and $75-90 for a suite. There is a minimum stay during special events and cancellation requires 72 hours' notice, one week for multinight stays or multiroom reservations.
CREDIT CARDS	American Express, Discover, MasterCard, Visa

BREAKFAST	Full breakfast is served in the dining room and includes fresh fruit, juice, homemade bread, entrées with meat, gourmet coffee, and fresh brewed teas. Lunch, dinner, and special meals are available at the on-site restaurant, Giuseppe's. Hot muffins and coffee are served in rooms on Sunday mornings.
AMENITIES	Complimentary soft drinks and popcorn, robes, hot tub in gazebo, balcony dining, room service from Giuseppe's restaurant, ceiling fans, central air conditioning, three rooms have fireplaces, back porch with swing, player piano.
RESTRICTIONS	No smoking inside, no pets. Rusty, the resident dachshund, sneezes for treats.
REVIEWED	Recommended Country Inns—The Southwest
MEMBER	Professional Association of Innkeepers International, Denton Area Bed & Breakfast Association, Texas Hotel and Motel Association
RATED	AAA 2 Diamonds

DICKINSON

NICHOLSTONE ON THE BAYOU

5000 Park Avenue, Dickinson, TX 77539   *281-337-1652*

DOSS

QUIET HILL RANCH

110 Quiet Hill Road, Doss, TX 78618   *830-669-2253*
WEBSITE www.quiethillranch.com

DRIPPING SPRINGS

SHORT MAMA'S HOUSE BED & BREAKFAST

101 College Street, Dripping Springs, TX 78620   *512-894-0023*

DUMAS

SERENDIPITY HOUSE

South Highway 287, Dumas, TX 79029   *806-935-0339*
WEBSITE www.wwirr.com/serendipity

EAGLE LAKE

Fifty miles west of Houston on Highway 90A, Eagle Lake is less than 10 miles from the Colorado River. Canoe the river or simulate a wild-river experience at Splashway Water Park. The Columbus Opry House and 8,000-acre Attwater Prairie Chicken Refuge are local sights to see. In April, the Prairie Chicken Festival honors this flightless fowl.

EAGLE HILL INN & RETREAT

307 East State Street, Eagle Lake, TX 77434   *800-324-3551*
WEBSITE www.texasguides.com/durninghouseb&b.html

THE FARRIS HOTEL

210 North McCarty, Eagle Lake, TX 77434　　　　　409-234-2546
Toy Kurtz, Innkeeper　　　　　　　　　　　　　　FAX 409-234-2548
Spanish spoken
EMAIL farrishotel@elc.net
WEBSITE www.farrishotel.com

LOCATION	Visit the website or call for detailed directions.
OPEN	All year
DESCRIPTION	Two 1912 two-story red-brick buildings, the main hotel and Farris Bentley House, both furnished entirely with turn-of-the-century antiques; large shaded terraces surround both buildings. Listed on the State Historic Register.
NO. OF ROOMS	One room with a private bathroom and 12 rooms share 15 bathrooms.
RATES	October through March, rates are $125 per person. April through September, rates are $85-95 for a single or double. There is no minimum stay and cancellation requires 10 days' notice.
CREDIT CARDS	American Express, Discover, MasterCard, Visa
BREAKFAST	Full breakfast is served in the dining room and includes bacon, eggs, potatoes, biscuits, fruit, juice, coffee, and tea. Lunch and dinner are also available.
AMENITIES	Hors d'oeuvres, fruit, fancy nuts, two large meeting/banquet rooms, common areas throughout both buildings, full-service dining, wine/beer licensed bar.
RESTRICTIONS	No pets. Charlie is the resident great Dane. Sophie is the Siamese mix.
REVIEWED	*The Texas Monthly: Texas Bed & Breakfast*

EDGEWOOD

Forty miles east of Dallas on Highway 80, Edgewood is a mere handful of miles north of Canton, site of the famous First Monday Trades Days. The Tyler Rose Garden, the Caldwell Zoo, and the antique malls in Mineola are close at hand, too. While in town, don't miss Edgewood's Heritage Park Museum, a circa-1900 village with 16 authentically restored, fully furnished buildings.

CROOKED CREEK FARM

Van Zandt County Road 3110, Edgewood, TX 75117   903-896-1284
H. B. & Dorthy Thornton, Innkeepers   800-766-0790

LOCATION	From I-20, go north on Highway 19 for 5 miles. Turn left onto County Road 3105, then left onto County Road 3110, and left again at the white entry.
OPEN	All year
DESCRIPTION	A 1977 traditional country brick host home with traditional decor and some antiques, situated on 100 acres.
NO. OF ROOMS	Two rooms with private bathrooms and four rooms share two bathrooms.
RATES	Year-round rates are $85-95 for a single or double with a private bathroom and $70-80 for a single or double with a shared bathroom. There is no minimum stay and cancellation requires seven days' notice.
CREDIT CARDS	Discover, MasterCard, Visa
BREAKFAST	Full breakfast is served in the dining room and includes sweet muffins and bread; an egg dish; hashbrowns or grits; fresh fruit; bacon, ham, or sausage; biscuits; gravy; jam and preserves; orange juice, coffee, tea, and milk.
AMENITIES	Evening dessert, wine, VCR and videos, candles in bathroom, robes, bubble bath, hot or cold drinks, cakes or cookies, air conditioning.
RESTRICTIONS	No smoking, no pets. Ask about a policy regarding children. B.B. is the retired cowdog, and there are numerous cattle and an Appaloosa horse named Jack.
REVIEWED	*The Official Guide to American Historic Inns, Inns & Outs*
MEMBER	East Texas Bed & Breakfast Association

HUMPHRIES HOUSE

201 South Main, Edgewood, TX 75117   903-896-4358
Henry & Pattizo Humphries, Innkeepers   *FAX 903-896-1381*
EMAIL *halhumphries@vznet.com*
WEBSITE *www.cantonfleamarket.com/humphries*

LOCATION	Fifty miles east of Dallas on Highway 80. Exit I-20 north onto Highway 859, go 9 miles to Highway 80, turn left, drive 1 block, and take a right onto South Main. The B&B is 1 block north of Highway 80.
OPEN	All year
DESCRIPTION	An 1894 two-story Victorian farmhouse with Victorian-era antiques and East Texas collectibles. Listed on the State Historic Register. "The home's quaint charm was carefully preserved to give visitors a physical record of a distinct time and place in rural East Texas."
NO. OF ROOMS	Four rooms with private bathrooms.
RATES	Year-round rate is $85 for a single or double. Ask about cancellation policy.
CREDIT CARDS	MasterCard, Visa
BREAKFAST	Full breakfast is served on Sundays. Continental is served the rest of the week.
AMENITIES	All rooms with central heat and air conditioning and ceiling fans.
RESTRICTIONS	No smoking, no pets, children over 12 are welcome.
MEMBER	Bed & Breakfast Texas Style, East Texas Bed & Breakfast Association

TEXAS STAR BED & BREAKFAST

County Road 3103, Edgewood, TX 75117   903-896-4277
WEBSITE *www.roomsplus.com/bb/tx/e/txe10047.htm*

Willow Pond Bed & Breakfast, Edgewood

WILLOW POND BED & BREAKFAST

Van Zandt County Road 3601, Edgewood, TX 75117   903-896-4594
Bob & Pattye Parker, Resident Owners   800-830-5822
WEBSITE *www.com.cantonfleamarket/willowpond*

LOCATION	From I-20, go north on Highway 19 for 8.2 miles, cross Highway 80 at the blinking light, and turn left at County Road 3601.
OPEN	All year
DESCRIPTION	A 1985 two-story Victorian farmhouse completely furnished with antiques. "We offer casual country atmosphere and a lot of friendly Texas hospitality."
NO. OF ROOMS	One room with a private bathroom and three rooms share two bathrooms. Try Papa's Room.
RATES	Year-round rates are $90 for a single or double with a private bathroom and $70 for a single or double with a shared bathroom. There is a two-night minimum stay during April and October and cancellation requires 10 days' notice.
CREDIT CARDS	No
BREAKFAST	Full country breakfast is served in the dining room and includes omelets, hashbrowns, biscuits, gravy, coffee, tea, juice, and a fruit dish. Special meals are available upon request.

AMENITIES	Fishing pond (great bass) and fishing equipment, jasmine arbor, old-fashioned bathtub, fresh flowers, gourmet fruit-and-cheese baskets for special occasions, coffee on the balcony overlooking the meadow, country walking trails, bicycles.
RESTRICTIONS	No smoking inside, no pets, children over 12 are welcome. Bobo is the resident outdoor cat. "She stays outside unless she can 'slip' in, which she delights in doing."
MEMBER	East Texas Bed & Breakfast Association

EDOM

Between Tyler and Canton on Highway 64, Edom is well positioned for exploring the rose gardens and festivals of Tyler, and scouring the world's biggest flea market at Canton's First Monday Trades Days. Drop by for the Art Festival in September and Azalea Trails in the spring.

WILD BRIAR—THE COUNTRY INN AT EDOM

625 FM 2339, Edom, TX 75754   903-852-3975
Max & Mary Scott, Innkeepers   FAX 903-852-5475
EMAIL mscotexas@aol.com

LOCATION	Located 1.5 miles off of Highway 279 on FM 2339, inside the Edom city limits.
OPEN	Closed February
DESCRIPTION	A 1986 two-story manor house decorated with British and American antiques, situated on 23 acres.
NO. OF ROOMS	Six rooms with private bathrooms.
RATES	Rates for a single or double are $135. There is no minimum stay and cancellation requires two weeks' notice. A full dinner is included in the price of the rooms.
CREDIT CARDS	No
BREAKFAST	Full breakfast is served in the breakfast room and includes fruit, muffins, cereal, juice, coffee, tea, eggs made to order, bacon or sausage, biscuits and gravy.
AMENITIES	Full dinners, robes, TV, central air conditioning and heat, 23 acres of woods to enjoy, patio, radios and clocks.
RESTRICTIONS	No pets, limited smoking, and "nice" children are welcome. Priscilla, the golden retriever, "runs the inn and us."

EL PASO

At the edge of the long ledge that juts out beneath New Mexico, El Paso is so far west it's in the Mountain Time Zone. This is home to the University of Texas at El Paso, Sun Bowl Stadium, Fort Bliss, and multitudes of missions. There are the traditional museums here, and a couple of non-traditional ones: Museum of the Noncommissioned Officer and the Border Patrol Museum. Juarez, Mexico, is a mere step across the Rio Grande.

SUNSET HEIGHTS BED & BREAKFAST INN

717 West Yandell Avenue, El Paso, TX 79902   915-544-1743
Mr. & Mrs. Mel Martinez, Innkeepers   FAX 915-544-5119
Spanish spoken
WEBSITE *www.bcity.com/sunsetheightsb_b*

LOCATION	Five blocks north of City Hall and 5 blocks south of the University of Texas at El Paso.
OPEN	All year
DESCRIPTION	A 1905 three-story southwestern Victorian furnished with antiques; listed on both the State and National Historic Registers.
NO. OF ROOMS	Five rooms with private bathrooms.
RATES	Year-round rates for a single or double are $85-150. Rates for holidays and during the Sun Bowl are higher. There is a minimum stay on holidays and cancellation requires 14 days' notice.
CREDIT CARDS	American Express, Discover, MasterCard, Visa
BREAKFAST	Full gourmet breakfast is served in the dining room. Luncheons, private parties, and gourmet dinners for six or more are available by reservation.
AMENITIES	Central air conditioning, swimming pool, cable TV/VCR, telephone, one room with a Jacuzzi, refreshments, fax.
RESTRICTIONS	No smoking, no pets, "mature" children welcome, no more than two people to a room.

ELGIN

Billed as the "Sausage Capital of Texas," Elgin celebrates its distinguished status during the Fireman's Barbecue Cook-off, Western Days, and the Hog-Eye Festival and Art Show. Elgin is 20 miles east of Austin on Highway 290.

BIGGER INN

100 West 11th Street, Elgin, TX 78621   512-285-9498

RAGTIME RANCH INN BED & BREAKFAST

Ragtime Ranch Road, Elgin, TX 78621   512-285-9599
Roberta Butler & Debbie Jameson, Innkeepers   800-800-9743
EMAIL *ragtimeinn@earthlink.net*   FAX 512-285-9651
WEBSITE *www.ragtimeinn.com*

LOCATION   At the stoplight in downtown Elgin, go east on FM 3000 for 3.2
                  miles, to Mundine Road. Turn right, go 1.3 miles to Ragtime Ranch
                  Road, and turn left. The road ends at the inn's front gate.

OPEN   All year

Ragtime Ranch Inn Bed & Breakfast, Elgin

DESCRIPTION	A 1995 Texas-style ranch with a wraparound porch, screened porches, private deck, natural pine, and casual western decor.
NO. OF ROOMS	Four rooms with private bathrooms. Try room 3.
RATES	Year-round rate is $95 for a single or double. There is no minimum stay and cancellation requires five days' notice.
CREDIT CARDS	American Express, Diners Club, Discover, MasterCard, Visa
BREAKFAST	Full breakfast is served in the guestrooms and includes breakfast tacos, muffins, cereal, milk, juices, coffee, and tea.
AMENITIES	Swimming pool, picnic tables, barbecue grills, fireplaces and firewood, stocked fishing pond, bait and tackle, TV/VCR, video library, stalls and private pastures for guests' horses, meeting room for up to 25 people, robes, refrigerator and ice-maker, microwave, hammocks.
RESTRICTIONS	Pets are welcome here. Rags, Muffin, Bluejean, and Tramp are the resident shelties; Char, Tiger, Cheetah, Lucky, and Soot are the cats; and there are 22 chickens and three Sicilian donkeys, named Belle, Dolly, and Cinco. "Take home a dozen fresh-laid eggs."
REVIEWED	*Texas Bed & Breakfast, Pets Welcome, Traveling Texas with Your Pets, Texas Dog Lover's Companion, A Lady's Day Out in Austin*
MEMBER	Bed & Breakfast Texas Style, Texas Hotel & Motel Association

EMORY

SWEET SEASONS BED & BREAKFAST

630 Honeysuckle Lane, Emory, TX 75440   903-473-3706
WEBSITE *www.bbchannel.com/bbc/p600904.asp*

FLOYDADA

HISTORIC LAMPLIGHTER INN

102 South 5th Street, Floydada, TX 79235   806-983-3035
Roxanna Cummings & Evelyn Branch, Resident Owners
WEBSITE *www.bbchannel.com/bbc/p212178.asp*

KUDOS/COMMENTS	"Good daily lunches; very quaint old hotel with 20 interesting theme rooms; sociable innkeepers."

FORT DAVIS

In west Texas, 60 beautiful miles south of Saragosa on Highway 17, Fort Davis is home to the McDonald Observatory, the Fort Davis Historic Site, the Overland Trail and Neill Doll Museums, and Davis Mountain State Park.

HISTORIC PRUDE RANCH

PO Box 1431, Fort Davis, TX 79734   800-458-6232
WEBSITE *www.prude-ranch.com*

INDIAN LODGE

PO Box 786, Fort Davis, TX 79734   915-426-3254
WEBSITE *www.tpwd.state.tx.us/park/indian/indian.htm*

NEILL HOUSE

PO Box 1034, Fort Davis, TX 79734   915-426-3838
Shirley Neill Vickers, Resident Owner

LOCATION	Seven blocks west of the courthouse at the end of Court Street.
OPEN	All year
DESCRIPTION	An 1898 Queen Anne Victorian furnished with antiques and surrounded on the north and west sides by huge volcanic boulders. The home is listed on the National and State Historic Registers.
NO. OF ROOMS	Two rooms with private bathrooms and two rooms share two bathrooms.
RATES	Year-round rates are $55-85, and cancellation requires 72 hours' notice.
CREDIT CARDS	No
BREAKFAST	Continental plus is served in the kitchen and includes coffee, tea, juice, cereal, muffins, biscuits, rolls, and bread.
AMENITIES	Air conditioning, patios, porches, gazebos, bird-watching, doll museum.
RESTRICTIONS	No smoking, no pets, no children

OLD TEXAS INN

PO Box 785, Fort Davis, TX 79734   915-426-3118
                                                   FAX 915-426-3023

THE VERANDA COUNTRY INN B&B

210 Court Avenue, Fort Davis, TX 79734   888-383-2847
Paul & Kathie Woods, Resident Owners
EMAIL info@theveranda.com
WEBSITE www.theveranda.com

LOCATION	One block west of the courthouse in the center of town.
OPEN	All year
DESCRIPTION	An 1883 adobe territorial country inn furnished with antiques, with 12-foot ceilings and hardwood floors, surrounded by walled gardens and courtyards. There are also a carriage house and garden cottage on the property.
NO. OF ROOMS	Fourteen rooms with private bathrooms.
RATES	Year-round rates for a single or double are $65-85, the carriage house is $100-145, and the garden cottage is $85. There is a minimum stay on major holidays and event weekends and advance reservations are suggested.
CREDIT CARDS	Discover, MasterCard, Visa
BREAKFAST	Full breakfast is served in the dining room and includes several juices; fresh fruit salad (seasonal); coffeecake or muffins; biscuits; bacon or sausage or Scotch eggs; omelets, soufflés, crepes, or French toast on homemade bread.
AMENITIES	Large living and reading room, robes, car service to and from the airport, facilities for small conferences and retreats.
RESTRICTIONS	No smoking, no pets
REVIEWED	*The Official Guide to American Historic Inns, Texas Bed & Breakfasts*
MEMBER	Historic Accommodations of Texas
KUDOS/COMMENTS	"Historic building with numerous rooms, high ceilings, engaging hosts, and stylish breakfasts. Garden and courtyard." "One of the oldest real hotels in Texas. Great breakfasts and good hosts."

WAYSIDE INN BED & BREAKFAST

400 West Fourth Street, Fort Davis, TX 79734   *915-426-3535*
      800-582-7510

LOCATION	Four blocks west of the Stone Village Grocery (that is on Highways 17 and 118) at the base of Sleeping Lion Mountain.
OPEN	All year
DESCRIPTION	A 1947 two-story country inn with country decor.
NO. OF ROOMS	Seven rooms with private bathrooms.
RATES	Please inquire about current rates and cancellation information.
CREDIT CARDS	American Express, Discover, MasterCard, Visa
BREAKFAST	Full breakfast is served in the dining room.
AMENITIES	Central heat and cooling, king- and queen-size beds.
RESTRICTIONS	No smoking, no pets
KUDOS/COMMENTS	"At the base of a spectacular mountain, this comfortable B&B is full of surprises, not the least of which is a hat collection in almost all of the rooms."

FORT WORTH

Dallas' sister city, Fort Worth boasts many worthwhile events and areas of interest all its own, including the Fort Worth Cultural District, Bass Performance Hall, Sundance Square, the Stockyards National Historic District, botanical gardens, and Trinity Park and Water Gardens. Fort Worth is also the home of Texas Christian University.

AZALEA PLANTATION BED & BREAKFAST

1400 Robinwood Drive, Fort Worth, TX 76111   *817-838-5882*
Martha & Richard Linnartz, Resident Owners   *800-687-3529*
WEBSITE *www.TexasSleepAways.com/azalea*

LOCATION	Take the Northside Drive/Yucca Avenue exit from I-35. Go east on Yucca through three lights. One block past the high school, turn left on Eagle and then right on Robinwood.
OPEN	All year
DESCRIPTION	A 1946 two-story southern plantation and cottage with traditional and antique furnishings.

NO. OF ROOMS	Four rooms with private bathrooms.
RATES	Year-round rates for a single or double are $110-159. There is no minimum stay and cancellation requires 72 hours' notice.
CREDIT CARDS	American Express, Discover, MasterCard, Visa
BREAKFAST	Full breakfast on weekends and continental plus on weekdays are served in the dining room.
AMENITIES	All rooms include terry robes, TV, reading material, clock radio, and air conditioning; wine, lemonade, soft drinks, and snacks are served on arrival; some rooms with Jacuzzis; early morning coffee service; meeting facilities for 30.
RESTRICTIONS	No smoking, no pets

BED & BREAKFAST AT THE RANCH

933 Ranch Road, Fort Worth, TX 76131   817-232-5522
Scott & Cheryl Stewart, Innkeepers   888-593-0352
EMAIL bbranch@home.com   FAX 817-656-1330
WEBSITE www.fortworthians.com/bbranch

LOCATION	Due north of downtown Fort Worth, just 10 minutes north of the Stockyards Historical District. Go north on I-35 west and exit onto NE Loop 820. Go 2.5 miles west to the Saginaw Main Street exit. Go north through town 3.5 miles. Turn right just past the Dairy Queen onto E Bailey Boswell Road and go 0.5 mile. Turn left onto Wagley Robertson, drive 0.5 mile, and take the first left onto Ranch Road. The B&B is at the very end of the drive.
OPEN	All year
DESCRIPTION	An 1896 two-story ranch-style country inn situated on 10 acres. The B&B is less than 10 minutes north of the stockyards.
NO. OF ROOMS	Five rooms with private bathrooms.
RATES	Year-round rates are $75-159 for a single or double. There is a minimum stay during special events and some holidays, and cancellation requires 72 hours' notice.
CREDIT CARDS	American Express, MasterCard, Visa
BREAKFAST	Full, ranch-style "stick-to-your-ribs" breakfast is served in the dining room on weekends and includes Mexican eggs, biscuits and gravy, spicy sausage in maple sauce, fresh fruit cup with crème fraiche. Early morning coffee and juice is available. Continental breakfast is available during the week.

AMENITIES	Thick fluffy robes in each room; extra towels for the spa; wine, cheese, and crackers at check-in; Sweetheart packages include beverage, two glasses on silver tray, chocolates, flowers, and Mylar balloon; butler's basket; laundry; fax; TV; telephone; two rooms with Jacuzzis; recreation room with a large spa and free pinball; gazebo. "We do luncheons, rehearsal dinners, parties, and host weddings."
RESTRICTIONS	No smoking, no pets, children are welcome.
REVIEWED	*Fort Worth Star Telegram*, Microsoft Sidewalk
MEMBER	Historical Accommodations of Texas, Professional Association of Innkeepers International, Fort Worth's Finest Bed & Breakfasts
RATED	AAA 3 Diamonds, Mobil 2 Stars

BLOOMSBURY HOUSE BED & BREAKFAST

2251 Lipscomb Street, Fort Worth, TX 76110   *817-921-2383*

THE COLONY BED & BREAKFAST

2611 Glendale Avenue, Fort Worth, TX 76106   *817-624-1981*
Gloria Sample, Resident Owner

MISS MOLLY'S HOTEL BED & BREAKFAST

109 1/2 West Exchange, Fort Worth, TX 76106   *817-626-1522*
Susan & Mark Hancock, Resident Owners
WEBSITE www.missmollys.com

THE TEXAS WHITE HOUSE BED & BREAKFAST

1417 Eighth Avenue, Fort Worth, TX 76104   817-923-3597
Jamie Sexton & Grover McMains, Resident Owners   800-279-6491
EMAIL *txwhitehou@aol.com*   *FAX 817-923-0410*

LOCATION	Southwest of downtown Fort Worth, about 1 mile south of I-30. Use the Summit/Ballinger exit (westbound) or the West Rosedale exit (eastbound).
OPEN	All year
DESCRIPTION	A restored 1910 two-story colonial revival built in 1910 and furnished in simple but elegant style.
NO. OF ROOMS	Three rooms with private bathrooms.
RATES	Year-round rates for a single or double are $100-125. There is no minimum stay and cancellation requires seven days' notice.
CREDIT CARDS	American Express, Discover, MasterCard, Visa
BREAKFAST	Full breakfast is served in the dining room or the guest rooms on antique china with sterling silver and crystal and includes fresh fruit or baked fruit in compote, baked egg specialties, fresh baked breads and muffins.
AMENITIES	Luxurious beds, bubble baths, relaxing sitting areas, snacks, TV and telephone on request, fresh flowers, candles, lotions, secretary and notary services available, laundry service for extended stays, off-street parking.
RESTRICTIONS	No smoking inside, no pets, no children
MEMBER	Historic Accommodations of Texas, Professional Association of Innkeepers International, Texas Hotel & Motel Association
RATED	AAA 3 Diamonds
AWARDS	1995, Pedestal Award for outstanding restoration, by the Tarrant County Historical Preservation Council

FREDERICKSBURG

A delightful, 150-year-old German tourist town in central Texas, 65 miles northwest of San Antonio, Fredericksburg and the surrounding area has much to offer. Hotspots include the LBJ Ranch and State Park, Enchanted Rock State Park (home of the second largest granite structure in North America), Admiral Nimitz and George Bush Museums, Weinachten Christmas Market, several flourishing wineries, and more. There are guided tours of the LBJ ranchlands and a Christmas Candlelight Tour of Homes. Major local festivals include Octoberfest, Food and Wine Fest, Gillespie County Fair, Night in Old Fredericksburg, Peach Jamboree, Fredericksburg Wine Festival, Spring Herb Fest, Founder's Day in May, and seasonal Country Peddler Shows.

AB BUTLER'S DOGTROT AT TRIPLE CREEK

801 Triple Creek Road, Fredericksburg, TX 78624   877-262-4366
EMAIL *abbutler@fbg.net*   WEBSITE *www.fbg.net/tce/abbutler.htm*

ALLEGANI'S LITTLE HORSE INN

307 South Creek, Fredericksburg, TX 78624   830-997-7448
Jane Schofield, Resident Owner

LOCATION	Turn off Main Street (Highway 290) onto Elk Street (beside the Sunday House Motel). Go two blocks, turn left onto East Creek and follow Creek across the low-water crossing to South Creek and up the hill. The B&B is on the left.
OPEN	All year
DESCRIPTION	A 1914 Texas gingerbread guesthouse, recently redone in Texas/Mexican decor.
NO. OF ROOMS	A private guesthouse with two rooms and one bathroom.
RATES	Year-round rates are $100 for two adults and $150 for four adults. There is no minimum stay required; three days' notice is needed for cancellations.
CREDIT CARDS	No
BREAKFAST	Continental plus is provided and includes fruit, juice, muffins, coffee, and milk.
AMENITIES	Coffee and teas, whirlpool bath, gardens, walking area, Longhorn cattle, old-fashioned kitchen, cable TV/VCR, telephone, air conditioning, books, and guitar.
RESTRICTIONS	Smoking on porch only, pets and children are welcome.

ALLEGANI'S SUNDAY HOUSE

418 West Creek, Fredericksburg, TX 78624   *830-997-7448*
Janie Schofield, Innkeeper

OPEN	All year
DESCRIPTION	A 1917 cottage decorated with antiques and collectibles.
NO. OF ROOMS	A private cottage with two bedrooms.
RATES	Year-round rates are $85 for a double and $110 for four. There is a two-day minimum stay on weekends and cancellation requires three days' notice.
CREDIT CARDS	No
BREAKFAST	Continental plus is provided in the kitchen.
AMENITIES	Coffee and tea, TV/VCR.
RESTRICTIONS	No smoking, children are welcome.

ALTE WELT GASTHAUS

PO Box 628, Fredericksburg, TX 78624   *830-997-0443*
EMAIL altewelt@fbg.net   *FAX 830-997-0040*
WEBSITE www.texas-bed-n-breakfast.com

ANNIE'S PLACE

Pfeiffer Road, Fredericksburg, TX   *830-997-4712*
WEBSITE www.bandbfbg.com

AUNT VIOLET'S MORNING GLORY INN

611 South Washington Street, Fredericksburg, TX 78624   830-997-0424
Melanie Edgecombe, Innkeeper   830-997-4712

LOCATION	On Highway 87, 6 blocks south of Main Street, 22 miles north of I-10.
OPEN	All year
DESCRIPTION	A 1913 Victorian gingerbread Painted Lady with period fixtures and shady porches, plus two log guesthouses and a full-service day spa.
NO. OF ROOMS	Three rooms with private bathrooms, plus two log homes with private bathrooms.
RATES	March through May and October through December, rates are $95 for a single or double in the main house and $125 for the log guesthouse. Rates are negotiable the remainder of the year. There is a minimum stay during high-season weekends and cancellation requires 10 days' notice.
CREDIT CARDS	American Express, Discover, MasterCard, Visa
BREAKFAST	Full breakfast is served in the main house and continental plus is delivered to the guesthouses and includes fresh-baked goods from the local bakery.
AMENITIES	Full-service day spa, private entrances to all rooms and cabins; main house features clawfoot tubs, porches, and swings; the cabins include stove fireplaces and Jacuzzis.
RESTRICTIONS	No smoking. Pets and well-behaved children are welcome. Delilah is the resident Rottweiler.

THE BACK FORTY OF FREDERICKSBURG

457 Bob Moritz Drive, Fredericksburg, TX 78264   830-997-6373
www.back40-fredericksburg.com/   830-997-1702
                                                     FAX 830-997-9986

Barbara's Bed & Breakfast

202 South Crockett, Fredericksburg, TX 78624   830-990-0033
Barbara Dover, Innkeeper   FAX 830-997-9514
EMAIL bdover@fbg.net   WEBSITE www.barbaras-b-and-b.com

LOCATION	Eighty-five miles west of Austin on Highway 290; 70 miles northwest of San Antonio, via Interstate 10 west and Highway 87 north; 1 block south of the first block of West Main Street (Highway 290).
OPEN	All year
DESCRIPTION	A 1928 stucco host home and cottage with art deco interiors.
NO. OF ROOMS	Three rooms with private bathrooms.
RATES	Year-round rates are $100-115 for a single or double. There is a minimum stay on weekends and cancellation requires seven days' notice.
CREDIT CARDS	No
BREAKFAST	Full breakfast is served in the dining room or on the porch or patio and includes homemade yogurt with homemade granola; juice; homemade breads and rolls; egg dishes; bacon, sausage, or ham; baked apples or poached pears in red wine sauce. The menu varies from day to day. Dinners or picnic baskets are available if ordered in advance.
AMENITIES	Fresh flowers, homemade "killer" brownies or cookies, air conditioning, backyard patio, front porch available for sitting and bird- or butterfly-watching, pecan and oak trees.
RESTRICTIONS	No smoking, no pets, children over 12 are welcome. Small, well-behaved children are welcome in the cottage.

Baron's Creek Inn

110 East Creek Street, Fredericksburg, TX 78624   210-997-9398
Brooke Schweers, Resident Owner   800-800-4082

THE BARRISTER'S GUEST QUARTERS

807 South Adams, Fredericksburg, TX 78624   830-997-3437
EMAIL econoldg@ktc.com   888-919-3437
WEBSITE www.ktc.net/econoldg   FAX 830-997-4405

BED & BREAKFAST AT PALO ALTO CREEK FARM

90 Palo Alto Lane, Fredericksburg, TX 78624   830-997-0088
Bill & Leigh Waller, Innkeepers   800-997-0089
EMAIL pacf@ktc.com   FAX 830-997-0088
WEBSITE www.paloaltocreekfarm.com

LOCATION	Take Main Street to Llano Street (Highway 16 north) and drive 1.5 miles north to Lower Crabapple Road. Turn left and go 3.5 miles to Palo Alto Lane.
OPEN	All year
DESCRIPTION	An 1855 pioneer-era log cabin and limestone barn decorated with comfortable local antiques, situated on a beautiful acreage with Texas longhorns grazing the property. This landmark German immigrant farm is listed on the State Historic Register.
NO. OF ROOMS	Two rooms with private bathrooms.
RATES	Year-round rates are $135-150 for a guesthouse. There is a minimum stay during local events and cancellation requires five days' notice.
CREDIT CARDS	MasterCard, Visa
BREAKFAST	Continental plus is available in the guesthouses and includes seasonal fruit, orange juice, bakery items, homemade granola, bagels, English muffins, milk, butter, jams and jellies. Catering is available upon request.
AMENITIES	King-size beds, fireplaces, Jacuzzi tubs for two, central heat and air conditioning, luxury linens, antiques, terry robes, home-baked chocolate-chip cookies, whole-bean gourmet coffee.
RESTRICTIONS	No smoking, no children, pets may be considered with prior approval. The property is populated with cattle, goats, three dogs, 10 cats, 40 to 50 deer ("which we feed every evening"), and our "almost tame" wild turkey.

BED & BREAKFAST ON KNOPP SCHOOL

Fredericksburg, TX 78624   830-997-3080
WEBSITE *www.nedry.com/knopp/*

BELL COTTAGE

503 East Morse, Fredericksburg, TX 78624   830-997-5612
Mr. & Mrs. Joe R. Bell, Innkeepers
EMAIL *gasthaus@ktc.com*
WEBSITE *www.sbglodging.com*

LOCATION	Seven blocks north of Main Street, out Llano Highway 16 north.
OPEN	All year
DESCRIPTION	A 1984 two-story wood-frame guesthouse with a porch and rustic country decor.
NO. OF ROOMS	Two rooms with private bathrooms.
RATES	Year-round rates are $72 for a single or double. Additional guests are $15 per person. There is a minimum stay during special event weekends and cancellation requires seven days' notice.
CREDIT CARDS	Discover, MasterCard, Visa
BREAKFAST	Continental plus is left in the cottage and includes tea, coffee, sweet rolls, sausage, breads, and fruit. Special diets can be accommodated. Guests do not receive the same breakfast twice.
AMENITIES	Outside entrances; one room with clawfoot tub, quilts, handmade braided rug, refrigerator, microwave, coffee-maker; one room with fully equipped kitchen; tandem and regular bikes; quiet streets to walk; swing set; barbecue; toys for children; games, croquet set, horse shoes; central heat and air conditioning; ceiling fans; cable TV; phone.
RESTRICTIONS	No smoking, no pets, children are welcome.
REVIEWED	*Texas Monthly: Texas Bed & Breakfast*

BELL HAUS

711 North Pine, Fredericksburg, TX 78624   830-997-5612
Mrs. & Mrs. Joe R. Bell, Resident Innkeepers   800-830-8282
EMAIL gasthaus@ktc.com   *WEBSITE www.sbglodging.com*

LOCATION	Seven blocks north of Main Street, off Llano Highway 16 north.
OPEN	All year
DESCRIPTION	A 1940 country ranch home of frame construction with country decor and antiques.
NO. OF ROOMS	One room with a private bathroom.
RATES	Year-round rate is $80 for a double. An extra guest is $15 more. There is a minimum stay on special event weekends and cancellation requires seven days' notice.
CREDIT CARDS	Discover, MasterCard, Visa
BREAKFAST	Full breakfast is served in the dining room or on the covered patio. Breakfast varies, but usually includes an egg dish, sausage, coffee, tea, milk, juice, jam, jelly, toast, rolls, pancakes, waffles, omelets, and oatmeal if requested. Special requests are honored. Breakfast is different each day.
AMENITIES	TV, air conditioning and heat, patio, large yard, bikes, quiet neighborhood, suggestions on where to eat.
RESTRICTIONS	No smoking, no pets, no children

BIRDSONG

1203 North Adams, Fredericksburg, TX 78624   830-997-0111
Mrs. Thompson, Resident Owner

BLUEBONNET BED & BREAKFAST

PO Box 930, Fredericksburg, TX 78624   830-997-8740
EMAIL bluebonnet@fbg.net   888-489-2149
WEBSITE www.fbg.net/bluebonnet/

Bluebonnet Cottage, Fredericksburg

BLUEBONNET COTTAGE

208 *South Edison, Fredericksburg, TX 78624*   830-997-4712
Dorothy Conlon, Innkeeper   FAX 830-990-0063
EMAIL *bandbfbg@ktc.com*   WEBSITE *ww.bandbfbg.com/*

LOCATION	From the courthouse on Adams Street, go 4 blocks west on Main Street, turn left onto Edison Street, and go one-and-a-half blocks, to the blue cottage on the right.
OPEN	All year
DESCRIPTION	A 1994 Fredericksburg Sunday house–style cottage with a stone foundation and walk, situated in a quiet neighborhood on a well-landscaped lot.
NO. OF ROOMS	One room with a private bathroom.
RATES	Year-round rate is $75 for the cottage. There is no minimum stay and cancellation requires 10 days' notice with a $10 fee.
CREDIT CARDS	American Express, Discover, MasterCard, Visa
BREAKFAST	The kitchen is stocked with juice, milk, cereal, eggs, bacon, bread, jams, coffee, and tea. Guests prepare breakfast.
AMENITIES	Front and back porches for sitting and sipping complimentary wine or soft drinks, central heat and air conditioning, ceiling fans, washer and dryer, microwave, full kitchen, TV, phone.
RESTRICTIONS	No smoking, no pets, no children

BLUMENTHAL FARMS B&B

9400 East US Highway 390, Fredericksburg, TX 78624 830-997-6327
WEBSITE www.blumenthalfarms.com FAX 830-990-4020

CREEKSIDE INN

304 South Washington Street, Fredericksburg, TX 78624 830-997-6316
Helen Smith, Innkeeper 888-997-6316
EMAIL creekside@fbg.net FAX 830-997-9864
WEBSITE www.fbg.net/creekside/

LOCATION	One-and-a-half blocks south of the Nimitz Museum on Main Street.
OPEN	All year
DESCRIPTION	A 1905 basse block inn and chalet-style guesthouse on 2 acres of natural landscaping. The guesthouse overlooks Baron's Creek.
NO. OF ROOMS	Seven rooms with private bathrooms.
RATES	Year-round weekend rate is $90 for a single or double. Midweek rate is $80. There is a two-night minimum stay during some weekends and cancellation requires 48 hours' notice.
CREDIT CARDS	American Express, Discover, MasterCard, Visa
BREAKFAST	Full breakfast is served in the dining room and includes casseroles, biscuits, pancakes, and fresh fruit.
AMENITIES	Plenty of coffee, teas, hot chocolate, cappucino; patio by the creek; koi pond.
RESTRICTIONS	No smoking, no pets, children over six are welcome.
MEMBER	Professional Association of Innkeepers International

DAS COLLEGE HAUS

106 West College Street, Fredericksburg, TX 78624 830-997-9047
Myrna Dennis, Innkeeper 800-654-2802
EMAIL myrna@hctc.net FAX 830-997-9047
WEBSITE www.dascollegehaus.com

LOCATION	From West Main Street, go north on North Milan 4 blocks to West College Street and turn right.

Das College Haus, Fredericksburg

OPEN	All year
DESCRIPTION	A 1912 two-story Greek revival Victorian inn furnished in Victorian country style with porches upstairs and downstairs, located in a quiet, historic district.
NO. OF ROOMS	Four rooms with private bathrooms.
RATES	Year-round rates for a single or double are $95-110. No minimum stay is required and cancellation requires seven days' notice.
CREDIT CARDS	American Express, MasterCard, Visa
BREAKFAST	Full breakfast is served in the dining room and includes such entrées as apple-pecan pancakes with bacon or sausage and fresh fruit. Special diets are accommodated upon request.
AMENITIES	Each room features mini-refrigerators stocked with refreshments, coffee-makers, cable TV/VCRs, videos, air conditioning; and handicapped accessible.
RESTRICTIONS	No smoking, no pets, children over six are welcome.
REVIEWED	*The Great Stays of Texas*
MEMBER	Fredericksburg Traditional Bed & Breakfast Associations, Historic and Hospitality Accommodations of Texas
RATED	AAA 2 Diamonds

Das Garten Haus, Fredericksburg

DAS GARTEN HAUS

604 South Washington Street, Fredericksburg, TX 78624   *830-990-8408*
Lynn & Kevin MacWithey, Innkeepers   *800-416-4287*
EMAIL *mac@hctc.net*   FAX *830-997-7377*
WEBSITE *www.dasgartenhaus.com*

LOCATION	About half a mile south of Main Street, on Washington Street.
OPEN	All year
DESCRIPTION	A 1945 two-story Dutch cottage with hardwood floors throughout, crown molding, traditional decor, and some antiques. The rooms overlook a New Orleans–style courtyard and perennial garden.
NO. OF ROOMS	Three rooms with private bathrooms.
RATES	March through December, rates are $105-175 for a single or double. January and February, rates are $95-150 for a single or double. There is a two-night minimum stay on most weekends. Ask about a cancellation policy.
CREDIT CARDS	Discover, MasterCard, Visa
BREAKFAST	Full breakfast is served in the formal dining room and includes fruit, breads or muffins, and a gourmet entrée served on china with silver.
AMENITIES	Two suites with kitchens and sitting areas; coffee, tea, juice, sodas available; flowers and homemade cookies in rooms; air conditioning.

RESTRICTIONS	No smoking. Children over 12 are welcome. Smokey and Stewie are the resident pooches, a Pomeranian and Lhasa apso respectively.
REVIEWED	*A Lady's Day Out, The Great Stays of Texas, Texas Bed & Breakfast Cookbook*
MEMBER	Historic Accommodations of Texas, Professional Association of Innkeepers International, Fredericksburg Traditional Bed & Breakfast Association

THE DELFORGE PLACE B&B INN

710 Ettie Street, Fredericksburg, TX 78624   830-997-6212
Betsy, George, & Pete Delforge, Innkeepers   800-997-0462
French spoken   FAX 830-997-7190
EMAIL *delplace@speakez.net*   WEBSITE *www.delforgeplace.com*

LOCATION	Fredericksburg is 90 miles due west of Austin, 70 miles northwest of San Antonio. From the intersection of Main Street (Highway 290) and Highway 16 south in the center of Fredericksburg, proceed south on Highway 16 for approximately 0.7 mile and turn left on Walnut Street (one full block after the fourth traffic light). On the corner is Fredericksburg Mirror and Glass. Go to the third cross street (Ettie Street). The B&B is on the northwest corner of Walnut and Ettie Streets.
OPEN	All year
DESCRIPTION	An 1898 one-and-a-half-story Victorian with historically themed suites and European, oriental, and early American decor.
NO. OF ROOMS	Four rooms with private bathrooms.
RATES	Year-round rates are $95 for a single or double and $95-125 for a suite. There is a two-night minimum stay on certain special event and holiday weekends. Cancellation requires seven days' notice with a $10 charge.
CREDIT CARDS	American Express, Discover, MasterCard, Visa
BREAKFAST	Full gourmet breakfast is served daily in the dining room or on the rock patio. Seven different breakfasts are served and dietary needs are accommodated with advance notice. Custom-designed picnic baskets are also available with advance notice
AMENITIES	Air conditioning; handicapped accessible; fresh flowers in rooms; homemade cookies at check-in; horse shoes, croquet, archery on the grounds; refrigerator with complimentary soft drinks and chilled spring water in each room; coffee corner in each room with house-blended coffee, teas, hot chocolate, and apple cider; toiletries in all bathrooms; Jacuzzi in one suite; ceiling fans in downstairs rooms/suites; email and fax services available; guest privileges at private swim and racquet club.

RESTRICTIONS	No smoking, no pets, children over six are welcome.
REVIEWED	*The Great Stays of Texas; Recommended Country Inns—The Southwest; The Southwest's Best Bed & Breakfasts; Gourmet* magazine; *Bon Appetit; The Texas Monthly—Texas Bed & Breakfasts; The Complete Guide to Bed & Breakfasts, Inns & Guesthouses in the United States, Canada and Worldwide; America's Most Charming Towns & Villages; Wake Up & Smell the Coffee—Southwest Edition; The Great Country Inns of America Cookbook; Texas Bed & Breakfast Cookbook*
MEMBER	Historic & Hospitality Accommodations of Texas, Texas Hotel & Motel Association
RATED	December 1994, Favorite Bed & Breakfast, Houston Chronicle travel editor, Harry Shattuck; 1997, Ann Ruff Award winner for the property that did the most to promote Historic and Hospitality Accommodations of Texas during the year, Historic & Hospitality Accommodations of Texas
KUDOS/COMMENTS	"Excellent food, each room decorated in a different theme." "Excellent breakfast. Wonderful antiques. Very good hosts."

DRACHE' HAUS BED & BREAKFAST

619 South Washington Street, Fredericksburg, TX 78624   830-997-7042
800-641-5006

ECHTE GEMUETLICHKEIT BED & BREAKFAST

314 West Travis Street, Fredericksburg, TX 78624   830-997-2262

ERNST HOUSE

102 South Cherry Street, Fredericksburg, TX 78624   830-997-4712
WEBSITE www.bandbfbg.com

FREDERICKSBURG BED & BREW

245 East Main Street, Fredericksburg, TX 78624   210-997-1646
WEBSITE www.yourbrewery.com

HAUS WILHELMINA

409 Cora Street, Fredericksburg, TX 78624   830-997-3997

HEIRATEN HAUS

623 South Washington, Fredericksburg, TX 78624   830-997-5612
WEBSITE www.fbglodging.com/heiraten.htm   830-997-5384
FAX 830-997-8282

THE HERB HAUS BED & BREAKFAST

401 Whitney, Fredericksburg, TX 78624   830-997-8615
Bill & Sylvia Varney, Resident Owners
WEBSITE www.fredericksburgherbfarm.com

HOFFMAN HAUS

608 East Creek Street, Fredericksburg, TX 78624   830-997-6739
WEBSITE www.hoffmanhaus.com   800-899-1672

KUDOS/COMMENTS "Three beautiful B&Bs in a beautiful setting with an interesting
host."

IMMEL COTTAGE

404 East Morse, Fredericksburg, TX 78624   830-997-5612
Mr. & Mrs. Joe R. Bell, Innkeepers
EMAIL *gasthaus@ktc.com*
WEBSITE *www.sbglodging.com*

LOCATION	Six blocks from Main Street, out Llano Highway 16 north.
OPEN	All year
DESCRIPTION	A 1929 bungalow, built from plans purchased from Sears and Roebuck, with a metal roof, wooden floors, period furnishings, antiques, and quilts.
NO. OF ROOMS	Two rooms with private bathrooms.
RATES	Year-round rate is $87 for a single or double. There is a minimum stay during special event weekends and cancellation requires seven days' notice.
CREDIT CARDS	Discover, MasterCard, Visa
BREAKFAST	Continental plus is supplied in the refrigerator and includes tea, coffee, locally made sausage, sweet rolls, breads, jelly, jam, fruit, and eggs. Breakfast changes each day of stay. Special requests are honored.
AMENITIES	Bikes, barbecue, picnic table, patio, quiet neighborhood, central heat and air conditioning, old books and games, porch swing, rocking chairs, ceiling fans, cable TV, telephone, microwave, full kitchen, refrigerator, coffee-maker, clawfoot tub with shower in both bathrooms.
RESTRICTIONS	No smoking, no pets, no children
REVIEWED	*The Texas Monthly—Texas Bed & Breakfast*

INN ON THE CREEK

107 North Washington, Fredericksburg, TX 78624   210-997-9585
Dianne Hauerland, Resident Owner
WEBSITE *www.inncreek.com*

THE KUENEMANN HOUSE INN

413 West Creek, Fredericksburg, TX 78624   *830-997-5612*
WEBSITE www.fbglodging.com/kuenemann.htm

KUDOS/COMMENTS "Beautifully restored mid-1800s home. Gracious innkeeper."

LONGHORN CORRAL & WESTERN STAR

207 South Bowie, Fredericksburg, TX 78624   *830-997-3049*
                                                 FAX 830-990-4171
WEBSITE www.sunnyside-b-and-b.com/longhorn-corral.htm

THE LUCKENBACH INN

HC 13, Box 9, Fredericksburg, TX 78624   *830-997-2205*
Captain Matthew &   *800-997-1124*
Eva Marie Carinhas, Resident Owners   *FAX 830-997-1115*
WEBSITE www.luckenbachtx.com

LOCATION	From Fredericksburg, go east on Highway 290 for 4.5 miles to Ranch Road 1376. Turn right and go 4.5 miles to Luckenbach Road, then go left for 0.5 mile. The inn is on the left.
OPEN	All year
DESCRIPTION	A restored 1867 two-story German pioneer country inn with elegant, rustic furnishings.
NO. OF ROOMS	Four rooms with private bathrooms and two rooms in the log cabin share a bathroom.
RATES	Year-round rate for a single or double with a private bathroom is $125; and a single or double with a shared bathroom is $95. There is a two-night minimum stay on weekends and cancellation requires 10 days' notice.
CREDIT CARDS	MasterCard, Visa
BREAKFAST	Full country breakfast is served in the dining room or on the patio.
AMENITIES	Central air conditioning; stone fireplace in the lobby; fresh flowers; fishing and swimming in South Grape Creek; corporate meeting facilities with fax and telephones; facilities for weddings, private parties, and banquets.

RESTRICTIONS	No smoking inside. Children and pets are welcome with prior notification.
MEMBER	Historic Accommodations of Texas, Texas Hotel & Motel Association, Fredericksburg Traditional Bed & Breakfast Association

MAGNOLIA HOUSE BED & BREAKFAST

101 East Hackberry, Fredericksburg, TX 78624 830-997-0306
Joyce & Patrick Kennstf, Innkeepers 800-880-4374
EMAIL *magnolia@hctc.net* FAX 830-997-0766
WEBSITE *www.magnolia-house.com*

LOCATION	From Main Street (Highway 290), turn north on Llano Street (Highway 16), drive to East Hackberry, turn left, and drive one block. The B&B is on the southeast corner of North Adams and East Hackberry.
OPEN	All year
DESCRIPTION	A restored 1923 two-story Craftsman-style European bungalow decorated with period pieces, antiques, and reproductions. Listed on the State Historic Register.
NO. OF ROOMS	Five rooms with private bathrooms. Try the Magnolia Suite.
RATES	Year-round rates are $95-140 for a single or double and $140 for a suite. There is a minimum stay during weekends and holidays and cancellation requires one week's notice, three weeks during holidays.
CREDIT CARDS	American Express, Discover, MasterCard, Visa
BREAKFAST	Full, bountiful breakfast is made from scratch and served on antique china and silver in the breakfast room. The buffet changes daily but includes a combination of waffles, French toast, or crepes, with fresh fruit, homemade muffins, juice, bacon, sausage, an egg entrée, sweet rolls, biscuits, and gravy.
AMENITIES	Fresh flowers; coffee; complimentary beverages; homemade snacks; monogrammed terry-cloth robes; Magnolia House soaps; each room has a TV with HBO and Encore, and air conditioning; patio with custom-designed fishpond and waterfall; wicker furniture on three porches.
RESTRICTIONS	No smoking, no pets. Cady is the resident pooch.
REVIEWED	*America's Favorite Inns, B&Bs and Small Hotels; Recommended Country Inns—The Southwest; America's Most Charming Towns and Villages; The Complete Guide to Bed & Breakfasts, Inns and Guesthouses in the United States, Canada & Worldwide*

Magnolia House Bed & Breakfast, Fredericksburg

MEMBER	Professional Association of Innkeepers International, Historic Accommodations of Texas, Fredericksburg Traditional Bed & Breakfasts
RATED	AAA 3 Diamonds, Mobil 2 Stars
KUDOS/COMMENTS	"Big, southern breakfast; house and grounds are beautifully kept; host and hostess are helpful and charming." "Beautiful. Excellent breakfasts and service. Warm hosts."

Main Street Bed & Breakfast

337 East Main, Fredericksburg, TX 78624   830-997-0153
Sharon Grona, Resident Owner

Mitchell's Guest House

PO Box 1172, Fredericksburg, TX 78624   830-997-5521
Jan Mitchell, Resident Owner

THE NAGEL HOUSE

106 West Creek Street, Fredericksburg, TX 78624   830-997-5612
WEBSITE www.nagelhaus.com/

OLD NEFFENDORF FARM

Route 1, Box 95, Fredericksburg, TX 78624   830-997-7227

THE ORCHARD INN

1364 South US Highway 87, Fredericksburg, TX 78624   830-990-0257
Annette & Mark Wieser, Innkeepers   800-439-4320
German spoken   FAX 830-990-0257
EMAIL orchard@ktc.com   WEBSITE www.orchard-inn.com

LOCATION	From the intersection of Highways 290 and 87 south, go 1.5 miles on Highway 87. The Orchard Inn will be on your right at the top of a small hill. Enter the parking lot between the Orchard Inn and Das Peach Haus, a roadside market for fresh peaches.
OPEN	All year
DESCRIPTION	A 1904 two-story Victorian inn with period decor.
NO. OF ROOMS	Four suites with private bathrooms.
RATES	Year-round rates are $115-140 for a single or double. There is a two-night minimum stay on weekends, and cancellation requires five days' notice with a $10 charge per night.
CREDIT CARDS	American Express, Discover, MasterCard, Visa
BREAKFAST	Full breakfast is served in the dining room and may include egg casserole, roasted potatoes, peach crepes, grilled pork tenderloins, and strawberry frappé; or eggs Benedict, poached pears, assorted fruits, peach frappé; or southwestern egg casserole served with roasted raspberry chipotle sauce, and hot mixed fruit. Breakfast always includes coffee or tea, home-baked breads, jams, and jellies.
AMENITIES	Fresh flowers in each room; pond on site for fishing, boating, and swimming; owners make preparations for picnics, assist in recommending restaurants and making reservations, booking horse-carriage tours, scheduling appointments with spas and massage therapists, suggesting country tours of the area's sights, and recommending the best stores for shopping.

RESTRICTIONS	No smoking, no pets, children over 12 are welcome. Families with children may be seated in a separate dining room. Chuzzlewit and Maggie are the resident dogs; Kitty Kat is the cat.
MEMBER	Historic Accommodations of Texas, Fredericksburg Traditionals, Fredericksburg Hospitality Association

PATSY'S BED & BREAKFAST OF FREDERICKSBURG

703 West Austin, Fredericksburg, TX 78624   *210-493-5101*
Patsy Swendosn, Innkeeper   *FAX 210-493-1885*
EMAIL *patsy@aisi.net*   WEBSITE *www.aisi.net/patsys-place*

LOCATION	One hour north of San Antonio and one-and-a-half hours from Austin.
OPEN	All year
DESCRIPTION	A 1987 two-story German-style guesthouse with sophisticated country decor.
NO. OF ROOMS	Three rooms with private bathrooms. Try Cook's Cottage.
RATES	Year-round rates are $110-135 for a single or double, $110-135 for a suite, and $135 for the cottage. There is a two-night minimum stay and cancellation requires two weeks' notice.
CREDIT CARDS	American Express, Diners Club, Discover, MasterCard, Visa

Patsy's Bed & Breakfast of Fredericksburg, Fredericksburg

BREAKFAST	Mondays and Saturdays, full breakfast is served and includes quiche, crepes, pastries, waffles, and more. The remainder of the week, a complimentary champagne brunch is available at the Oak House.
AMENITIES	Double whirlpool, fresh flowers, robes, homemade bath salts, sachets to pack in bags when going home, wine and appetizers upon arrival, desserts on nightstand, chocolates on pillows, chocolate-dipped spoons, hot chocolate, cider, plates of home-baked pastries and cookies, gardens (herb, flower, and butterfly) to explore, porch swing and swing in the old oak tree in the front yard, peace and quiet, air conditioning, screened porch, refrigerators, microwaves, coffee bars, double-chocolate muffins, dinner reservation and carriage ride service, massage therapist available, special-occasion packages or a la carte, weddings in garden, anniversary and honeymoon packages, small meeting facilities, library, CD library, antiques, wine tour services, antiquing services.
RESTRICTIONS	No smoking inside, no pets, no children.
REVIEWED	*Travel and Leisure* magazine, *Country Almanac* magazine, *Country Home*

RAZORHORN BED & BREAKFAST

---

463 Heritage Lane, Fredericksburg, TX 78624   830-685-3589

RIVERVIEW INN AND FARM

---

402 West Main Street, Fredericksburg, TX 78624   830-997-7227
830-997-8555

THE SCHANDUA SUITE

---

205 East Main Street, Fredericksburg, TX 78624   830-990-1415
Sharla & Jonathan Godfrey, Innkeepers   888-990-1415
WEBSITE *www.schandua.com/*

LOCATION	At the southeast corner of the intersection of Highways 290 and 16 in downtown Fredericksburg.
OPEN	All year

The Schandua Suite, Fredericksburg

DESCRIPTION	An 1897 two-story hand-hewn native limestone Victorian host home decorated with antiques. Listed on the National and State Historic Registers.
NO. OF ROOMS	One suite with a private bathroom.
RATES	Year-round rates are $150-200. There is a two-night minimum stay on weekends and cancellation requires seven days' notice, three weeks during holidays.
CREDIT CARDS	Discover, MasterCard, Visa
BREAKFAST	Continental plus is served in the guestrooms and includes German pastries, fresh fruit, cereals, specialty coffee and tea, and fresh juices.
AMENITIES	Fresh flowers, evening beverage and hors d'oeuvres, robes, chocolates, private balcony, private courtyard, rooftop cactus garden, air conditioning, phone, TV, king-size bed, skylight, walk-in closet, pullman kitchen in library.
RESTRICTIONS	No smoking, no pets, no children
REVIEWED	*The Great Stays of Texas*
MEMBER	Historic & Hospitality Accommodations of Texas, Fredericksburg Traditional Bed & Breakfasts, Professional Association of Innkeepers International
KUDOS/COMMENTS	"Beautiful, large, and elegant suite. Wonderful for a honeymoon."

Schildknecht–Weidenfeller House

Fredericksburg, TX 78624
EMAIL *gasthaus@ktc.com*

830-997-5612
WEBSITE *www.speakez.net/schildknecht*

Settlers Crossing Bed & Breakfast

Fredericksburg, TX
WEBSITE *www.texassleepaways.com/settlerscrossing/*

800-874-1020

Town Creek Bed & Breakfast

304 North Edison Street, Fredericksburg, TX 78624
David Ross & Brent Waldoch, Innkeepers
Spanish spoken

830-997-6848
FAX 830-990-0115

LOCATION	Two blocks off Main Street in Fredericksburg's Historic District.
OPEN	All year
DESCRIPTION	An 1898 two-story Victorian inn and cottage with Victorian and antique decor. The inn sits in a parklike setting on an acre with a creek.
NO. OF ROOMS	Four rooms with private bathrooms. Try the Garden Cottage.
RATES	Year-round rates are $110-160 for a single or double. The cottage rents for $135. There is no minimum stay and cancellation requires seven days' notice.
CREDIT CARDS	Discover, MasterCard, Visa
BREAKFAST	A full gourmet breakfast is served in the dining room.
AMENITIES	All suites include private entrances and private baths. Other amenities include gardens, flowers, creekside setting.
RESTRICTIONS	No smoking, no children. Pets are allowed in the cottage. Dixie and Duke are the resident terriers.
MEMBER	Fredericksburg Bed & Breakfast Association

VINTAGE ROSE BED & BREAKFAST

511 West Main Street, Fredericksburg, TX 78624   800-997-1952
WEBSITE *www.vintage-rose.com/*   FAX 830-997-4065

VOGEL SUNDAY HOUSE

418 West Austin, Fredericksburg, TX 78624   512-997-4712
WEBSITE *www.ktc.net/gschmidt/vogelsun.htm*

WAY OF THE WOLF RANCH

HC 12 Box 92H, Fredericksburg, TX 78624   830-997-0711
EMAIL *wawolf@ktc.com*   888-929-9653
WEBSITE *www.wayofthewolf.com/*

FREEPORT

BANKERS INN BED & BREAKFAST

224 West Park Street, Freeport, TX 77541   409-233-4932

FULTON

CYGNET—A NATURAL BED & BREAKFAST

Fulton, TX 78358   512-790-7992

GAINESVILLE

Sixty miles north of Dallas on I-35, 7 miles south of the Oklahoma border, Gainesville hosts the annual Peanut Festival the third weekend in October. Lake Texoma and the Hagerman Wildlife Refuge are brief excursions to the northeast. Gainesville features outlet malls and plenty of antiquing too.

ALEXANDER BED & BREAKFAST

3692 County Road 201, Gainesville, TX 76240   903-564-7440
Jimmy & Pamela Alexander, Innkeepers   800-887-8794
EMAIL *abba@texoma.net*   FAX 903-564-7440 *(call first)*
WEBSITE *www.bbhost.com/alexanderbbacres*

LOCATION	Take Highway 82 to the Whitesboro exit for Highway 377. Travel south 4.6 miles, turn right onto County Line Churd Road, and turn right again onto West Line Road. Go 1.5 miles to Chaparral, turn left, and go to the dead end.
OPEN	All year
DESCRIPTION	A 1994 three-story Queen Anne country inn and guesthouse with eclectic furnishings, situated on 65 acres of woods and meadows.
NO. OF ROOMS	Five rooms with private bathrooms.

Alexander Bed & Breakfast, Gainesville

RATES	Year-round rates are $60-100 for a single or double and $125 for the guesthouse. There is no minimum stay and cancellation requires 72 hours' notice with a $10 fee.
CREDIT CARDS	American Express, Discover, MasterCard, Visa
BREAKFAST	Full breakfast is served in the dining room or delivered to guestrooms by request (for an additional $10) and includes quiche, omelets, egg casseroles, or homemade pancakes; bacon or sliced ham; a fruit dish; homemade rolls; coffee, tea, and juice. Dinner is also available by reservation for $15 per person.
AMENITIES	Robes, meeting area with private kitchenette, TV/VCR and video library, barn and farm animals, porch swings, spa, pool, hiking trails, stargazing, geothermal heat and air conditioning, three wood-burning fireplaces.
RESTRICTIONS	No smoking, children are welcome in the guesthouse. Allie and Freckles are the resident mixed beagles, Mr. G and Miss Buttons are the cats, and there are three horses, a donkey, and six head of cattle.
REVIEWED	*Bed & Breakfast Texas Style; Stash Tea Bed & Breakfast Guide; The Complete Guide to Bed & Breakfasts, Inns and Guesthouses in the United States, Canada & Worldwide*
MEMBER	Professional Association of Innkeepers International, Denton Area Bed & Breakfast Association, Red River Valley Bed & Breakfast Association

HONEY HUSH BED & BREAKFAST

321 South Dixon Street, Gainesville, TX 76240   817-665-1010

ROSE HOUSE BED & BREAKFAST

321 South Dixon Street, Gainesville, TX 76240   940-665-1010
Guy & Kay George, Innkeepers   FAX 940-665-1010 *(call first)*
EMAIL *RoseHouse@aol.com*
WEBSITE *www.innsite.com/inns/A002217.html*

LOCATION	Sixty miles north of Dallas/Fort Worth on I-35. The B&B is about a mile from the intersection of I-35 and California Street. Go east on California to the third traffic light, turn south on Dixon, and go two-and-a-half blocks. The B&B is the first two-story Victorian on the west side of Dixon, south of the courthouse.

Rose House Bed & Breakfast, Gainesville

OPEN	All year
DESCRIPTION	An 1898 two-story Queen Anne Victorian inn decorated with Victorian antiques.
NO. OF ROOMS	Five rooms with private bathrooms and one room shares one bathroom. Try the Aviary Suite.
RATES	Year-round rates are $60-110 for a single or double with a private bathroom, $45-65 for a single or double with a shared bathroom, and $80-110 for a suite. There is no minimum stay and cancellation requires seven days' notice, 14 days when the entire house is reserved.
CREDIT CARDS	American Express, MasterCard, Visa
BREAKFAST	Full Brennan's of New Orleans–style gourmet breakfast is served in the dining room; starts with a soup and ends with a flaming dessert. The main course includes fresh fruit, an egg dish, meat, stuffed French toast, coffee, and a choice of juices. Lunch or dinner can be catered when a group rents the entire house.

AMENITIES	Red and white Texas wines, homemade peach liqueur, early morning coffee and biscotti, gowns, nightshirts, terry robes, sleep machines, rubber duckies, antique pool table, player piano, crank phonograph.
RESTRICTIONS	No smoking, no pets, children over 12 are welcome. Miss Freckles is the resident German short-haired pointer; Ki-Ki is the cat. Both are outside animals.
REVIEWED	*Texas Bed & Breakfast Cookbook*
MEMBER	Texas Hotel & Motel Association, Denton Area Bed & Breakfast Association, Red River Valley Bed & Breakfast Association
KUDOS/COMMENTS	"This is a true B&B, owned and operated by a lovely couple."

GALVESTON

Southeast of Houston on I-45, Galveston is a long sliver of an island with much to offer. Stroll historic Strand Street, wander miles of beaches, explore Moody Gardens and Rainforest Pyramid, and check out the 1873 lighthouse on Bolivar Peninsula and the Texas Heroes Monument. Three museums of note are the Rice Straw, Texas Seaport, and Lone Star Flight Museums. Dickens on the Strand is a major event during Christmas, Mardi Gras is celebrated in style, and May's Crab Festival is a tasty event.

AWAY AT SEA INN

1127 Church Street, Galveston, TX 77550   *409-762-1668*
Larry Pithan, Innkeeper   *800-762-1668*
EMAIL *awayatsea@aol*   WEBSITE *awayatseainn.com*

LOCATION	After the bridge, I-45 turns into Broadway. Take Broadway to 10th Street, turn left, go to Church, and turn left again.
DESCRIPTION	An 1888 two-story Victorian inn decorated with period antiques, listed on the National Historic Register.
NO. OF ROOMS	Three rooms with private bathrooms.
RATES	Year-round rates are $85-165 for a single or double. There is a two-night minimum stay on weekends and cancellation requires five days' notice.
CREDIT CARDS	American Express, MasterCard, Visa
BREAKFAST	Full gourmet breakfast is served in the dining room.
AMENITIES	Bicycles, Jacuzzi
RESTRICTIONS	No smoking, no pets, no children.
REVIEWED	*Southern Living*

CAROUSEL INN

712 10th Street, Galveston, TX 77550   409-762-2166
Jim & Kathy Hughes, Resident Owners
Spanish spoken
WEBSITE www.sat.net/~jhughes

LOCATION	From Houston take I-45 south to Galveston. Do not exit off I-45 south as it becomes Broadway Street. Continue on Broadway to 10th Street and turn left. The inn is one-and-a-half blocks ahead on the right.
OPEN	All year
DESCRIPTION	An 1886 two-and-a-half-story Victorian decorated with period antiques, named for a handcarved carousel horse in the living room.
NO. OF ROOMS	Four rooms with private bathrooms.
RATES	Year-round rates for a single or double are $95-135. A minimum stay is required the first weekend in December (during the Dickens in the Strand celebration), and 72 hours' notice is required for cancellation.
CREDIT CARDS	American Express, Discover, MasterCard, Visa
BREAKFAST	Full breakfast is served in the dining room or guestrooms and includes a breakfast casserole, home-baked coffeecakes, muffins, biscuits, cinnamon rolls or sweet rolls; seasonal fresh fruit; fresh-squeezed orange juice and other beverages.
AMENITIES	Off-street lighted parking, central heat and air conditioning, antique player piano, antique phonograph with records, anniversary discounts, Jacuzzi in one room, space for small functions.
RESTRICTIONS	No smoking, no pets, children are welcome with prior approval.

COPPERSMITH INN BED & BREAKFAST

1914 Avenue M, Galveston, TX 77550   409-763-7004
Lisa Hering, Resident Owner   800-515-7444
WEBSITE cimarron.net/usa/tx/copper.html

THE GARDEN INN, CIRCA 1887

1601 Ball Street, Galveston, TX 77550   409-770-0592
Susan Milligan & Angela Whorton, Innkeepers
EMAIL as1231@aol.com   WEBSITE www.galveston.com/gardeninn

LOCATION	From Houston, take I-45 south to Galveston. I-45 will become Broadway (Highway 87). From Broadway, turn left onto 16th Street and go north 2 blocks. Turn right onto Ball Street. The inn will be on your right at the end of the block.
OPEN	All year
DESCRIPTION	An 1887 high Victorian chalet decorated with a garden theme, family heirlooms, antiques, and period reproductions.
NO. OF ROOMS	Two rooms with private bathrooms and two rooms share one bathroom. Try the Rose Room.
RATES	May through September, rates are $125-140 for a single or double with a private bathroom, $75-125 for a single or double with a shared bathroom, and $165-180 for a suite. October through April, rates are $89-140 for a single or double with a private bathroom, $75-125 for a single or double with a shared bathroom, and $165-180 for a suite. There is a minimum stay during special event and holiday weekends. Cancellation requires 72 hours' notice, seven days during special event and holiday weekends.
CREDIT CARDS	American Express, Discover, MasterCard, Visa
BREAKFAST	Full breakfast is served in the dining room and includes gourmet coffee, baked goods (breads, muffins, or biscuits), egg and potato dishes, fresh fruit, hot tea, and an assortment of jams and jellies.
AMENITIES	Flowers, swimming pool, hot tub, TV/VCR, videos, wine and cheese served on Friday and Saturday evenings, a coffee bard easily accessible to the rooms, off-street parking, central heat and air conditioning, porches, fireplaces.
RESTRICTIONS	No smoking, no pets, children over 12 are welcome. Monica is the resident Border collie; Moushka, Mick, and Katarina are the bichon frise dogs.
MEMBER	Galveston Bed & Breakfast Association

The Gilded Thistle, Galveston

THE GILDED THISTLE

1805 Broadway, Galveston, TX 77550   409-763-0194
Helen & Pat Hanemann, Resident Owners   800-654-9380
WEBSITE www.gildedthistle.com

LOCATION	From Houston, take I-45 south 45 minutes to Galveston.
OPEN	All year
DESCRIPTION	An 1892 two-story Queen Anne inn with elegant but homey decor.
NO. OF ROOMS	One room with a private bathroom and two rooms share two bathrooms.
RATES	Year-round rates are $165 for a single or double with a private bathroom and $145-155 for a single or double with a shared bathroom. There is a minimum stay during some weekends and cancellation requires seven days' notice.
CREDIT CARDS	Discover, MasterCard, Visa
BREAKFAST	Full breakfast includes fresh fruits, butter croissants, eggs, biscuits, bacon, glazed ham, potatoes, and waffles with roasted pecans and whipping cream. Dinner is also available.

AMENITIES	Flowers, robes, books and magazines, TV/VCR, videos, antique furnishings, teddy bears, air conditioning, parlor and verandas, candy, ice water, snacks, cold drinks, and homemade cheesecake.
RESTRICTIONS	No smoking inside, no pets
REVIEWED	*Best Places to Stay in the South, Best Places to Stay in the Southwest*
KUDOS/COMMENTS	"Excellent."

GOLDEN EAGLE RETREAT

12427 East Ventura Drive, Galveston, TX 77554   409-737-2112

HARBOR HOUSE

Pier 21, No. 28, Galveston, TX 77550   409-763-3321
EMAIL *hhouse@galveston.com*   800-874-3721
WEBSITE *www.harborhousepier21.com/*

HOLLYWOOD AT GALVESTON

3028 Seawall Boulevard, Galveston, TX 77550   409-750-8900
WEBSITE *www.galveston.com/hollywood*   888-899-0899
        FAX 409-750-8926

INN AT 1816 POSTOFFICE

1816 Postoffice, Galveston, TX 77550   409-765-9444
Bettye Hall & Judy Wilkie, Innkeepers
EMAIL *inn1816@aol.com*
WEBSITE *www.bbonline.com/tx/1816/*

LOCATION	Take I-45 south from Houston to Galveston. I-45 becomes Broadway after crossing the causeway. Continue on Broadway to 19th Street, turn left, go 5 blocks to Postoffice, and turn right.

The Inn at 1816 Postoffice, Galveston

OPEN	All year
DESCRIPTION	An 1886 two-story Victorian inn decorated with Victorian and fine furnishings and located in Galveston's East End Historic District.
NO. OF ROOMS	Five rooms with private bathrooms.
RATES	Year-round rates are $110-145 for a single or double and $195 for a suite. There is a minimum stay during special events and holidays. Ask about a cancellation policy.
CREDIT CARDS	American Express, Discover, MasterCard, Visa
BREAKFAST	Full breakfast is served in the dining room. Picnic baskets are also available for an extra charge.
AMENITIES	Jacuzzis, pool table, game room, afternoon refreshments, bicycles.
RESTRICTIONS	No smoking, no pets, children over 12 are welcome. Star and P. B. are the resident cats.
MEMBER	Galveston Bed & Breakfast Association

KEY LARGO

5400 Seawall Boulevard, Galveston, TX 77550   800-833-0120

OUT BY THE SEA BED & BREAKFAST

2134 Vista Drive, Crystal Beach TX 77650   409-684-1555
Jerry Reitz & Jim Winslett, Innkeepers   888-522-5926
Limited German spoken   FAX 409-684-1555 (call first)
EMAIL reitz-cbi@juno.com   WEBSITE www.outbythesea.com

LOCATION	On the Bolivar Peninsula across from Galveston Island. Take Highway 87 into Crystal Beach. From the Bolivar ferry landing, travel east 11.5 miles. Turn right at the sign for the B&B.
OPEN	All year
DESCRIPTION	A 1998 two-story beach house with antiques and English and beach decor, located 1 block from the Gulf of Mexico.
NO. OF ROOMS	Two rooms with private bathrooms.
RATES	May through September, rates are $80-150 for a single or double. October through April, rates are $60-100 for a single or double. There is no minimum stay. Please ask about a cancellation policy.
CREDIT CARDS	Diners Club, MasterCard, Visa
BREAKFAST	Full breakfast is served in the dining room and might include scrambled eggs, bacon, hashbrowns, toast, and fruit; or blueberry pancakes, sausage, and fruit. "We never serve the same breakfast to the same guest twice." Picnic lunch baskets are also available for taking to the beach.
AMENITIES	Complimentary beverage at check-in (wine, beer, soda, iced tea, lemonade, et cetera), tray of apples and cheese with crackers, cable TV/VCR in rooms, videos, fireplace (cocoa served in winter), air conditioning, beach umbrellas, beach towels, sand castle toys.
RESTRICTIONS	No smoking, no pets, children over 12 are welcome.
MEMBER	Galveston Bed & Breakfast Association

THE QUEEN ANNE BED & BREAKFAST

1915 Sealy Avenue, Galveston, TX 77550   409-763-7088
Ron & Jackie Metzger, Innkeepers   800-472-0930
EMAIL queenann@phoenix.net   FAX 409-765-6525
WEBSITE www.phoenix.net/~queenann

LOCATION   From downtown Houston, take I-45 south to Galveston
                   (approximately one hour out of Houston). After crossing the bridge
                   onto the island, I-45 becomes Broadway. Proceed down Broadway
                   to 20th Street and turn left. Go 1 block to Sealy Avenue and turn
                   right. The B&B is the fourth house on the right.

OPEN   All year

DESCRIPTION   A 1905 three-story late Victorian Queen Anne–style host home with
                   elegant Victorian decor, including antique furniture, 10-foot pocket
                   doors, stained glass, inlaid wood parquet floors, and four porches.
                   Listed on the National Historic Register.

NO. OF ROOMS   Three rooms with private bathrooms and two rooms share one
                   bathroom. Try the Cape Fear Room.

RATES   Rates are $100-125 for a single or double with a private bathroom,
                   $85-100 for a single or double with a shared bathroom, and $125-
                   145 for a suite. There is a minimum stay from May through
                   September and cancellation requires 48 hours' notice.

CREDIT CARDS   American Express, Discover, MasterCard, Visa

BREAKFAST   Full gourmet breakfast is served in the dining room.

AMENITIES   Robes, bicycles, afternoon refreshments, coffee served on upstairs
                   porch before breakfast, climate-controlled rooms, map of island
                   and brochures.

RESTRICTIONS   No smoking, no pets, children over 15 are welcome.

REVIEWED   *The Complete Guide to Bed & Breakfasts, Inns & Guesthouses in
                   the United States, Canada & Worldwide; Victorian Voyages: U.S.
                   Travel Guide for Victorian Era Enthusiasts; Bed & Breakfast Guest
                   Houses and Inns of America*

MEMBER   Galveston Bed & Breakfast Association

ROSE HALL

2314 Avenue M, Galveston Island, TX 77550   409-763-1577
WEBSITE www.galveston.com/rosehall/

KUDOS/COMMENTS   "Very caring hosts."

The Victorian Inn Bed & Breakfast

511 17th Street, Galveston, TX 77550   409-762-3235
Marcy Hanson, Manager   FAX 409-762-6351
WEBSITE *www.bestinns.net/usa/tx/vi.html*

LOCATION	In the Historic District, less than 1 mile from the Strand and 0.1 mile from the beach.
OPEN	All year
DESCRIPTION	An 1899 four-story Italianate Victorian inn with veranda and gardens and Victorian furnishings.
NO. OF ROOMS	Three suites with private bathrooms and three rooms share one central-hallway bathroom.
RATES	Year-round rates are $100 for a room with a shared bathroom and $150 for a suite. There is a two-night minimum stay during weekends and cancellation requires 72 hours' notice.
CREDIT CARDS	American Express, MasterCard, Visa
BREAKFAST	Full breakfast buffet is served in the dining room.
AMENITIES	Horse-drawn carriage, butler's pantry full of snacks, homemade cookies, wine, toiletries, robes, private verandas, all rooms have king-size brass beds, and air conditioning.
RESTRICTIONS	No smoking, no pets, no children

Georgetown

A mere 20 miles north of Austin on I-35, Georgetown features a few local points of interest and events all its own. Check out the Candle Factory and Inner Space Caverns. Enjoy Mayfair and the Christmas Stroll.

Claibourne House

912 Forest Street, Georgetown, TX 78626   512-930-3934
Clare Easley, Innkeeper   FAX 512-869-0202
WEBSITE *bbonline.com*

LOCATION	Twenty-five minutes north of Austin. From I-35, take the Highway 29 exit east. At the second stoplight (Austin Avenue), take a left, drive to 10th Street, take another left, and go 2 blocks to Forest Street. The B&B is on the corner of 10th and Forest, two blocks from the historic square in the heart of Georgetown.

OPEN	All year
DESCRIPTION	A restored 1896 two-story asymmetrical Victorian host home on three lots, with wood floors, five fireplaces, 12-foot ceilings, big windows, a wraparound porch, and a brick terrace.
NO. OF ROOMS	Four rooms with private bathrooms.
RATES	Year-round rates are $85-125 for a single or double. There is no minimum stay and cancellation requires one week's notice.
CREDIT CARDS	MasterCard, Visa
BREAKFAST	Continental plus is served in the dining room and includes breads, biscuits, croissants, fruit, cereal, and bacon.
RESTRICTIONS	No smoking, children over 12 are welcome. Daisy is the resident cat.
MEMBER	Professional Association of Innkeepers International
AWARDS	1989, Beautify Georgetown Award, for restoration, from the City of Georgetown

HERON HILL FARM BED & BREAKFAST

1350 County Road 143, Georgetown, TX 78628   *512-863-0461*
WEBSITE www.touringtexas.com

INN ON THE SQUARE BED & BREAKFAST

104 1/2 West 8th Street, Georgetown, TX 78628   *512-868-2203*

PAGE HOUSE

1000 Leander Road, Georgetown, TX 78628   *512-863-8979*
Paula Arand, Resident Owner

RIGHT AT HOME BED & BREAKFAST

1208 Main Street, Georgetown, TX 78626
Barbara Shepley, Resident Owner

512-930-3409
800-651-0021
FAX 512-869-0694

GILMER

SARAH'S BED & BREAKFAST

104 North Montgomery Street, Gilmer, TX 75644
WEBSITE www.sarahsbedandbreakfast.com/

903-843-6203

GLADEWATER

A hundred miles northeast of Dallas, Gladewater features the Helen Lee Estate Daffodil Gardens, the East Texas Gusher Days, the Gladewater Round-Up Rodeo (a PRCA-sanctioned event since 1937), a major arts and crafts festival with over 200 exhibitors, and Christmastime in Gusherville.

HONEYCOMB SUITES

111 North Main Street, Gladewater, TX 75647
Bill & Susan Morgan, Resident Owners
EMAIL sho4go@internetwork.net

903-845-4430
FAX 903-845-2448
WEBSITE honeycombsuites.com

LOCATION	Gladewater is 13 miles north of I-20 on Highway 271 (Main Street). Honeycomb Suites is located in the center of the Antique District, one block north of the railroad tracks, and one-and-a-half blocks south of the intersection of Highways 80 and 271.
OPEN	All year
DESCRIPTION	A 1933 two-story commercial brick building. The owners operate a bakery/restaurant on the first floor and five suites on the second floor. There are two additional suites in a separate building in the same block. All suites are decorated in different themes such as Victorian country cottage, art deco, nautical, and Americana.

NO. OF ROOMS	Seven rooms with private bathrooms.
RATES	Year-round rates for a single or double are $75-130. A minimum stay is required during holidays and festival weekends and for rooms with whirlpools, and cancellation requires seven days' notice.
CREDIT CARDS	American Express, Discover, MasterCard, Visa
BREAKFAST	Full breakfast is served in the dining room and includes seasonal fresh fruit, an entrée such as quiche, crepes, or apple-puffed pancakes, and fresh-baked bread. Lunch, dinner, and special meals are available. On Saturday evenings, carriage rides and candlelight dinners are available by reservation.
AMENITIES	All suites have queen-size beds, cable TV, and individual heat and air conditioning. Four of the seven suites have whirlpool tubs for two.
RESTRICTIONS	No smoking, no pets, no children.
MEMBER	Professional Association of Innkeepers International

PRIMROSE LANE

116 East Glade Avenue, Gladewater, TX 75647   *903-845-5922*

GLEN ROSE

In the Texas Hill Country, southwest of Fort Worth on Highway 67, Glen Rose features the Fossil Rim Wildlife Center, Dinosaur Valley State Park, bluegrass and Celtic festivals, and Barnard's Mill Arat Museum.

BUSSEY'S SOMETHING SPECIAL B&B

202 Hereford Street, Glen Rose, TX 76043   *254-897-4843*
Morris & Susan Bussey, Innkeepers

LOCATION	From Glen Rose, take FM 56 south for 0.4 mile. The B&B is on the left.
OPEN	All year
DESCRIPTION	A 1986 inn with a two-story guesthouse and one-story cottage, with Arts & Crafts and antique decor.
NO. OF ROOMS	Two rooms with private bathrooms.

Bussey's Something Special B&B, Glen Rose

RATES	Year-round rates for the guesthouse are $80-100. There is no minimum stay and cancellation requires 48 hours' notice.
CREDIT CARDS	American Express, Discover, MasterCard, Visa
BREAKFAST	Continental plus includes eggs, milk, bread, muffins, fruit, juices, coffee, teas, hot chocolate, cereal, bagels, pancakes, and waffles. Special meals are available at an extra cost.
AMENITIES	Heat and air conditioning, whirlpool tub, flowers, garden and porches, games, toys, puzzles, crib, playpen, highchairs, cassette players and tapes, magazines and books, fossil hunts, tours, tennis.
RESTRICTIONS	No smoking, no pets
MEMBER	Texas Hotel & Motel Association

INN ON THE RIVER

205 Barnard Street, Glen Rose, TX 76043   *254-897-2929*
Ernest & Shirley Reinke, Innkeepers   *800-575-2101*
Spanish spoken   *FAX 254-897-7729*
EMAIL *inn@innontheriver.com*   WEBSITE *www.innontheriver.com*

LOCATION	Fifteen miles south of Granbury, 30 miles west of Cleburne, and 30 miles east of Stephenville.
OPEN	All year
DESCRIPTION	A 1906 two-story inn decorated with traditional elegance and antique furnishings, located on the banks of the Pulasky River. Listed on the State Historic Register.

NO. OF ROOMS	Twenty-two rooms with private bathrooms. Try the Garden Room Suite.
RATES	Year-round rates are $115-195 for a single or double and $155-195 for a suite. There is a minimum stay during holiday weekends and cancellation requires 48 hours' notice. "No-shows will be charged the full rate."
CREDIT CARDS	American Express, Discover, MasterCard, Visa
BREAKFAST	Full breakfast is served in the dining room and includes Columbian coffee, fresh-squeezed orange juice, fresh fruit, raspberry poppyseed muffins, Belgian waffles with seasonal fruit and whipped cream, and fresh sausage links. Dinner is also available.
AMENITIES	Swimming pool, mountain bikes, featherbeds, state-of-the-art meeting facilities, one room is handicapped accessible.
RESTRICTIONS	No smoking, no pets, no children
RATED	ABBA 3 Crowns
KUDOS/COMMENTS	"Beautiful sites on the Pulasky River with Adirondack chairs, excellent food service, gracious hospitality." "Wonderful, tranquil setting, delicious food, attention to detail."

LILLY HOUSE

611 Northeast Barnard Street, Glen Rose, TX 76043   *254-897-9747*

POPEJAY HAUS

PO Box 2023, Glen Rose, TX 76043   *254-897-3521*
Kody & Klare Popejoy, Resident Owners

KUDOS/COMMENTS	"Very unique German decor. Cabins in the woods. Great getaway, very clean."

WHITE GABLES INN

101 Vine, Glen Rose, TX 76043   *254-897-2149*

KUDOS/COMMENTS	"Friendly, great food, privacy, takes families, in town, very clean."

THE WILD ROSE INN

401 Grace Street, Glen Rose, TX 76043   254-897-4112
Sheilah Keeling, Resident Owner

KUDOS/COMMENTS "Lovely Victorian home, lots of keepsakes displayed, good food."

YE OLE MAPLE INN B&B

1509 Van Zandt, Glen Rose, TX 76043   817-897-3456
Roberta Maple, Resident Owner
WEBSITE ivillage.bbchannel.com/bbc/p217435.asp

KUDOS/COMMENTS "Fluff and fancy, gourmet breakfast, friendly host and hostess, very
clean and comfortable." "Beautiful rooms, excellent food."

GONZALES

The first shot fired in Texas' war for independence from Mexico rang out in
Gonzales. The Chisolm Trail Gathering in April honors the history of the cattle
industry in Texas. Visit the Old Jail Museum and Pioneer Village. Gonzales is east
of San Antonio on Alternate Highway 90.

HOUSTON HOUSE BED & BREAKFAST

621 Saint George Street, Gonzales, TX 78629   830-672-6940
WEBSITE www.houstonhouse.com   888-477-0760

ST. JAMES INN

723 St. James, Gonzales, TX 78629   830-672-7066
Ann & J. R. Covert, Resident Owners
EMAIL st.james@gvec.net

LOCATION   Three blocks from downtown.

OPEN   All year

DESCRIPTION	A 1914 three-story 10,000-square-foot Greek revival inn. The house was a former Texas cattle baron's mansion.
NO. OF ROOMS	Five rooms with private bathrooms.
RATES	Year-round rates for a single or double are $65-125 and a suite is $150 and up. A two-night minimum stay is required on weekends and cancellations require three days' notice.
CREDIT CARDS	American Express, MasterCard, Visa
BREAKFAST	Full gourmet breakfast is served in the dining room and includes banana or apricot bread, fruit, omelets, crepes, or "mile-high" French pancakes (the house speciality), and desserts. Lunch, dinner and special meals are available by arrangement.
AMENITIES	Air conditioning, fireplace, lemonade, tea and cookies.
RESTRICTIONS	No smoking, no pets, children over 12 are welcome.
MEMBER	Historic Accommodations of Texas, Texas Hotel & Motel Association
RATED	AAA 3 Diamond, Mobil 2 Stars

GRANBURY

About 30 miles southwest of Fort Worth on Highway 377, Granbury's Historic Town Square was recently voted "Best in Texas." The town's myriad draws are headlined by the Granbury Opera House and Theater. Built in 1893, the opera and theater house draws sell-out crowds every weekend for drama, comedy, and musical performances. The Civil War Re-enactment in September is another major event. Other happenings of note include the Old-Fashioned Fourth of July celebration, the Harvest Moon Festival in October, and the Candlelight Tour of Homes in December. For a real taste of Texas, check out the General Granbury Bean and Rib Cook-off in March. Granbury's drive-in movie theater is one of only eight still operating in Texas.

ALFONSO'S LOFT

137 East Pearl, Granbury, TX 76048

817-573-3308
FAX 817-573-3308

Angel of the Lake

606 East Bridge Street, Granbury, TX 76048   817-573-3143
Mike & Helen Pemberton, Innkeepers   800-641-0073
EMAIL *arbor@itexas.net*   WEBSITE *www2.itexas.net/angel*

LOCATION	Granbury is 35 miles southwest of Fort Worth, 70 miles southwest of Dallas on Highway 377. Four blocks east of the historic Granbury Square on Business Highway 377 (Pearl Street).
OPEN	All year
DESCRIPTION	A 1998 Victorian host home with uncluttered, Victorian interior decor, situated with panoramic views of Lake Granbury.
NO. OF ROOMS	Three rooms with private bathrooms. Try the Angel's Loft.
RATES	Year-round rates are $165 for a single or double. There is a minimum stay during holidays and special events, and cancellation requires seven days' notice.
CREDIT CARDS	American Express, Discover, MasterCard, Visa
BREAKFAST	Full breakfast is served on china in the dining room and includes homemade pastries, eggs, meat, and fruit.
AMENITIES	Each room with cable TV, king-size bed, ceiling fan, six-foot marble Jacuzzi, central air conditioning and heat; guest refrigerator stocked with complimentary soft drinks and ice cream; horse-drawn carriage will pick you up curbside.
RESTRICTIONS	No smoking, no pets, no children. Penny is the resident pooch. "Penny lives at the Arbor House just across the garden. You may see her basking in the sun or resting on the porch of the big house."

Annabelle's Victorian Rose Bed

404 West Bridge Street, Granbury, TX 76048   817-579-7673
WEBSITE *www.annabellesrose.com*

Apple Gate Bed and Breakfast

221 West Pearl Street, Granbury, TX 76048   817-573-2811
WEBSITE *www.applegatebb.com*

ARBOR HOUSE LAKESIDE INN B&B

530 East Pearl Street, Granbury, TX 76048   817-573-0073
Mike & Helen Pemberton, Innkeepers   800-641-0073
WEBSITE arbor@itexas.net   *WEBSITE www2.itexas.net/~arbor*

LOCATION	Granbury is 35 miles southwest of Fort Worth, 70 miles southwest of Dallas on Highway 377. Four blocks east of the historic Granbury Square on Business Highway 377 (Pearl Street).
OPEN	All year
DESCRIPTION	A 1995 two-story Queen Anne Victorian host home with an uncluttered, Victorian interior decor.
NO. OF ROOMS	Seven rooms with private bathrooms. Try Victoria's Suite.
RATES	Year-round rates are $100-165 for a single or double. There is a minimum stay during holidays and special events, and cancellation requires seven days' notice.
CREDIT CARDS	American Express, Discover, MasterCard, Visa
BREAKFAST	Full breakfast is served on elegant china in the formal dining room and includes homemade pastry, egg casseroles, fruit, and homemade bread and jelly.
AMENITIES	Central air conditioning and heat; ceiling fans; cultured marble showers; guest refrigerator in the kitchen stocked with soda, milk, juice, and ice cream ("Guests are invited to 'raid the frig'"); home-baked chocolate-chip brownies served hot from the oven in the afternoon; flowers and cards in rooms for anniversaries, birthdays, and other special occasions; specialize in church retreats, corporate planning meetings, and adult reunions. "In conjunction with our other B&B (next door), we can provide 10 guestrooms and meeting facilities for up to 30 persons. We work with other B&B's to accommodate groups of over 20 persons."
RESTRICTIONS	No smoking, no pets, children over 12 are welcome. Penny is the resident pooch.
REVIEWED	*Southern Living, The Romantic Southwest, The Texas Monthly: Texas Bed & Breakfast*
MEMBER	Texas Hotel & Motel Association

THE CAPTAIN'S HOUSE ON THE LAKE

123 West Doyle, Granbury, TX 76048   817-579-6664
Julia Pannell, Innkeeper
Some Spanish spoken
EMAIL captain@itexas.net
WEBSITE www.virtualcities.com/ons/tx/d/txd2801.htm

LOCATION	From the historic town square, go 1 block west to Lambert, turn left, and drive to a stop sign. The B&B is on West Doyle across from the stop sign.
OPEN	All year
DESCRIPTION	An 1880s two-story Queen Anne Victorian host home with period decor and excellent lake views. There is also a 1920 cottage.
NO. OF ROOMS	Five rooms with private bathrooms. Try the Mary Kate Doyle Suite.
RATES	Year-round rates are $98-141 for a single or double and $115-141 for a suite. There is a two-night minimum stay on summer weekends, two to three nights during festivals and holidays.
CREDIT CARDS	No
BREAKFAST	Continental breakfast is delivered to the guestrooms and includes hot breads, fruit, juice, coffee, and more. Continental breakfast is left in the cottage. Brunch and lunch are available in the bakery.
RESTRICTIONS	No smoking, no pets, children over 13 are welcome in the Captain's House. Children of all ages are welcome in the cottage. Sweet Pea is the resident Maltese.
REVIEWED	*Historic Accommodations of Texas, Texas Highways*
MEMBER	Granbury Association of Bed & Breakfasts

DABNEY HOUSE

106 South Jones, Granbury, TX 76048   817-579-1260
John & Gwen Hurley, Innkeepers   800-566-1260
EMAIL safe-dabney@flash.net

LOCATION	Take the Business Highway 377 exit to downtown Granbury. From the downtown courthouse square, go west on West Pearl Street (Business 377) for 7 blocks to the traffic light. Continue 1 block past the light and turn left onto South Jones. The B&B is on the corner of West Pearl Street and South Jones.
OPEN	All year

DESCRIPTION	A 1907 Craftsman host home with hardwood floors, beveled and stained glass, large exposed ceiling beams, and a limestone fireplace, and decorated with antiques, Gwen's cross-stitch, German paper art, and quilts.
NO. OF ROOMS	Five rooms with private bathrooms. Try the Dabney Suite.
RATES	Year-round rates are $60-105 for a single or double. There is a minimum stay during holidays and cancellation requires 48 hours' notice, two weeks for a whole-house rental.
CREDIT CARDS	American Express, MasterCard, Visa
BREAKFAST	Full breakfast is served in the dining room and includes pecan waffles with ham (the specialty of the house), baked blueberry French toast, or baked egg fluff with sausage and homemade biscuits and jam. Candlelight dinner packages are also available. Room service is available in the suite.
AMENITIES	Complimentary cold drinks and juice, anniversary or birthday cakes with advance notice, hot tub in the backyard, each room individually heated and cooled, two front porch swings, VCR and videos.
RESTRICTIONS	No smoking inside, no pets, children over 10 are welcome. Buster is the resident dachshund; Patches is the calico. "Buster is kept mostly upstairs in our private quarters. Patches is an outside cat and likes to sit in your lap on the porch swing. Neither are ever allowed in the guestrooms."
REVIEWED	*Texas Bed & Breakfast, Quick Escapes from Dallas/Fort Worth*
MEMBER	Texas Hotel & Motel Association, Granbury Area Bed & Breakfast Association

DERRICK–HOFFMAN FARM

7030 Thorp Spring Road, Weatherford, TX 76087 817-573-9952
Jean D. Hoffman, Resident Owner 800-573-9953
EMAIL *jhoffman@hcnews.com* FAX 817-573-3542

LOCATION	Between Granbury and Weatherford on FM 2580. From Granbury take Highway 51, then go north on Highway 4 for 4 miles and turn right on FM 2580. Drive 6.9 miles.
OPEN	All year
DESCRIPTION	A late 1800s farmhouse-style guesthouse furnished with antiques, on a 260-acre operating farm. There is also one suite in the main house.
NO. OF ROOMS	The guesthouse has two rooms that share one bathroom. The main house has one suite with a private bathroom.

RATES	Year-round rates for a single or double begin at $80. There is no minimum stay. "Cancellation is based on honesty and integrity."
CREDIT CARDS	No
BREAKFAST	Full breakfast is served in the host's home and includes fruit juice, fresh fruit, breakfast meat, eggs, homemade biscuits, sweet bread, coffee, tea, and milk.
AMENITIES	Fresh flowers, walking paths in pasture, bicycle surrey. Suite in the main house is handicapped accessible.
RESTRICTIONS	No smoking. Pets and children are welcome. The farm animals include a "mutt" called Susie, a herd of cows, a horse, and a donkey.

THE DOYLE HOUSE BED & BREAKFAST

205 West Doyle, Granbury, TX 76048   817-573-6492
Linda Stoll, Innkeeper
EMAIL *doylehse@hcnews.com*   WEBSITE *www.doylehouse.com*

LOCATION	Two blocks from the town square. Turn south on Houston Street, which turns into Doyle.
OPEN	All year
DESCRIPTION	An 1880 two-story estate featuring three separate accommodations with traditional decor, situated on the banks of Lake Granbury.
NO. OF ROOMS	Three rooms with private bathrooms. Try the Emily Suite or the Pool Cottage.
RATES	Year-round rates are $105-130 for a single or double. There is a minimum stay during summer and festival weekends, and cancellation requires 48 hours' notice.
CREDIT CARDS	American Express, Diners Club, Discover, MasterCard, Visa
BREAKFAST	Full breakfast is served in the dining room and includes a main entrée with fruit, meat, juice, sweet breads, and beverages.
AMENITIES	Snack tray, flowers in rooms, individual climate control, pool, fishing dock, yard games, two suites with Jacuzzi tubs.
RESTRICTIONS	No smoking. Clover is the resident cocker spaniel, and Barrington and Gracie are the cats.
REVIEWED	*Texas Bed & Breakfast, Recommended Country Inns—The Southwest, Texas Bed & Breakfast Cookbook, The Great Stays of Texas, Specialties of the House—A Country Inn B&B Cookbook*
MEMBER	Historic Accommodations of Texas, Granbury Area Bed & Breakfasts

ELIZABETH CROCKETT BED & BREAKFAST

201 West Pearl Street, Granbury, TX 76048   817-573-7208
WEBSITE www2.itexas.net/~crockettb&b   FAX 817-573-7209

THE IRON HORSE INN

616 North Thorp Spring Road, Granbury, TX 76048   817-579-5535
Bob Atkinson, Resident Owner
WEBSITE www.theironhorseinn.com/

KUDOS/COMMENTS   "Exceedingly comfortable, breakfast was fantastic, and the
                  innkeepers were friendly and hospitable beyond our expectations."

THE NUTT HOUSE HOTEL

121 East Bridge Street, Granbury, TX 76048   817-279-9457

OAK TREE FARM

6415 Charmichael Court, Granbury, TX 76049   817-326-5595
Jeanette & Michael Charmichael and   800-326-5595
Jeanne Bennett, Resident Owners

PEARL STREET INN BED & BREAKFAST

319 West Pearl Street, Granbury, TX 76048   817-579-7465
Danette Hebda, Resident Owner   888-732-7578
EMAIL danette@itexas.net   WEBSITE www2.itexas.net/~danette

LOCATION   Three blocks west of Granbury's historic square.

OPEN   All year

Pearl Street Inn Bed & Breakfast, Granbury

DESCRIPTION	A 1911 two-story prairie-style four-square home with Victorian touches and antiques, pocket doors, two porches, a massive front entry, winding wisteria, and 42 windows.
NO. OF ROOMS	Five rooms with private bathrooms. Danette recommends the English Garden Suite.
RATES	Year-round weekend rates are $74-109 for a single or double. Weekday rates are $20 less. There is a minimum stay during special events and some holidays, and cancellation requires seven days' notice.
CREDIT CARDS	No
BREAKFAST	Full breakfast is served in the dining room and includes an egg dish, breads, fruit, meat, coffee, tea, and juice. Special meals are available for parties of six or more with reservations.
AMENITIES	Complimentary instant coffee, tea, cocoa, and cookies; clawfoot tubs, king-size beds.
RESTRICTIONS	No smoking, no pets, children over 10 are welcome.
REVIEWED	*Texas Bed & Breakfast, Texas Bed & Breakfast Cookbook, The Great Stays of Texas, Quick Escapes from Dallas/Fort Worth*
MEMBER	Professional Association of Innkeepers International, Historic Accommodations of Texas, Texas Hotel & Motel Association

POMEGRANATE HOUSE

1002 West Pearl Street, Granbury, TX 76048   817-279-7412
Alden & Billie Moore, Innkeepers   888-503-7659
WEBSITE *www.pomegranatehouse.com*

LOCATION	Eight blocks west of historic Granbury Square, 35 miles southwest of Fort Worth, 70 miles southwest of Dallas on Highway 377.
OPEN	All year
DESCRIPTION	A 1906 Victorian host home that features a unique collection of antiques and romantic decor. The home is shaded by majestic oaks.
NO. OF ROOMS	Four rooms with private bathrooms. Try the Lilacs & Lace Suite.
RATES	Year-round rates are $89-129 for a single or double. There is a minimum stay during holidays and special events, and cancellation requires three days' notice.
CREDIT CARDS	American Express, MasterCard, Visa
BREAKFAST	Full breakfast is served in the dining room or is delivered to the Lilacs & Lace Suite and includes baked egg casseroles, bacon or ham, fruit, and waffles or pastries.
AMENITIES	Twenty-four-hour beverage bar with house specialty "Sweetie" cookies; central air conditioning and heat; sunroom; parlor with TV, phone, and fresh flowers; sitting areas in the garden; koi pond.
RESTRICTIONS	No smoking, no pets, children over 12 are welcome. Buddy is the resident Mexican redhead parrot.

GRAND SALINE

East of Dallas on Highway 80, Grand Saline is a mere dozen miles northeast of Canton and the wildly popular flea market, First Monday Trades Days. The Salt Palace is a noteworthy local attraction.

AUNTIE DOT'S B&B

421 Waldrip Street, Grand Saline, TX 75140   903-567-5410
Dorothy Miller, Resident Owner   800-256-7460

LOCATION	From Highway 80 at Waldrip Street in Grand Saline, turn north on Waldrip and go 2 blocks. The B&B is on the left, a green house with white trim.
OPEN	All year

DESCRIPTION	A 1950 one-story guesthouse with country and Victorian decor. Dorothy recommends the Victorian Room.
NO. OF ROOMS	Three rooms with private bathrooms.
RATES	Year-round rates are $65 for a single or double and $125 for a suite that sleeps six. There is a two-night minimum stay during Canton First Monday weekends.
CREDIT CARDS	American Express, Discover, MasterCard, Visa
BREAKFAST	Continental plus breakfast is served in the dining room and includes fruit, yogurt, sweet rolls, toast, jellies, homemade cookies, coffee, milk, and juice.
AMENITIES	Teas, coffee, and cookies; fresh flowers; air conditioning; two porches; full kitchen privileges.
RESTRICTIONS	No smoking indoors, no pets

LIT'L FANNIE'S

4564 State Highway 110, Grand Saline, TX 75140   903-962-3737
Beth Swint Fisher, Innkeeper   903-962-5675

LOCATION	From the only stoplight in Grand Saline, go south on Highway 110 for 5 miles and take a left to the B&B.
OPEN	All year
DESCRIPTION	A main house with a room and a suite that sleeps five to eight people, and five additional buildings: the Bunk House, School House, Farm House, Hen House, and Meetin' House (a converted house).
NO. OF ROOMS	Two rooms in the main house with private bathrooms; guesthouses have two rooms and one bathroom.
RATES	Year-round rates for a single or double are $65-100. There is no minimum stay and cancellation requires seven days' notice.
CREDIT CARDS	No
BREAKFAST	Continental breakfast is served in the main house and includes coffee, juice, muffins, and donuts.
AMENITIES	Air conditioning, swimming pool, fishing, quiet country setting, beautiful sunsets and wildflowers.
RESTRICTIONS	Smoking on porches only

GRANITE SHOALS

ISLAND VIEW BED & BREAKFAST

1710 Lakecrest Drive, Granite Shoals, TX 78654   *512-244-7126*

GRAPEVINE

On Highway 114, Grapevine celebrates its namesake fruit in both spring and fall. The annual Texas New Vintage Festival kicks off the third weekend in April, and Grapefest gets underway the second weekend in September. The Heritage Festival takes place in May. Tiny downtown Grapevine features a lovely historical main street.

1934 BED & BREAKFAST

322 East College Street, Grapevine, TX 76051   *817-424-4207*
Willie & Wanda Livingston, Innkeepers   *FAX 817-251-1934*
WEBSITE *www.home1.gte.net/the1934*

LOCATION	Take Highway 114 into Grapevine, exit onto Main Street (Spur 103), go north to East College Street, and turn east.
OPEN	All year
DESCRIPTION	A restored 1934 redbrick Craftsman with art deco and period furnishings, tiger oak and birdseye maple hardwood, beveled glass, and large shady porches; situated on 1.5 acres, 1 block from historic Main Street.
NO. OF ROOMS	Three rooms with private bathrooms.
RATES	Year-round rates are $95-115 for a single or double and $115 for a suite. There is no minimum stay and cancellation requires 72 hours' notice.
CREDIT CARDS	American Express, Discover, MasterCard, Visa
BREAKFAST	Full five-course gourmet breakfast is served on sterling silver in the dining room.
AMENITIES	Fresh flowers in rooms; hospitality area with mineral water, soft drinks, and snacks; porches and wooden deck; private parking; central heat and air conditioning.
RESTRICTIONS	No smoking, no pets, children over 12 are welcome.

GREENVILLE

IRON SKILLET INN BED & BREAKFAST

664 Forrester Street, Greenville, TX 75401   *903-455-0074*

HAMILTON

About 75 miles west of Waco at the junction of Highways 281 and 36, this sleepy town features year-round antiquing and gift shopping on the town square. The Dove Festival takes flight over Labor Day Weekend. Wonder from whence you came? Check out Hamilton's Genealogy Research Library.

HAMILTON GUEST HOTEL

109 North Rice, Hamilton, TX 76531   *254-386-8977*

ROOM WITH A VIEW

203 South College, Hamilton, TX 76531   *254386-3089*
Patt Bartlett, Innkeeper   *800-401-4100 (pin: 2080)*
EMAIL *pmoore@htcomp.net*   WEBSITE *bbchannel.com*

LOCATION	Located 1 block west of the post office in the center of Hamilton.
OPEN	All year
DESCRIPTION	A 1908 two-story prairie farmhouse decorated with antiques and unique furnishings, situated on 1.5 secluded acres in the Hamilton Cultural District with views of the town square.
NO. OF ROOMS	Two rooms with private bathrooms and two rooms share one bathroom. Try Sylvia's Suite.

RATES	Year-round rates are $75-85 for a single or double with a private bathroom, $65 for a single or double with a shared bathroom, and $95 for a suite. There is no minimum stay. Ask about a cancellation policy.
CREDIT CARDS	No
BREAKFAST	Full breakfast is served in the breakfast room and includes egg pie (an egg, sausage, and cheese casserole), biscuits, seasonal fruit, juice, and coffee.
AMENITIES	Central heat and air conditioning; ceiling fans in all rooms; portable CD player; access to computer, Internet, and email; cozy library upstairs and even more books downstairs.
RESTRICTIONS	No smoking, no pets, children over 12 are welcome.

HARLINGEN

THE ROSS HAUS

PO Box 3306, Harlingen, TX 78551   512-425-1717
Darrel & Grace Johnson, Resident Owners

HASKELL

THE BEVERS HOUSE ON BRICK STREET B&B

311 North Avenue F, Haskell, TX 79521   940-864-3284
Ruby Turner, Resident Owner   800-580-3284
WEBSITE *www.westex.net/rturner*

HENDERSON

Back in the 1930s, Henderson was the site of the world's largest oil field. November brings the great Heritage Syrup Festival, East Texas' largest folk-art festival. Henderson is about 50 miles west of the Louisiana border, southwest of Shreveport on Highway 79.

LAZY STAEHS BED & BREAKFAST

1816 Millville Drive, Henderson, TX 75652   903-655-6680
WEBSITE www.lazystaehs.com

TREE HOUSE BED & BREAKFAST

1305 Westwood Drive, Henderson, TX 75654   903-655-1210
Mary Jackson & Gizmo (the Shih Tzu), Innkeepers
EMAIL trehouse@ballistic.com
WEBSITE www.texas-treehouse-inn.com

LOCATION	From the intersection of Highways 64/43 and 259/79, take Highway 259/79 south. Drive 3.4 miles to South Evenside (the seventh stoplight from the traffic star). Turn right, travel north for 0.4 mile, and turn right onto Westwood Drive (across from Emmanuel Baptist church). The B&B is the fourth house on the right.
OPEN	All year
DESCRIPTION	A 1975 ranch-style host home with an interior "modern enough for comfort, antique enough for charm," with a dance hall–size covered deck out back overlooking a stream and woods below.
NO. OF ROOMS	Two rooms with private bathrooms. Try the Blue Room, with a king-size bed.
RATES	Year-round rates are $75-85 for a single or double. There is a two-night minimum stay on holiday and festival weekends, and cancellation requires 48 hours' notice with a $10 charge. Reservations neither kept nor canceled (no shows) forfeit deposit.
CREDIT CARDS	American Express, MasterCard, Visa
BREAKFAST	Full breakfast is served in the dining room or on the deck and includes coffee or tea; fresh-squeezed orange juice; a ham and egg casserole with cheese, mushroom, and scallion sauce; fluffy biscuits with Henderson's famous ribbon-cane syrup; poached pears topped with caramel sauce and whipped cream. Dinner is available on Civic Theater weekends, with dessert and coffee afterward.

AMENITIES	Refreshments on arrival, fresh flowers and chocolate-chip cookies in rooms, in-room TVs, ceiling fans, air conditioning, down pillows and electric blankets, hair dryers, irons and ironing boards, coffee trays with morning paper set outside rooms each morning, guest passes to local fitness center, certified backyard habitat for birders, binoculars provided.
RESTRICTIONS	No smoking, no pets. There is a good local kennel for pets nearby. Gizmo is the resident Shih Tzu. "Gizmo loves company. When guests arrive, she presents them with her favorite toy."
REVIEWED	*Texas Highways*

HIGH ISLAND

BIRDER'S HAVEN

PO Box 309, High Island, TX 77623   *409-286-5362*
Glendaweena Llast, Resident Owner
WEBSITE *www.intur.net/website/birds/html/b_b.html*

HILLSBORO

Sixty miles south of Dallas on I-35, Hillsboro is a dozen miles east of Lake Whitney. The town boasts over 250 homes on the National Historic Register and over 200 antique dealers.

THE COUNTESS ROSE HOUSE 1910

301 East Franklin, Hillsboro, TX 76645   *254-582-7673*
Nancy Lamar Countess, Innkeeper   *888-233-8066*
Spanish spoken   *FAX 254-582-0211*

LOCATION	Exit I-35 at Hillsboro. Take Old Brandon Road to the west. Stay on Old Brandon Road to the stop sign, and continue on Franklin Street 3 blocks from the courthouse.
OPEN	All year
DESCRIPTION	A 1910 three-story prairie-style inn decorated in a rose theme with period antiques and a wraparound porch. Rose gardens surround the home.

NO. OF ROOMS	Five rooms with private bathrooms.
RATES	Year-round rates are $86-120 for a single or double and $120 for a suite. There is no minimum stay and cancellation requires 72 hours' notice.
CREDIT CARDS	American Express, Discover, MasterCard, Visa
BREAKFAST	Full country breakfast is served in the dining room and includes eggs, bacon, sausage, grits, gravy, biscuits, and juices. Sunday breakfast includes champagne and eggs Benedict with all the trimmings. Lunch, dinner, and special meals are available with advance notice.
AMENITIES	Robes, wine, cookies and milk at bedtime, turndown service, meeting room, rehearsal dinners, bridge parties, individual air conditioning and gas heaters, tea room, early morning coffee served, high tea available by reservation.
RESTRICTIONS	No smoking inside. Pets and children are permitted on a case-by-case basis. Sugar is the resident bichon frise dog.

TARLTON HOUSE OF 1895

211 North Pleasant Street, Hillsboro, TX 76645   817-582-7216
Gene & Mary Smith, Resident Owners   800-823-7216
WEBSITE *triab.com/tarlton*

WINDMILL BED & BREAKFAST

Route 2, Box 448, Hillsboro, TX 76645   972-871-8709
WEBSITE *www.hillsboro.net/windmillbb*   800-951-0033
      FAX 972-871-7809

HITCHCOCK

VOLK RANCH

7425 Memorial Drive, Hitchcock, TX 77563   409-986-5443
Tommy & Sharon Barber, Resident Owners

HOUSTON

Though 50 miles inland from the gulf, Houston is one of the country's most important seaports, thanks to the Houston Ship Channel. Most notably, this is the home of the Houston Space Center—it's the Houston of "Houston, we have a problem" fame. Take a stroll through pretty Sam Houston Park. Enjoy the International Festival in April and International Quilt Show in October.

ANGEL ARBOR BED & BREAKFAST INN

848 Heights Boulevard, Houston, TX 77007   713-863-4654
Marguerite Swanson, Resident Owner   800-722-8788
EMAIL b-bhoutx@wt.net   FAX 713-861-3189
WEBSITE www.angelarbor.com

LOCATION	Five blocks north of I-10 at the corner of Heights Boulevard and 9th Street.
OPEN	All year
DESCRIPTION	A 1923 three-story redbrick Georgian inn with traditional furnishings. Manicured garden and arbor, spacious guest rooms, formal dining room, and solarium. "Classic but comfortable."
NO. OF ROOMS	Five rooms with private bathrooms.
RATES	Year-round rates for a double are $95-125. There is no minimum stay and cancellation requires 72 hours' notice.
CREDIT CARDS	American Express, Discover, MasterCard, Visa
BREAKFAST	Full breakfast is served in the dining room and typically includes an egg dish and a breakfast meat, baked items, juice, fresh fruit, coffee, tea, and milk.
AMENITIES	Robes, small library, magazines, jogging trail along the boulevard, candy, soft drinks, tea and coffee, cable TV/VCR, video library; three rooms have whirlpool tubs for two; small meeting facility, in-room telephones.
RESTRICTIONS	No smoking, no pets, children 12 and over are welcome.
MEMBER	Professional Association of Innkeepers International, Historic Accommodations of Texas

CAPTAIN'S QUARTERS

701 Bay Avenue, Kemah, TX 77565   713-474-2042
Mary & Royston Patterson, Resident Owners

KUDOS/COMMENTS "Elegant, comfortable, and hospitable."

GAR-DEN SUITES

2702 Crocker, Houston, TX 77006   713-528-2302
Dennis Stoeckel & Gary Walter, Innkeepers   800-484-1036 (2669)
Spanish spoken
EMAIL garden2@earthlink.net
WEBSITE www.webspawer.com/users/gardensuites

LOCATION	West of downtown Houston, in the Montrose area.
OPEN	All year
DESCRIPTION	A 1916 Craftsman cottage decorated with plantation, southwest, and beach themes.
NO. OF ROOMS	Three rooms with private bathrooms.
RATES	Year-round rates are $75-110 for a single or double. There is no minimum stay and cancellation requires seven days' notice for a full refund.
CREDIT CARDS	American Express, Discover, MasterCard, Visa
BREAKFAST	Continental breakfast is served in the guestrooms and includes cold cereal, muffins, juice, fruit, bagel, yogurt, Danish, milk, and coffee.
AMENITIES	Microwaves, refrigerators, TV/VCR, coffee-makers, air conditioning, video library, outdoor spa/hot tub, pool, common sun deck, bicycles.
RESTRICTIONS	No smoking, no pets, no children. Tibby is the resident poodle, Noble is the Lab/springer mix, and Eartha Kitty is the black cat.

HIDDEN OAKS BED & BREAKFAST

7808 Dixie Drive, Houston, TX 77087   713-640-2457
                                                           888-305-0204
                                                     FAX 713-640-2505

THE HOUSTONIAN HOTEL

111 North Post Oak Lane, Houston, TX 77024
WEBSITE www.houstonian.com

713-680-2626
FAX 713-680-2992

THE LANCASTER

701 Texas Avenue, Houston, TX 77002
WEBSITE www.slh.com

713-228-9500
FAX 713-223-4528

THE LOVETT INN

501 Lovett Boulevard, Houston, TX 77006
Tom Fricke, Resident Owner
Spanish spoken
EMAIL lovettin@aol.com

713-522-5224
800-779-5224
FAX 713-528-6708
WEBSITE www.lovettinn.com

LOCATION	Located 2.5 miles from downtown in the museum district, and 3 blocks east of Montrose.
OPEN	All year
DESCRIPTION	A 1924 three-story colonial inn with traditional antique furnishings.
NO. OF ROOMS	Eight rooms with private bathrooms, and two rooms share one bathroom.
RATES	Year-round rates for a single or double with a private bathroom are $75-150, a single or double with a shared bathroom is $75, and a suite rents for $85-120. Ask about minimum stay and cancellation policy.
CREDIT CARDS	American Express, MasterCard, Visa
BREAKFAST	Continental breakfast is served in the dining room and includes fresh fruit, coffee, tea, milk, juice, muffins, and cereal. Special meals can be catered by request.
AMENITIES	Pool, hot tub, TV/VCRs, videos, telephones, parking, meeting facilities, fax.
RESTRICTIONS	Smoking is limited, ask about pets and children.
MEMBER	Texas Hotel & Motel Association
RATED	AAA 2 Diamonds

Montrose Inn

408 Avondale Street, Houston, TX 77006   *713-520-0206*
Henry McClug, Resident Owner

The Patrician Bed & Breakfast Inn

1200 Southmore Avenue, Houston, TX 77004   *713-523-1114*
Pat Thomas, Resident Owner   *800-553-5797*
EMAIL southmor@swbell.net   *FAX 713-523-0790*
WEBSITE www.texasbnb.com

LOCATION	From Highway 59 south, take the Fannin exit just past downtown Houston. Turn left at the second light, which is Southmore. The inn is on the corner of Southmore Avenue and San Jacinto.
OPEN	All year
DESCRIPTION	A 1919 three-story brick colonial revival inn with early 20th-century interior decor. Two of the guestrooms are two-room suites.
NO. OF ROOMS	Four rooms with private bathrooms.
RATES	Year-round rates for a single or double are $70-125. There is no minimum stay and cancellation requires five days' notice.
CREDIT CARDS	American Express, Discover, Diners Club, MasterCard, Visa
BREAKFAST	Full breakfast is served in the dining room and includes juice, fresh fruit, pear compote, sticky buns, French toast with cream cheese and strawberries, apple pancakes, or cheesy egg bake.
AMENITIES	Fluffy robes, cable TV, CD players, telephones, fireplace in one room, complimentary refreshments, meeting room, fax machine, whirlpool tubs in two rooms, air conditioning.
RESTRICTIONS	No smoking, no pets, children over eight are welcome.
MEMBER	Professional Association of Innkeepers International, Texas Hotel & Motel Association
RATED	AAA 2 Diamonds, ABBA 3 Crowns

ROBIN'S NEST BED & BREAKFAST INN

4104 Greeley, Houston, TX 77006
Robin Smith, Resident Owner
WEBSITE www.houstonbnb.com/

713-528-5821
FAX 713-521-2154

KUDOS/COMMENTS "Lovely, cozy inn."

SARA'S BED & BREAKFAST INN

941 Heights Boulevard, Houston, TX 77008
Connie McCreight, Innkeeper
Spanish spoken
EMAIL stay@saras.com

713-868-1130
800-593-1130
FAX 713-868-3284
WEBSITE www.saras.com

LOCATION	About 5 miles northwest of downtown Houston and 6 blocks north of I-10. Take the Heights/Yale exit.
OPEN	All year
DESCRIPTION	An 1898 two-story Queen Anne Victorian inn decorated with antiques and collectables, located in the heart of Houston.
NO. OF ROOMS	Eleven rooms with private bathrooms and two rooms share two bathrooms. Try the Austin Suite.
RATES	Year-round rates are $70-150 for a single or double with a private bathroom and $75-80 for a single or double with a shared bathroom. There is a minimum stay during holidays and special events. Ask about a cancellation policy.
CREDIT CARDS	American Express, Diners Club, Discover, MasterCard, Visa
BREAKFAST	Full breakfast is served on the weekdays in the dining room and includes eggs or French toast, sausage, bread, and fruit. Continental plus is served on the weekends and includes fruit, granola and yogurt, sticky buns, coffeecake, and cream puffs.
AMENITIES	Telephones; voice mail; data ports; TV/VCR; video library; patio; on-site parking; jogging trail; complimentary soft drinks, coffee and tea.
RESTRICTIONS	No smoking, no pets, children under 12 are welcome in the Balcony Suite, children 12 and over are welcome at the rest of the inn.
REVIEWED	Bed & Breakfast USA, Historic Inns, Bed & Breakfasts and Country Inns
RATED	AAA 3 Diamonds, Mobil 2 Stars
KUDOS/COMMENTS	"Beautifully furnished and appointed rooms, historic neighborhood near downtown, great hospitality."

HUBBARD

Twenty-five miles northeast of Waco and about 60 miles south of Dallas on Highway 31, Hubbard lies at the southern end of Navarro Mills Lake.

BELL HOUSE BED & BREAKFAST

200 North 3rd Street West, Hubbard, TX 76648   254-576-2107
Anne Bell, Resident Owner
EMAIL *bell_house@go.com*   WEBSITE *www.home.earthlink.net/~igoe*

LOCATION   From Dallas, take I-35 60 miles south to Hillsboro, then take
                   Highway 171 southeast for 24 miles.

OPEN   All year

DESCRIPTION   A 1900 three-story Victorian host home decorated with Victorian
                   furnishings and antiques.

NO. OF ROOMS   One suite with a private bathroom and four rooms share two
                   bathrooms.

RATES   Year-round rates are $125 for a single or double in the suite and
                   $60 for a single or double with a shared bathroom. There is no
                   minimum stay. Please ask about a cancellation policy.

CREDIT CARDS   American Express, Discover, MasterCard, Visa

Bell House Bed & Breakfast, Hubbard

BREAKFAST	Full breakfast is served in the dining room and includes sausage, eggs, bacon, biscuits, gravy, fruit, orange juice, and coffee.
AMENITIES	Complimentary bottle of wine.
RESTRICTIONS	No smoking, no pets, children over 12 are welcome. Prissy is the resident cocker spaniel.

HUNTSVILLE

LONGHORN HOUSE BED & BREAKFAST

Route 1, Box 681, Huntsville, TX 77340   *409-295-1774*
Claire Jordan, Resident Owner
WEBSITE www.lonestar.texas.net/~jjordan

NELSON'S BLUE BONNET BED & BREAKFAST

1704 Avenue O, Huntsville, TX 77340   *409-295-2072*
John & Bette Nelson, Resident Owners

THE WHISTLER B&B

906 Avenue M, Huntsville, TX 77340   *409-295-2834*
Mary Clegg, Resident Owner
WEBSITE www.geocities.com/heartland/ridge/3155

KUDOS/COMMENTS	"Wonderful family homeplace converted by daughter who grew up in the home—original furnishings, toys, etc. Antiques are exquisite."

INGRAM

Sixty-six miles northwest of San Antonio via I-10 and Highway 27, Ingram is an art center on the northern bank of the Guadalupe River. The Hill Country Arts Foundation presents art workshops and theater by famous professionals. Over Memorial Day weekend, check out the Texas Arts and Crafts Fair. Ingram is home to the Cowboy Artist Museum.

RIVER OAKS LODGE

HCR 78 Box 231A, Ingram, TX 78025	*830-367-4214*
Gilda & Byron Wilkinson, Innkeepers	*800-608-2596*
WEBSITE *www.riveroakslodge.com*	*FAX 830-367-3545*

LOCATION	From the stoplight in Ingram, go west on Highway 39 for 3.7 miles.
OPEN	All year
DESCRIPTION	A 1920s two-story limestone lodge with a wraparound porch, and four cottages, located on 5 acres with live oak trees.
NO. OF ROOMS	Ten rooms with private bathrooms.
RATES	Year-round rates for a double are $85-125. There is a two-night minimum stay and cancellation requires 14 days' notice.
CREDIT CARDS	American Express, Discover, MasterCard, Visa
BREAKFAST	Full breakfast is served in the dining room and includes orange juice and other beverages, homemade breads, fruits, and a main entrée.
AMENITIES	Air conditioning, TV, telephone, access to the Guadalupe River with inner tubes and rafts provided, each suite has a deck or covered porch with views of the Texas Hill Country.
RESTRICTIONS	No smoking, no pets

IRAAN

Home of west Texas' finest crude, Iraan was a boomtown of early oil exploration in west Texas. Its setting in the Pecos River valley is warm and sunny and full of desert beauty. Check out Fort Lancaster, a frontier fort along the Pecos. Iraan is 14 miles north of I-10 on Highway 190.

PARKER RANCH BED & BREAKFAST

PO Box 1320, Iraan, TX 79744
Dickie Dell Ferro, Innkeeper
Spanish spoken
EMAIL *parker.ranch.bb@apex2000.net*

915-639-2850
877-639-2850

LOCATION	From the east edge of Iraan on Highway 190, drive east for 2 miles, cross the Pecos River, and take an immediate left onto a dirt road. Pass through the gate and drive 2 miles to the B&B.
OPEN	All year
DESCRIPTION	A 1929 two-story Spanish colonial revival host home with a blend of Spanish-style and 1930s-era "modern" decor, situated in the Pecos River Valley surrounded by buttes. Listed on the State Historic Register.
NO. OF ROOMS	Two rooms with private bathrooms and two rooms share one bathroom. Try Wendell's Room.
RATES	Year-round rate is $65 for a single or double with a private or shared bathroom. There is no minimum stay and cancellation requires 48 hours' notice.
CREDIT CARDS	No
BREAKFAST	Full breakfast is served in the dining room and includes hot bread, biscuits or muffins, eggs and bacon or sausage, fruit, juices, cereals, toast, perked coffee, teas, and milk.

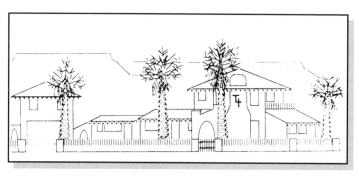

Parker Ranch Bed & Breakfast, Iraan

AMENITIES	Bird-watching, riding trails for riders who bring their own horses, many varieties of cacti and other desert plants, clear skies and black nights for stargazing, hiking and mountain biking trails.
RESTRICTIONS	No smoking, no pets, children over 10 are welcome. Slick is the resident cat and there are about 20 head of cattle on the property.
REVIEWED	*Country* magazine, *Texas Highways, Bed & Breakfast USA*

JACKSONVILLE

TREE HOUSE BED & BREAKFAST

501 El Paso Street, Jacksonville, TX 75766   903-589-2958
WEBSITE *www.travelpick.com/tx/treehouse*   888-tree-555

JASPER

THE BELLE–JIM HOTEL

160 North Austin, Jasper, TX 75951   409-384-6923

JEFFERSON

A major port town in the 1880s, with a population larger than that of Dallas, Jefferson's chief claim to fame today is its reputation as the undisputed "Bed & Breakfast Capital of Texas." A storybook town of antebellum and Greek revival homes on Big Cypress Bayou, between Caddo Lake and Lake o' the Pines, it is also known as the "Williamsburg of the Southwest." Significant events that take place year-round include Mardi Gras in February, Pilgrimage Tour of Homes the first weekend in May, Fireworks on the Riverfront in July, Founders Day in October, and the Christmas Candlelight Tour the first two weekends in December. Explore the historic downtown riverport area, take a riverboat tour or the J. Gould Railroad Car Tour, or enjoy a romantic carriage ride through town.

AZALEA INN

203 East Dixon, Jefferson, TX 75657   903-665-2051
Bill & Jo West, Resident Owners
WEBSITE *www.jeffersontx.com*

BAKER STREET INN

409 East Baker Street, Jefferson, TX 75657   903-665-3662
Beth Meyer, Resident Owner
WEBSITE *jefferson-texas.com/5-bsin.htm*

CAPTAIN'S CASTLE BED & BREAKFAST

403 East Walker Street, Jefferson, TX 75657   903-665-2330
Buck & Barbara Hooker, Resident Owners   800-650-2330
WEBSITE *www.jeffersontx.com/captainscastle*

LOCATION	Fifteen miles north of Marshall on Highway 59. At the stoplight on Highway 59 in Jefferson, turn right and go 3 blocks to Alley. Turn right and go 2 blocks. The inn is on the corner of Alley and Walker.
OPEN	All year
DESCRIPTION	An 1850s-era two-story Tennessee planter–style host home with 20-foot columns, with a cottage and carriage house overlooking the garden. The house is listed on both the National and State Historic Registers.

NO. OF ROOMS	Seven rooms with private bathrooms.
RATES	Year-round rates for a single or double with a private bathroom are $95-110. A two-night minimum stay is required on holiday weekends, and cancellation requires seven days' notice, 30 days for special weekends.
CREDIT CARDS	MasterCard, Visa
BREAKFAST	Full breakfast is served in the dining room or the temperature-controlled gazebo and includes juice, coffee, fruit, egg casserole and other casseroles, and bread.
AMENITIES	Coffee and muffins are brought to rooms prior to breakfast; all rooms have heat and air conditioning; meeting facilities available for up to 14.
RESTRICTIONS	No smoking, no pets, children over 12 are welcome.
KUDOS/COMMENTS	"Historic home, very popular." "Antiques from the 1700s, large outdoor dining, great!!"

CHAPELRIDGE BED & BREAKFAST

Route 1, Box 2695, Jefferson, TX 75657　　　　　*903-665-6730*
EMAIL chapelridge@jeffersontx.com
WEBSITE jeffersontx.com/chapelridge

THE CHARLES HOUSE

209 East Clarksville Street, Jefferson, TX 75657　　　*903-665-1773*
WEBSITE jefferson-texas.com/5-tcho.htm

CHEZ LAFAYETTE

305 West Lafayette, Jefferson, TX 75657　　　　*903-665-3145*
Beth Crawford, Innkeeper　　　　　　　*FAX 903-665-3144*
EMAIL ChezLafaye@aol.com　　*WEBSITE jeffersontx.com/chezlafayette*

LOCATION	From Highway 59, go east on Highways 49 and 134 to downtown. Turn right onto Lafayette Street. Go past Sterne Fountain (at the intersection of Market and Lafayette) to the inn, next door to Carnegie Library.

OPEN	All year
DESCRIPTION	An elegant 1937 traditional southern-style inn decorated with antiques, with a double front entry.
NO. OF ROOMS	Two rooms with private bathrooms.
RATES	Year-round rates are $95-110 for a single or double. There is a minimum stay during holidays and special events and cancellation requires seven days' notice, 30 days during special events.
CREDIT CARDS	Discover, MasterCard, Visa
BREAKFAST	Full gourmet breakfast is served in the dining room and includes such specialties as sausage crepes and baked apple pancakes. Orange juice and muffins are delivered to the rooms each morning.
AMENITIES	Beautifully landscaped garden, conveniently located so guests can enjoy parades and festivities from the front porch, air conditioning, ceiling fans, TV/VCR, video library, refrigerator, coffee-maker, telephone in all rooms.
RESTRICTIONS	No smoking, no pets, children over 12 are welcome. Sterling is the resident Persian cat.

THE CLAIBORNE HOUSE

312 South Alley, Jefferson, TX 75657   903-665-8800
Elaine Holden, Innkeepers   877-385-9236
EMAIL *claiborne@jeffersontx.com*   FAX 903-665-9335
WEBSITE *jeffersontx.com/claiborne*

LOCATION	At the intersection of Highways 59 and 49, go east on Highway 49 (Broadway Street). Go 3 blocks and turn right onto South Alley. The B&B is 3 blocks up, on the left.
OPEN	All year
DESCRIPTION	An 1872 two-story Greek revival inn with elegant Victorian decor. "Romanticism and elegance are our main themes both in decor and attitude."
NO. OF ROOMS	Six rooms with private bathrooms.
RATES	Year-round rates are $95-140 for a single or double. There is a minimum stay during holidays and special events, and cancellation requires seven days' notice, 30 days during special events.
CREDIT CARDS	American Express, MasterCard, Visa
BREAKFAST	Full breakfast is served in the dining room and includes coffee, juice, tea, a main entrée, meat, and fruit. Sometimes cold soup is served before the main entrée; other times a dessert is included.

AMENITIES   Fresh flowers in each room, wine and snacks in the afternoon, full
                   office amenities, bubble bath in rooms with tubs.

RESTRICTIONS   No smoking, no pets

CLARKSVILLE STREET INN

107 East Clarksville, Jefferson, TX 75657   903-665-6659
Jo-Lynn Darnell, Innkeeper
WEBSITE *www.jefferson-texas.com/5-csin.htm*

COTTONWOOD INN

209 North Market Street, Jefferson, TX 75657   903-665-2080
EMAIL *the4jays@worldnet.att.net*   FAX 903-665-2080
WEBSITE *www.angelfire.com/biz/cottonwoodinn/cotton1.html*

LOCATION   In Jefferson, take Highway 49 east (Broadway Street) for five-and-
                   a-half blocks. Veer right at a small traffic island onto Polk Street
                   and drive south for 5 blocks. Turn right at the first stoplight, onto
                   Lafayette Street. Go west on Lafayette for 2 blocks until you reach
                   a statue in the center of the street. Turn right onto Market Street.

OPEN   All year

DESCRIPTION   A restored 1855 Louisiana raised cottage–style inn with Greek
                   revival architecture, Victorian heirloom antiques, hardwood floors,
                   and wood-burning fireplaces.

NO. OF ROOMS   Four rooms with private bathrooms. Try the Benefield/Bullard
                   Room.

RATES   Year-round rates are $60-95 for a single or double. There is a
                   minimum stay during holidays and special events, and cancellation
                   requires seven days' notice, 14 days for holidays, 30 days for special
                   events.

CREDIT CARDS   Discover, MasterCard, Visa

BREAKFAST   Full breakfast includes a variety of fresh-baked breads and pastries,
                   omelets, coffee, and juice.

AMENITIES   Cool lemonade in summer; warm mug of cocoa or cider in chilly
                   months; cookies, cheese and crackers, and other snacks; silver tray
                   with sparkling cider and champagne glasses in the room for special
                   occasions.

RESTRICTIONS   No smoking, no pets, children over 13 are welcome.

1992, Historical Preservation Award, Jefferson Historic
Foundation; 1991–1996, 1998, Christmas decorations awards,
Historic Jefferson Foundation

THE EXCELSIOR HOUSE

211 West Austin Street, Jefferson, TX 75657   *903-665-2513*
EMAIL *excelsior@jeffersontx.com*
WEBSITE *www.excelsior@jeffersontx.com*
KUDOS/COMMENTS   "Excellent in every way."

THE FADED ROSE

1101 South Line Street, Jefferson, TX 75657   *903-665-2716*
Merlene R. Meek, Resident Owner

FALLING LEAVES

304 Jefferson Street, Jefferson, TX 75657   *903-665-8803*
Joe & Barbara Bell, Innkeepers
EMAIL *fallingleaves@tyler.net*
WEBSITE *www.jeffersontx.com/fallingleaves*

LOCATION   If entering Jefferson on Highway 59 from the north, Jefferson
                     Street is the first street past the Best Western. Turn left and drive 2
                     blocks. If entering Jefferson on Highway 59 from the south,
                     Jefferson Street is the first street inside the city limits. Turn right
                     and drive 2 blocks.

OPEN   All year

DESCRIPTION   An 1855 Greek revival inn with 13-foot ceilings and columns in
                     front, decorated with antiques, and listed on the National and State
                     Historic Registers.

NO. OF ROOMS   Four rooms with private bathrooms. The Magnolia is the best
                     room.

RATES	Year-round rates are $90-100 for a single or double. Midweek rates are $10 less except during holidays and festivals. Ask about a cancellation policy.
CREDIT CARDS	Discover, Mastercard, Visa
BREAKFAST	Full breakfast includes sausage and egg quiche with apple-raisin crepes; eggs Benedict; or a country breakfast with bacon, scrambled eggs, biscuits, and cream gravy; plus homemade banana bread, and more. The menu varies daily.
AMENITIES	Wine, soft drinks, cable TV, air conditioning, central heat, library, screened porch with rocking chairs, flowers for special occasions, a trophy room for visiting with friends.
RESTRICTIONS	No smoking inside, no pets, no children.
MEMBER	Texas Hotel & Motel Association
RATED	Mobil 2 Stars
AWARDS	1998, Commercial Garden of the Month, awarded by Jessie Allen, Wise Garden Club of Jefferson

THE FAMILY TREE AT THE MARSH PLACE

202 South Friou, Jefferson, TX 75657　　　　903-665-7055
Jim & Betty Carroll, Innkeepers　　　　FAX 903-665-9882
EMAIL *familytree@jeffersontx.com*
WEBSITE *www.jeffersontx.com/familytree*

THE GINGERBREAD HOUSE AND HONEY DO GUEST INN

601 East Jefferson Street, Jefferson, TX 75657　　　　903-665-8994
Norma & Douglas Horn, Resident Owners
WEBSITE *www.jefferson-texas.com/5-ghhd.htm*

GOVERNOR'S HOUSE

321 North Walnut, Jefferson, TX 75657   903-665-7933
Bill & Llwanda Golden, Resident Owners   800-891-7933
EMAIL rooms@thegovernorshouse.com
WEBSITE www.thegovernorshouse.com/

KUDOS/COMMENTS   "Tastefully renovated Greek revival home."

THE GUEST HOUSE PRIVATE COTTAGE

509 West Austin Street, Jefferson, TX 75657   903-665-2080
EMAIL the4jays@worldnet.att.net

LOCATION	In Jefferson, take Highway 49 east (Broadway Street) for five-and-a-half blocks. Veer right at a small traffic island onto Polk Street and drive south for 6 blocks. Turn right at the second stoplight, onto Austin Street. Go west on Austin Street for four-and-a-half blocks.
OPEN	All year
DESCRIPTION	A restored 1920 saltbox-style cottage with Victorian antiques.
NO. OF ROOMS	One cottage with a private bathroom.
RATES	Year-round rates are $110-160 for the cottage. There is a minimum stay during holidays and special events. Cancellation requires seven days' notice, 14 days during holidays, 30 days during special events.
CREDIT CARDS	No
BREAKFAST	Full breakfast includes a variety of fresh-baked breads and pastries, omelets, coffee, and juice.
AMENITIES	Private cottage with living room, TV, phone, kitchen and dining area, refrigerator, microwave, coffee-maker, washer/dryer, within walking distance to shops and restaurants, snacks including soft drinks and fresh-baked breads.
RESTRICTIONS	No smoking, no pets, children are welcome.

HALE HOUSE

702 South Line Street, Jefferson, TX 75657   903-665-8877
L. D. & Joyce Barringer, Resident Owners
WEBSITE www.jeffersontx.com:80/halehouse/

HODGE PLANTATION

Route 1, Box 2562, Jefferson, TX 75657   903-665-7442
Sammie DeSpain, Resident Owner

HOLCOMB LODGE

Kim Street, Crestwood Addition   903-665-3236
Lake O' The Pines, Jefferson, TX 75657
Bobbie Holcomb, Innkeeper
EMAIL holcomb@jeffersontx.com
WEBSITE www.jeffersontx.com/holcomb

LOCATION	At the intersection of Highways 59 and 49, take Highway 49 west for 5 miles to Highway 729. Turn left and go 7 miles to Crestwood Addition, then take a left. Bear to the right and the inn will be the third house on the right, on Kim Street.
OPEN	All year
DESCRIPTION	A 1950 cottage with rustic decor.
NO. OF ROOMS	Two rooms share one bathroom. Bobbie recommends the Maple Room.
RATES	Year-round rate is $95 per night for couples, and $10 for each additional person. Cancellation requires seven days' notice.
CREDIT CARDS	None
BREAKFAST	A continental breakfast is left in the refrigerator and includes orange juice, rolls, cereal, milk, and coffee.
AMENITIES	Fireplace, TV/VCR, air conditioning and central heat, microwave, coffee-maker, deck, grill, picnic table, radio, bird sanctuary, porch swing, park, marina, fishing pier, boat dock, and beach.
RESTRICTIONS	No smoking, no pets
REVIEWED	Texas Bed & Breakfast
MEMBER	Marion County Bed & Breakfast Association

THE HOUSE OF THE SEASONS—THE SEASONS GUEST HOUSE BED AND BREAKFAST

409 South Alley Street, Jefferson, TX 75657
Kirby & Cindy Childress, Innkeepers
EMAIL *houseoftheseasons@jeffersontx.com*
WEBSITE *jeffersontx.com/houseoftheseasons*

903-665-1218
FAX 903-665-1218

LOCATION	Six blocks from historic downtown Jefferson. From Marshall, take Highway 59 north to Jefferson. Turn right at Highway 49 (Broadway Street), stay in the right-hand lane, and travel 3 blocks. Turn right on South Alley Street, drive 4 blocks, and you will be sitting in front of the House of the Seasons. Turn right on Delta Street and come to the large driveway by The Seasons' Guest House.
OPEN	All year
DESCRIPTION	An 1872 two-story Greek revival/Italianate host home and carriage house furnished with family antiques and heirlooms dating back through five generations, with Victorian and country Victorian decor; listed on the State and National Historic Registers.
NO. OF ROOMS	Four rooms with private bathrooms.
RATES	Year-round rates are $125-135 for a single or double. There is a minimum stay during holidays and local events, and cancellation requires two weeks' notice.
CREDIT CARDS	MasterCard, Visa
BREAKFAST	Full gourmet breakfast is served in the dining room of the main house.
AMENITIES	Private entrances; whirlpool tubs for two in each room; cable TV; ceiling fans; individual heating and cooling units; complimentary tour of the main house; brownies and cookies in rooms upon arrival; strawberry lemonade and tea during warm months; hot chocolate and spiced cider during cool months; large garden area with two ponds, pavilion, and arbor; coffee and tea served before breakfast; off-street parking with monitored driveway; within walking distance of historic homes, restaurants, antique shops, and museums; carriage rides can be arranged; requests for flowers, cakes, fruit plates can be left in rooms on arrival.
RESTRICTIONS	No smoking, no pets, no children
REVIEWED	*National Geographic Traveler, Southern Living, Victorian Homes, Destinations* magazine, *A Texas Christmas*
KUDOS/COMMENTS	"Filled with antiques; featured on daily tours." "Very beautiful."

Kennedy Manor

217 West Lafayette Street, Jefferson, TX 75657   903-665-2528
Larry & Mary Bill Royder, Innkeepers
EMAIL kennedymanor@jeffersontx.com
WEBSITE www.jeffersontx.com:80/kennedymanor/

Laura Anna Bed & Breakfast

1105 South Line Street, Jefferson, TX 75657   903-665-2447

The Lodge on Busy B Ranch

1100 West Prospect, Jefferson, TX 78657   903-665-7448
Jason & Shannon Bonner, Resident Owners

Maison-Bayou Plantation

300 Bayou Street, Jefferson, TX 75657   903-665-7600
Jan & Pete Hochendel, Resident Owners   FAX 903-665-7100
EMAIL cabins@maisonbayou.com   WEBSITE www.maisonbayou.com

LOCATION	From Highway 59 going north, turn right onto FM 2208 just after the Chevy dealership. Go 1 mile to the intersection, bear left, continue 0.25 mile to Bayou Street, turn left, and the road dead-ends at the entrance gate.
OPEN	All year
DESCRIPTION	A 1991 two-story reproduction of a Greek revival plantation overseer's home with cabins, plus a steamboat paddlewheeler and converted railcars, all on 55 acres.
NO. OF ROOMS	Eleven rooms with private bathrooms.
RATES	Year-round rates for a single or double are $69-135. There is a two-night minimum stay during holidays and festivals. Holiday cancellation requires 30 days' notice, all other days require seven days' notice.
CREDIT CARDS	Discover, MasterCard, Visa

BREAKFAST	Full breakfast is served in the dining room and includes juice, coffee, tea, milk, seasonal fresh or baked fruit, sausage or ham, egg dishes, pancakes, or waffles.
AMENITIES	Fishing in pond or river, handicapped shower, individual heat and air conditioning, walking distance to town.
RESTRICTIONS	No smoking, no pets. There is a llama called Dakalooloo, peacocks, ducks, and horses.
REVIEWED	*London Times, Dallas Morning News, Shreveport Times, Richmond Dispatch*
MEMBER	Texas Hotel & Motel Association

McKay House Bed & Breakfast Inn

306 East Delta Street, Jefferson, TX 75657　　　　　903-665-7322
Lisa & Roger Cantrell, Innkeepers　　　　　　　　　800-468-2627
EMAIL *McKayHouse@aol.com*　　　　　　　　　FAX 903-665-8551
WEBSITE *www.bbonline.com/tx/mckayhouse/*

LOCATION	Three blocks east of Highway 59, 4 blocks south of Highway 49 (Broadway Street), and across the street from the House of the Seasons—the most popular tour home in historic Jefferson.
OPEN	All year
DESCRIPTION	A restored 1851 two-story, high-raised Greek revival inn and a classic Victorian cottage decorated with documented wallpaper and fine period antiques, surrounded by an authentic Williamsburg picket fence. Listed on the National and State Historic Registers.
NO. OF ROOMS	Seven rooms with private bathrooms. Try the Grand Gable Suite.
RATES	Rates during weekends, holidays, and festivals are $139-149 for a single or double, $169 for a suite, and $139 for the cottage. Midweek rates are $89 for a single or double, $99 for a suite, and $89 for the cottage. Corporate rates are also available. There is a minimum stay during Mardi Gras and other festivals. Cancellation requires one week's notice.
CREDIT CARDS	American Express, MasterCard
BREAKFAST	Full "gentleman's breakfast" is served in the sunny garden conservatory and includes fresh fruit, yogurt parfait, shirred eggs with honey-baked ham, orange-pecan French toast with genuine maple syrup or strawberries, cheese blintz, fresh-baked pineapple-zuchini muffins, homemade preserves and fresh juices. A crackling fire keeps the conservatory warm on chilly mornings.

McKay House Bed & Breakfast, Jefferson

AMENITIES   Pillared veranda; English tea with refreshments upon arrival; innkeeper provides a brief tour of the historic inn that has welcomed Lady Bird Johnson, Alex Haley, Martin Jurow, Fabio, George Bush's staff, and thousands of discriminating individuals; Victorian nightclothes; choice books and good reading lamps; cable TV; plenty of information about local points of interest; innkeeper will be pleased to direct you to a fine dining spot or to make reservations; garden balcony; horse-drawn carriage for early morning drives about the historic village (breakfast in a picnic basket and lap robes available).

RESTRICTIONS   No smoking, no pets.

REVIEWED   *Texas Highways, Vacation* magazine, *Victorian Homes, Country Inns, Southern Living, Country Homes* magazine

MEMBER   Professional Association of Innkeepers International

RATED   Mobil 3 Stars

KUDOS/COMMENTS   "Very sweet and neatly done." "Beautiful, interesting innkeepers, comfortable, great town." "Excellent."

OLD MULBERRY INN

209 Jefferson Street, Jefferson, TX 75657   903-665-1945
Donald & Gloria Degn, Innkeepers   800-263-5319
EMAIL *mulberry@jeffersontx.com*   FAX 903-665-9123
WEBSITE *jeffersontx.com/oldmulberryinn*

LOCATION   From Highway 59, turn east onto Jefferson Street. The inn is 2 blocks south of Highway 59, approximately 0.3 mile south of the intersection with Highway 49.

OPEN	All year
DESCRIPTION	A 1997 Greek revival inn with upscale, eclectic decor, including antiques and family pieces, crown molding, antique flooring, custom bed coverings and window treatments.
NO. OF ROOMS	Five rooms with private bathrooms.
RATES	Year-round rates are $100-125 for a single or double. There is a minimum stay during holidays and special events. Cancellation requires seven days' notice, 30 days during special events.
CREDIT CARDS	American Express, Discover, MasterCard, Visa
BREAKFAST	Full breakfast is served in the dining room and includes juice, fresh fruit, a variety of gourmet egg dishes and side dishes, bacon, coffeecake, muffins, biscuits, coffee, and tea.
AMENITIES	Quiet heating and air conditioning with eletronic air cleaners, king- and queen-size beds, ceramic tile baths, clawfoot tubs, upscale toiletries, library with fireplace, rockers and swings on large porches, early morning coffee and biscotti, drinks and snacks available 24 hours a day.
RESTRICTIONS	No smoking, no pets, children over 12 are welcome. "The inn and grounds are designated tobacco-free."
MEMBER	Bed & Breakfast Texas Style
RATED	AAA 3 Diamonds

THE PACE HOUSE

402 North Polk Street, Jefferson, TX 75657   903-665-1433
Geraldine Pace Mason, Resident Owner   FAX 903-665-1433

LOCATION	From Highway 59 in Jefferson, go east on Broadway Street for 0.25 mile to the Y in the street. Turn left onto North Polk Street and look for Haley's Antique Shop. The Pace House is on the right, at the corner of Polk and Orleans Streets.
OPEN	All year
DESCRIPTION	A 1923 brick home decorated in country and Victorian style.
NO. OF ROOMS	Two rooms with private bathrooms.
RATES	Year-round rate for a single or double is $80. There is a minimum stay during holidays and cancellation requires 48 hours' notice.
CREDIT CARDS	Discover, MasterCard, Visa
BREAKFAST	Full gourmet breakfast is served in the dining room.
AMENITIES	Sun porch, common area with television.
RESTRICTIONS	No smoking, no pets, children over 12 are welcome.

PINE NEEDLE LODGE

Route 3, Box 447, Jefferson, TX 75657   *903-665-2911*
WEBSITE www.shreve.net/~caddo_lk/

THE PRIDE HOUSE

409 Broadway, Jefferson, TX 75657   *903-665-2675*
Carol Abernathy & Christel Frederick, Innkeepers   *800-894-3526*
German spoken   *FAX 903-665-3901*
EMAIL jefftx@mind.net   *WEBSITE www.jeffersontexas.com*

LOCATION	Three hours east of Dallas, 4 hours north of Houston, and 1 hour west of Shreveport.
OPEN	All year
DESCRIPTION	An 1889 two-story stick Victorian mansion with an Italianate roof, a two-story bay window, a wraparound front porch with gingerbread trim, original woodwork, and over 30 original stained-glass windows. Listed on the State Historic Register.
NO. OF ROOMS	Eleven rooms with private bathrooms.
RATES	Year-round rates are $85-150 for a double and $15 per additional guest. There is a minimum stay when a Saturday night is involved and cancellation requires seven days' notice.
CREDIT CARDS	American Express, Discover, MasterCard, Visa
BREAKFAST	Full breakfast is served in the dining room and includes an elegant fruit course such as poached pears, praline-banana parfait, or peaches Amaretto; a main course such as egg olé and ham or eggs Galveston; sausage or bacon; croissants; Texas bluebonnets; strawberry butter; homemade marmalade; coffee and juice. A French picnic is also available.
AMENITIES	Hot and cold drinks any time, off-street parking, hand-painted footed tubs with bubbles and bath pillows, triple sheets, fireplaces, cake on arrival Fridays and Saturdays, hair dryers, fresh flowers, phones and TVs on request, private balcony, porch swings, original art, air conditioning, ceiling fans, antiques and heirlooms, steamboat memorabilia and literature, French picnic (free to those who arrive Friday instead of Saturday).
RESTRICTIONS	No smoking indoors, no pets
REVIEWED	*The Complete Guide to Bed & Breakfasts, Inns and Guesthouses in the United States, Canada and Worldwide; Romantic Northeast Texas; The Official Guide to American Historic Inns; The Great Stays of Texas*

| RATED | Mobil 2 Stars |

| KUDOS/COMMENTS | "Beautiful; said to be the first B&B in Texas." "Very well done. Good full breakfast." |

SECRETS OF LAKE CLABORN

Highway 59 North, No. 1 Lois Lane, Jefferson, TX 75657   906-665-8518
Lois Smith, Innkeeper

THE STEAMBOAT INN

114 North Marshall, Jefferson, TX 75657   903-665-8946
Lou & Mary Castleman, Resident Owners
EMAIL *steamboat@jeffersontx.com*
WEBSITE *www.jeffersontx.com/steamboat/*

LOCATION	One-and-a-half blocks from the downtown area.
OPEN	All year
DESCRIPTION	A 1992 one-story Greek revival period home constructed of material from old historic homes.
NO. OF ROOMS	Four rooms with private bathrooms.
RATES	Year-round rate for a single or double is $95. Cancellation requires seven days' notice.
CREDIT CARDS	American Express, MasterCard, Visa
BREAKFAST	Full breakfast is served in the dining room.
AMENITIES	Complimentary beverages upon arrival; coffee and homemade muffins delivered to guestrooms one hour before breakfast.
RESTRICTIONS	No smoking, no pets, children over 12 are welcome.
KUDOS/COMMENTS	"Lovely home, wonderful breakfasts."

STILLWATER INN

203 East Broadway, Jefferson, TX 75657   903-665-8415
Bill & Sharon Stewart, Resident Owners   FAX 903-665-8416
EMAIL theinn@stillwaterinn.com   WEBSITE *www.stillwaterinn.com*

KUDOS/COMMENTS   "Beautiful accommodations and great food served by friendly
host/chef Bill Stewart." "Fine evening dining. Four-star food. Nice
rooms, too."

TERRY–McKINNON HOUSE

109 West Henderson Street, Jefferson, TX 75657   903-665-1933
Ted & Kay McKinnon, Innkeepers   FAX 903-665-9003
EMAIL terrymc@jeffersontx.com
WEBSITE *www.jeffersontx.com/terrymc/*

LOCATION   Take I-20 to the Marshall exit onto Highway 59. Stay on Highway
59 into Jefferson and turn right onto Highway 49. Go to Polk
Street, turn right, and drive to Henderson Street. The house is
immediately on the right.

OPEN   All year

Terry–McKinnon House, Jefferson

DESCRIPTION	An 1870 two-story Queen Anne Victorian with a classic front porch, original architecture, and decorated with antiques. Listed on the National and State Historic Registers.
NO. OF ROOMS	Four rooms with private bathrooms. Try the Rose Room.
RATES	Year-round rates are $105-125 for a single or double. There is a minimum stay during special events, and cancellation requires seven days' notice, 30 days during tours and festivals.
CREDIT CARDS	American Express, Discover, MasterCard, Visa
BREAKFAST	Full gourmet breakfast is beautifully presented in the dining room and includes eggs, meat, fresh fruit, biscuits, sticky buns. The menu varies according to what is fresh and in season.
AMENITIES	Evening dessert and coffee served upstairs, bubble bath and special soaps, soft drinks, hot tea, hot chocolate, ice machine, wine glasses and buckets, air conditioning, down comforters.
RESTRICTIONS	No smoking inside, no pets, children over 12 are welcome. Mary Margaret is the resident yellow Lab, Molly is the mini-dachshund, and Alex and Scarlett are the cats.
REVIEWED	*The Great Stays of Texas, Quick Escapes from Dallas/Fort Worth*
MEMBER	Historic Accommodations of Texas

THE TOWN HOUSE

504 Polk, Jefferson, TX 75657   903-665-6927
Monique Phillips & Sue Summers, Innkeepers

TWIN OAKS COUNTRY INN

Twin Oaks Plantation, Highway 134 S, Jefferson, TX 75657 903-665-3535
Vernon & Carol Randle, Resident Owners   800-905-7751
EMAIL *randle@twinoaks.inn.com*   FAX 903-665-1800
WEBSITE *www.twinoaksinn.com*

LOCATION	On Highway 1345 across from the Big Cypress River, 1.4 miles from the center of Jefferson.
OPEN	All year
DESCRIPTION	A one-story 1890 Victorian inn, with "bright and cheery" interior decor of antiques, lace and quilts.

NO. OF ROOMS	Six rooms with private bathrooms. Vernon suggests the Harrison–Lee Room.
RATES	Year-round rates for a single or double are $100 during Friday and Saturday nights and $90 during midweek. A minimum stay is required during special local holidays. Cancellation requires seven days' notice, and 30 days during holidays.
CREDIT CARDS	American Express, Discover, MasterCard, Visa
BREAKFAST	Full breakfast is served in the dining room and includes coffee, orange juice, meat and egg casserole, Virginia cheese grits, apple dumplings, biscuits, jelly, and sometimes blueberry muffins.
AMENITIES	Swimming pool, 7 acres of wooded grounds, tree swings, hammocks, badminton, croquet, horseshoes, picnic tables, rose arbor for weddings, and a special meeting room with refrigerator and coffee. All rooms have air conditioning, TV, and a snack basket.
RESTRICTIONS	No smoking, no pets, children over 12 are welcome.

URQUHART HOUSE OF ELEVEN GABLES

301 East Walker Street, Jefferson, TX 75657   903-665-8442
Joyce Jackson, Innkeeper   888-922-8442
EMAIL llgables@jeffersontx.com
WEBSITE www.jeffersontx.com/llgables

LOCATION	From the intersection of Highways 49 and 59 in Jefferson, go east on Highway 49 for 2 blocks to Friou Street. Turn right and drive 2 blocks to East Walker Street.
OPEN	All year
DESCRIPTION	An 1890 three-story Queen Anne host home with Victorian decor that includes period antiques, stained- and leaded-glass windows, and wraparound porches.
NO. OF ROOMS	Two suites with private bathrooms. Try the Founder's Suite.
RATES	Year-round rate is $130 for a single or double. There is a minimum stay on holidays and during special events, and cancellation requires seven days' notice, 30 days during holidays or special events.
CREDIT CARDS	American Express, Diners Club, Discover, MasterCard, Visa
BREAKFAST	Full breakfast is served on crystal and china in the parlor or on the porch and includes eggs, sausage, homemade biscuits, fresh-baked sweet breads, juice, fruit, and coffee.

WHITE OAK MANOR BED & BREAKFAST

502 Benners, Jefferson, TX 75657   903-665-1271
Larry & Cindy Pinkerton, Innkeepers   903-665-1048
EMAIL etr@iamerica.net   FAX 903-665-7820
WEBSITE www.bbonline.com/tx/whiteoak/ (sent)

WINBORN HAVEN AND GUEST COTTAGE

408 Houston, Jefferson, TX 75657   903-665-7745
Carolyn & Dwight Winborn, Resident Owners   FAX 903-665-1067
EMAIL winbornhaven@jeffersontx.com
WEBSITE www.jeffersontx.com:80/winbornhaven/ (sent)

WISE MANOR

408 Houston, Jefferson, TX 75657   903-665-2386

JOHNSON CITY

Forty-five miles west of Austin on Highway 281, Johnson City has a population that hovers right around 1,000. Visit the Feed Mill Complex, a restored 1800s feed mill converted into restaurants, shops, and venues for live entertainment. Nearby points of interest and events include Pedernales Falls State Park, LBJ National and State Parks (as well as LBJ's boyhood home), the Stonewall Peach Jamboree, Blanco City Fair and Rodeo, Blanco State Park, and Lights Spectacular. Market Days are the third weekend of each month.

BED & BREAKFAST—JOHNSON CITY

100 North Nugent, Johnson City, TX 78636   830-868-4548

CAROLYNE'S COTTAGE

103 Avenue D, Johnson City, TX 78636   830-868-4374
Carolyn & Tom Holler, Innkeepers

LOCATION	Located 0.25 mile west of the intersection of Highways 290 and 281. Turn west onto Highway 290 and drive 2 blocks to Avenue D. Go south to the second house.
OPEN	All year
DESCRIPTION	A pre-1900 one-story cottage, reminiscent of a German Sunday house, constructed of native stone. The interior is decorated with lace, chintz, and period furnishings.
NO. OF ROOMS	One room with a private bathroom.
RATES	Year-round rate for the cottage is $85 for a double, $10 for each additional guest up to four. Children under six are free. Ask about a cancellation policy.
CREDIT CARDS	Discover, MasterCard, Visa
BREAKFAST	Continental breakfast is stocked in the cottage and includes fresh fruit, homemade breads, jams, jellies, juice, and gourmet coffee. Special meals are available on request.
AMENITIES	Air conditioning, fresh flowers, barbecue pit.
RESTRICTIONS	Smoking on porch only

HOPPE'S GUEST HOUSE

404 Avenue N, Johnson City, TX 78636   830-868-7359
Janette Hoppe, Resident Owner

LOCATION	Located 0.5 mile from the center of town. Turn right on Highway 290 and go two-and-a-half blocks. The house is on the left.
OPEN	All year
DESCRIPTION	A 1925 guesthouse furnished with antiques, quilts, and crockery.
NO. OF ROOMS	Two rooms share one bathroom.
RATES	The guesthouse rents for $75 for a single or double and $15 per night for each additional person.
CREDIT CARDS	Discover, MasterCard, Visa
BREAKFAST	Continental plus is left in the kitchen and includes coffee, tea, sweets, and homemade bread.
AMENITIES	Fully equipped kitchen, flowers, fresh-baked cookies.
RESTRICTIONS	No smoking, no pets
MEMBER	Texas Hotel & Motel Association

SMITH'S TIN HOUSE

204 North Avenue G, Johnson City, TX 78636   830-868-4870
Cynthia Smith, Owner
EMAIL csmith@moment.net

LOCATION	One mile from the intersection of Highway 290 west and Highway 281 north. From Highway 290, turn north and go 1 block to Blanco County Courthouse Square. The B&B is on the square, on the east side of the courthouse.
OPEN	All year
DESCRIPTION	A 1904 one-story guesthouse with pressed-tin exterior and decorated with antiques, wicker, and iron beds. The two-bedroom guesthouse sleeps five people.
NO. OF ROOMS	Private guesthouse with two rooms and a private bathroom.
RATES	Year-round weekend rate is $125 for a double; each additional guest is $15. Midweek rates are $95. There is a two-night minimum stay during the month of December and during holidays.
CREDIT CARDS	Discover, MasterCard, Visa

BREAKFAST	Continental plus is left in the kitchen and includes a choice of fresh-baked pastries and breads, quiche, breakfast tacos, fresh fruit, coffee, tea, and juice.
AMENITIES	Air conditioning and heat, ceiling fans, deck, barbecue, front porch swing.
RESTRICTIONS	No smoking, no pets
MEMBER	Texas Hotel & Motel Association, Historic Hotels of Texas

JUNCTION

SHADY REST AT THE JUNCTION

101 North 11th Street, Junction, TX 76849   *915-446-4067*

KARNACK

This tiny East Texas town is just west of Caddo Lake on Highway 43. Jefferson, the "Williamsburg of the Southwest," and Lake o' the Pines are about a dozen miles to the northeast. Nearby Marshall celebrates Stagecoach Days in May, the Fireant Festival in October, and the Wonderland of Lights Christmas Festival.

BELLE'S VIEW OF THE BAYOU ON CADDO LAKE

213 Kings Road, Karnack, TX 75661   *903-679-3234*
Amy & Bob Bell, Innkeepers
WEBSITE www.texassleepaways.com/bellsview/

LOCATION	Take I-20 to Marshall, take Highway 59 north to Highway 43 north, and drive 14.6 miles to FM 2198. Turn right toward Caddo Lake State Park, drive 4 miles, turn left onto County Road 2415 (Mound Pond Road), and drive 2.3 miles, following the signs.
OPEN	All year
DESCRIPTION	A 1989 two-story brown-cedar lodge with vaulted ceilings and aspen walls.
NO. OF ROOMS	Two rooms share one bathroom.
RATES	Year-round rates are $80 for a single or double. There is a two-night minimum stay. Ask about a cancellation policy.

CREDIT CARDS	No
BREAKFAST	Continental breakfast is served in the dining room or the sunroom and includes fresh fruit, banana bread, muffins, bagels, juice, and coffee.
AMENITIES	Hot tub enclosed in gazebo, deck overlooking Mound Pond, fishing pier, air conditioning, corner fireplace, sunroom with eight windows and two skylights.
RESTRICTIONS	No smoking inside, children over 12 are welcome. Ask about a pet policy.

KAUFMAN

CHRISTMAS HILL BED & BREAKFAST

11291 County Road 104, Kaufman, TX 75142   972-932-7593
WEBSITE www.christmashousebnb.com   800-268-4187

KEMAH

GATEWAY BOAT & BREAKFAST

585 Bradford Avenue, A, Kemah, TX 77565   281-334-4606
WEBSITE www.gatewaycharters.com

KERRVILLE

Along the Guadalupe River, 20 miles southwest of Fredericksburg on I-10, Kerrville was the trailhead of the great Chisholm Trail. Today it is the home of the Cowboy Artists of America Museum and the Riverside Nature Center. Lost Maples State Park is just to the south, and LBJ State and National Parks are close to the northeast. In spring, enjoy the peculiar pairing that is the Easter Chili Cook-off and Bicycle Race. Local fetes include the Kerrville Folk Music Festival and Texas Arts and Crafts Fair.

JOY SPRING RANCH BED & BREAKFAST

Route 1, Box 174-A, Hunt, TX 78024   830-238-4531
June & Don Price, Innkeepers   FAX 830-238-4531 *(call first)*

LOCATION	From Hunt, take FM 1340 west for 11 miles. Turn left onto Rock Bottom Road, about 50 yards beyond Mo-Ranch entrance. Go another 1.3 miles.
OPEN	All year
DESCRIPTION	A 1984 log cabin with rustic, early American furniture, located on a working ranch.
NO. OF ROOMS	One room with a private bathroom.
RATES	Year-round rates are $90 for a single or double for a single night's stay and $75 for multiple-night stays. There is no minimum stay.
CREDIT CARDS	No
BREAKFAST	Full ranch-style breakfast is served in the ranch house and features fresh eggs, homemade biscuits and gravy, and venison. Dinner is also available.
AMENITIES	Hiking, bird-watching, wildlife tours, air conditioning, wood-burning stove, close to the Guadalupe River.
RESTRICTIONS	No smoking, no pets, children over 12 are welcome. Brangus cattle and Corsican sheep populate the property. Gracie is the resident pooch, and Fluffy is the cat.

MORNING GLORY INN

Harper Road, Kerrville, TX 78028   830-895-5606

River Run Bed & Breakfast, Kerrville

RIVER RUN BED & BREAKFAST

120 Lemos Street, Kerrville, TX 78028
Ron & Jean Williamson, Innkeepers
Some Spanish spoken
EMAIL riverrun@ktc.com

830-896-8353
800-460-7170
FAX 830-896-5402
WEBSITE riverrunbb.com

LOCATION	Take exit 508 off I-10 and take Highway 16 into Kerrville. The highway becomes Sidney Baker Street. Turn right onto Water Street, go 4 blocks to the stoplight at Lemos Street, and turn left. The inn is on the right.
OPEN	All year
DESCRIPTION	A 1996 two-story classic Texas Hill Country stone inn with a metal roof, wide porches across the front and sides, and situated on 3 landscaped acres.
NO. OF ROOMS	Six rooms with private bathrooms. Try the Dobie Suite.
RATES	Year-round rates are $98 for a single or double and $134 for a suite. There is a minimum stay on weekends and cancellation requires five days' notice.
CREDIT CARDS	American Express, Discover, MasterCard, Visa
BREAKFAST	Full country breakfast includes Southwest casserole, Guadalupe River fries, fruit compote, homemade bread, juices, coffee, and teas.

AMENITIES	Small meeting facilities, air conditioning, handicapped accessible, large library, tea and cookies, soft drinks, picnic baskets, whirlpool hot tubs in each room, recommendations and reservations made to local restaurants.
RESTRICTIONS	No smoking, no pets, no children
REVIEWED	*A Lady's Day Out in the Texas Hill Country, Texas Bed & Breakfast Cookbook, Romantic Texas*
MEMBER	Professional Association of Innkeepers International, Historic Accommodations of Texas

KINGSVILLE

About 30 miles south of Corpus Christi on Highway 77, Kingsville is a designated bird-watching site and home to Kings Ranch and Texas A&I University. Check out the Kings Ranch Museum and Saddle Shop. Local celebrations include the Ranching Heritage Festival and La Pasada Festival. Matamoros, Mexico, is a couple hours' drive to the south.

B BAR B RANCH INN

325 East CR 2215, Kingsville, TX 78363　　　512-296-3331
Luther & Patti Young, Innkeepers　　　888-222-7246
EMAIL *bbarb@rivnet.com*　　　FAX 512-296-3337
WEBSITE *www.b-bar-b.com*

LOCATION	Eight miles south of Kingsville. Take Highway 77 south to County Road 2215 and turn left. Follow the paved road 1 mile, make a right at the sign for the inn, and drive 0.5 mile.
OPEN	All year
DESCRIPTION	Originally part of historic King Ranch, the restored ranch house retains the look and feel of the old west and is decorated with lodge-style furnishings.
NO. OF ROOMS	Sixteen rooms with private bathrooms.
RATES	Year-round rates are $85 for a single or double and $110-125 for a suite. There is no minimum stay. Ask about a cancellation policy.
CREDIT CARDS	Discover, MasterCard, Visa
BREAKFAST	Full gourmet breakfast is served. Lunch, dinner, and special meals are available upon request.
AMENITIES	Pool, hot tub, gazebo, picnic area, phones in rooms, satellite TV, laundry facilities, pet kennels, meeting facilities, air conditioning, complete catering.

B Bar B Ranch Inn, Kingsville

RESTRICTIONS	No smoking, children over 12 are welcome. Pets are allowed in the outside kennels. There are dozens of cattle on the property, a dog named Megan, and two pigs named Omar and O.P.
MEMBER	Professional Association of Innkeepers International
KUDOS/COMMENTS	"A beautiful ranch setting. Quiet country experience near world-famous King Ranch. The innkeepers are happy to make touring arrangements and the food is excellent." "Great birding. Good, relaxing pool."

KOUNTZE

Visit the Big Thicket Preserve, canoe Village Creek, or cruise down Ghost Light Road. Kountze is 20 miles north of Beaumont on Highway 69.

LOG CABIN BED & BREAKFAST

103 South Williford Road, Kountze, TX 77625   409-246-3978
Bill & Ann Etheridge, Innkeepers   FAX 409-246-3978

LOCATION	Three miles south of Kountze at the junction of Highway 69 and FM 327. Turn northeast on South Williford Road and follow it 2.2 miles to the gates.
OPEN	All year
DESCRIPTION	A 1910 log cabin furnished with antiques and country decor, situated among tall pine and giant magnolia trees.

NO. OF ROOMS	One room with a private bathroom and one room shares one bathroom.
RATES	Year-round rates are $95-150 for a single or double. There is no minimum stay. Ask about a cancellation policy.
CREDIT CARDS	No
BREAKFAST	Full country breakfast is served in the dining room and includes eggs, meat, fruit, homemade biscuits and jelly, sausage gravy, coffee, and orange juice. Special meals are available with advance notice.
AMENITIES	Air conditioned, 16-foot vaulted ceilings, "giant" fireplace, large deck with spa, flowers, picking fruit (blueberries, blackberries, citrus, and pears).
RESTRICTIONS	No smoking indoors, no pets, children over 10 are welcome. The resident dogs are Bear and Foxy.

KYLE

Kyle is 20 miles south of Austin and 10 miles north of San Marcos on I-35. During the dog days, cool off at Aquarena Springs, and celebrate Chilympiad in September. The factory shops off I-35 are a big draw to the area.

NEW TRACKS LLAMA RANCH BED & BREAKFAST

PO Box 128, Kyle, TX 78640
David & Shyrle Allen, Resident Owner
Spanish spoken
EMAIL NancieAatEarthlink.net
WEBSITE www.texhillcntry.com/wimberley

512-268-3211
800-460-3909
FAX 512-847-2004

LOCATION	From I-35, take exit 213 and drive west through town on Center Street, which becomes County Road 225 at the edge of town. Continue straight west for 3.5 miles. The road will dead-end at the ranch.
OPEN	All year
DESCRIPTION	A 1973 rock cottage built with native fieldstone, double rock walls, massive hand-hewn beams, saltillo tile floors, and southwestern decor, and an authentically restored 1840 log cabin with primitive decor and a wide rock porch. Both are situated on a working llama ranch.
NO. OF ROOMS	Each facility has two rooms with one shared bathroom.

RATES	Year-round rates are $100 for a double in the cabin and $120 for a double in the rock cottage. Add $20 for each additional guest up to four. There is a two-night minimum stay on weekends, three nights on holidays. Forty-eight-hour notice for cancellations is appreciated.
CREDIT CARDS	MasterCard, Visa
BREAKFAST	Full breakfast is supplied in the facilities and includes fresh breads, muffins, fruit, juice, coffee, farm-fresh eggs, bacon, breakfast casseroles, milk, and cereal.
AMENITIES	Access to Blanco River for swimming, canoeing, tubing, picnicking, hiking; feeding and petting llamas and miniature donkeys; central heat and air conditioning; fireplaces; full kitchen in rock cottage; microwave, refrigerator in log cabin; clawfoot tubs; rock showers.
RESTRICTIONS	No smoking, no pets, children over 12 are welcome. There are llamas, miniature donkeys, and pygmy goats on the property.
REVIEWED	*Texas Bed & Breakfast, Best Bed & Breakfast Inns in Texas, A Lady's Day Out in Austin and Surrounding Areas*

LA GRANGE

Between Austin and Houston at the junction of Highways 77 and 71, La Grange is home to the Winedale Historical Center and Music Festival, Fayette Heritage Museum, Monument Hill State Park, and the Kreische Brewery (oldest in Texas).

WALDHUTTE

1613 Guenther Road, La Grange, TX 78945   409-247-4802

Y KNOT BED & BREAKFAST

2819 Frank Road, La Grange, TX 78945   409-247-4529
Peggy Edwards, Resident Owner

KUDOS/COMMENTS   "Separate cottage, pond. Excellent."

LAKE TEXOMA

TERRALAK B&B ON LAKE TEXOMA

39 Tanglewood Drive, Lake Texoma, TX 75076   *214-532-8062*
WEBSITE www.terralak.com

LAMPASAS

About 30 miles west of Killeen, at the junction of Highways 183 and 281, Lampasas is close to Colorado Bend State Park, the Vanishing Texas River Cruise, Native American sites, the Chisholm and Phantom Hill Trails, and the Moses Hughes Rendezvous.

COUNTRY INN AT THE PARK

1802 South Highway 281, Lampasas, TX 76550   *512-556-5615*

HISTORIC MOSES HUGHES BED & BREAKFAST

Route 2, Box 31, Lampasas, TX 76550   *512-556-5923*
Al & Beverly Solomon, Innkeepers
French and Spanish spoken
WEBSITE www.bestinns.net/usa/tx/moseshughes.html

LOCATION	Seven miles west of Lampasas on Highway 580 west.
OPEN	All year
DESCRIPTION	An 1856 two-story native limestone house furnished with period antiques and collectibles, nestled among ancient oaks on 45 parklike acres in the heart of the Texas Hill Country. Listed on the State Historic Register.
NO. OF ROOMS	Three rooms with private bathrooms. Try the Courtyard Casita.
RATES	Year-round rates for a single or double are $75-85. There is a two-night minimum stay on weekends and major holidays. Ask about a cancellation policy.
CREDIT CARDS	MasterCard, Visa

Historic Moses Hughes Bed & Breakfast, Lampasas

BREAKFAST	Full gourmet breakfast is served in the dining room and includes such themes as French country and Italian.
AMENITIES	Spring-fed creek on acreage that is an official Texas Wildscape; central heat and air conditioning, ceiling fans, small refrigerators stocked with complimentary drinks, stationery, complimentary tourist bag with information on the area.
RESTRICTIONS	No smoking, no pets, children over 15 are welcome. There are six resident outdoor cats and a herd of deer. The deer are fed from the front porch.
REVIEWED	*Texas Bed & Breakfast, The Official Guide to American Historic Inns*
MEMBER	Association of American Historic Inns, Association of Hill Country Bed & Breakfasts

LEALEY

WHISKEY MOUNTAIN INN

HCR 1, Box 555, Leakey, TX 78873   830-232-6797
Darrell & Judy Adams, Resident Owner
WEBSITE *ivillage.bbchannel.com/bbc/p217469.asp*

LEANDER

CASA DE ESPERANZA

21511 Perry Cv, Leander, TX 78645   512-267-2060

TRAILS END BED & BREAKFAST

12223 Trails End Road #7, Leander, TX 78641   512-267-2901
JoAnn & Tom Patty, Resident Owners
WEBSITE austin.citysearch.com/E/V/AUSTX/0001/00/88/

LEDBETTER

LEDBETTER BED & BREAKFAST
AND CONFERENCE CENTER

Corner of FM 1291 and East Brenham,   409-249-3066
Ledbetter, TX 78946   FAX 409-249-3330
Chris & Jay Jervis, Resident Owners
WEBSITE www.ledbetter-tx.com/ledbb.htm

LIVINGSTON

Nearby attractions include Big Thicket National Preserve, Lake Livingston and Lake Livingston State Park, the Alabama-Coushatta Indian reservation, and Heritage Village. The annual Pine Cone Festival gets underway in October. Livingston is 70 miles north of Houston on Highway 59.

THE MILAM HOME BED & BREAKFAST

412 West Milam Street, Livingston, TX 77351   409-327-1173
Debra Nelson, Innkeeper   888-551-1173
EMAIL *milambb@livingston.net*   FAX 409-327-4165
WEBSITE *www.bbhost.com/milamhome/*

LOCATION	From Houston, take Highway 59 north approximately 70 miles to the Business 59 exit at Livingston. Stay on Business 59 to Milam Street and turn west. The B&B is the sixth house on the right.
OPEN	All year
DESCRIPTION	A Victorian inn with a wraparound porch, beautifully restored wooden floors and shutters, and decorated with antiques from the antebellum era.
NO. OF ROOMS	Three rooms with private bathrooms. Try the Warren Room.
RATES	Year-round rates are $95 for a single or double and $125 for a suite. There is no minimum stay and cancellation requires 72 hours' notice.
CREDIT CARDS	Discover, MasterCard, Visa
BREAKFAST	Full breakfast is served in the dining room and includes fruit, eggs, three meats, potatoes or grits; homemade biscuits, blueberry muffins, or cinnamon rolls; juice, milk, and coffee.
AMENITIES	Snack of choice upon arrival and choice of soft drinks or coffee.
RESTRICTIONS	Smoking restricted to the porch. Children over 12 are welcome.
MEMBER	Professional Association of Innkeepers International, Texas Hotel & Motel Association

MY HEART'S DESIRE—A BED & BREAKFAST

1200 South Houston Avenue, Livingston, TX 77351   409-327-3358

LLANO

Near Enchanted Rock State Natural Area and Texas' wine country, Llano celebrates the Blue Bonnet Festival, Crawfish Open, Heritage Days, and Monarch Madness. Take the Vanishing Texas River Cruise or loiter along the quiet streets of historic downtown Llano. On scenic Highway 16, Llano is about 70 miles northwest of Austin.

THE BADU HOUSE

601 Bessemer Street, Llano, TX 78643   915-247-4304
WEBSITE www.highlandlakes.com   FAX 915-247-3262

DABBS RAILROAD HOTEL

112 East Burnet Street, Llano, TX 78643   915-247-7905
Gary Smith, Resident Owner

FORD STREET INN

1119 Ford Street, Llano, TX 78643   915-247-1127
Bruce & Kris Rohnstock, Innkeepers
Spanish spoken
EMAIL fsi@moment.net
WEBSITE www.fordstreetinn.com

LOCATION	Three blocks south of historic Llano Square, 70 miles northeast of Austin.
OPEN	All year
DESCRIPTION	A 1919 colonial hill-country inn with international eclectic decor, on grounds that include many 100-year-old pecan trees.
NO. OF ROOMS	Two rooms with private bathrooms.
RATES	Year-round rate is $100 for a single or double. There is a minimum stay during certain holiday special event weekends. Cancellation requires seven days' notice.
CREDIT CARDS	Discover, MasterCard, Visa

BREAKFAST	Full breakfast is served in the dining room and includes homemade muffins or scones; fresh seasonal fruit salad or plate; international egg dishes such as Breton crepes, eggs Benedict with lime-spiked ancho-chile hollandaise sauce, huevos rancheros with homemade chorizo, or Scottish farmhouse eggs; fresh-ground gourmet coffee; assorted teas; juice.
AMENITIES	Afternoon social hour with homemade hors d'oeuvres, canapes, cheese plate; evening sweets and treats; saloon and game room with darts, backgammon, TV/VCR; air conditioning; ceiling fans; old-fashioned front porch with swing; occasional live music provided by resident musician.
RESTRICTIONS	No smoking, no pets. Rooms accommodate two people—no age limits.
REVIEWED	*Great Destinations: Texas Hill Country Book—A Complete Guide, A Lady's Day Out in the Texas Hill Country*
MEMBER	Professional Association of Innkeepers International

THE PHOENIX NEST BED & BREAKFAST

804 Birmingham, Llano, TX 78643
EMAIL *contact@phoenixnest.com*

915-247-4985
WEBSITE *www.phoenixnest.com/*

LOCKHART

ALBION BED & BREAKFAST

604 West San Antonio Street, Lockhart, TX 78644

512-376-6775

LONGVIEW

From Thanksgiving through New Years, the Longview courthouse is covered in lights, creating the quintessential small-town-for-the-holidays experience. The Great Texas Balloon Race takes off in July. Longview celebrates Alley Fest in June and Dalton Days in September. Longview is about 30 miles west of the Louisiana border, 5 miles north of I-20.

LONGVIEW ARMS BED & BREAKFAST

110 West Methvin Street, Longview, TX 75601   903-236-3000
Laurie Gillespie, Innkeeper   888-321-4720
WEBSITE *longviewarms.com*   FAX 903-236-0643

LOCATION	Within walking distance of the Gregg County Courthouse in the heart of historic downtown Longview.
OPEN	All year
DESCRIPTION	A restored 1931 two-story old-world hotel oasis located in the heart of historic downtown Longview and reminiscent of the finest Old World inns.
NO. OF ROOMS	Five rooms with private bathrooms.
RATES	Year-round rates are $95-120 for a single or double. There is no minimum stay and cancellation requires 24 hours' notice.
CREDIT CARDS	American Express, Discover, MasterCard, Visa
BREAKFAST	Full breakfast is served in the dining room or guestrooms and includes specialties such as Dutch babies served with Grand Marnier syrup, bacon, coffee, tea, and fresh juice. Catering is available upon request.
AMENITIES	Elegant rooms with fine linens, plush bathrobes, and custom bath amenities; each suite is equipped with fax and data ports for the business traveler; complimentary wine on the romantic garden patio.
RESTRICTIONS	No smoking, no pets
MEMBER	Professional Association of Innkeepers International, Texas Hotel & Motel Association

LOVELADY

LOG CABIN BED & BREAKFAST

Route 4, Box 106K, Crockett, TX 75835   409-636-2002
Greta Hicks, Resident Owner
WEBSITE *www.holidayjunction.com/usa/tx/ctx0012.html*

LUBBOCK

Buddy Holly hailed from Lubbock, and the town has not forgotten its local hero. The annual Buddy Holly Festival pays tribute to the man and his music. Lubbock attractions include the Ranching Heritage Center, Texas Tech Museum, Llano Estacado and Caprock wineries, and the Cowboy Symposium. Lubbock is a couple hours south of Amarillo on I-27.

BROADWAY MANOR BED & BREAKFAST

1811 Broadway, Lubbock, TX 79401   806-749-4707
Michael & Darlia Sommermeyer, Resident Owners   800-749-4707

COUNTRY PLACE BED & BREAKFAST

16004 County Road 1600, Wolfforth TX 79382   806-863-2030
Pat Conover, Resident Owner
French and German spoken

LOCATION	In Lubbock, take 82nd Street west to Upland Avenue, which becomes County Road 1600. The B&B is the last house on the west side of the road.
OPEN	All year
DESCRIPTION	A 1992 two-story contemporary host home in a rural setting with comfortable, contemporary furnishings and many original paintings and souvenirs from world travels.
NO. OF ROOMS	One room with a private bathroom and four rooms share two bathrooms. Pat suggests the Master Suite.

RATES	Year-round rates are $100 for a single or double with a private bathroom and $70 for a single or double with a shared bathroom. There is a minimum stay during university events and cancellation requires one week's notice.
CREDIT CARDS	MasterCard, Visa
BREAKFAST	Full gourmet breakfast is served in the dining room or outside in the summer and always includes an egg dish, meat, fruit, homemade breads, coffee, and juice. Special meals for groups of 8 to 30 are available by reservation.
AMENITIES	Robes, beach towels, outdoor hot tub, Jacuzzi tub in Master Suite, lap pool, conference room, complimentary beverages, ice and snacks always available, games, books, satellite TV/VCR.
RESTRICTIONS	No smoking, no pets, no children. Inky is the resident dog and there is a quarter horse on the property.
REVIEWED	*Specialties of the House*
MEMBER	Texas Hotel & Motel Association, Bed & Breakfasts of the South Plains
KUDOS/COMMENTS	"Very sweet lady."

WOODROW HOUSE

2629 19th Street, Lubbock, TX 79410
David & Dawn Fleming, Innkeepers
EMAIL innkeeper@woodrowhouse.com
WEBSITE www.woodrowhouse.com

806-749-3330
800-687-5234
FAX 806-793-7676

LOCATION	Across from Texas Tech University at the southeast corner of Boston Avenue and 19th Street.
OPEN	All year
DESCRIPTION	A 1995 three-story Southern colonial-style inn with traditional decor and theme rooms.
NO. OF ROOMS	Eight rooms with private bathrooms.
RATES	Year-round rates are $85 for a single or double and $104 for a suite. There is a minimum stay during football-game weekends and graduations, and cancellation requires two weeks' notice with a $15 fee.
CREDIT CARDS	American Express, MasterCard, Visa
BREAKFAST	Full breakfast is served buffet style in the dining room and includes eggs, bacon, sausage, biscuits, gravy, pancakes, waffles, fresh fruit, cinnamon rolls, milk, coffee, and juice.

Woodrow House, Lubbock

AMENITIES	Air conditioning, harp concerts in the foyer, sodas in an old-fashioned Coke machine, fruit and snacks in the kitchen.
RESTRICTIONS	No smoking, no pets. Chip is the resident chinchilla.
MEMBER	Texas Hotel & Motel Association

MABANK

BIRD HOUSE BED & BREAKFAST

103 East Kaufman Street, Mabank, TX 75147   *903-887-1242*
WEBSITE *www.inn-guide.com/birdhouse*

GUEST HOUSE

121 Excalibur Circle, Mabank, TX 75147   *903-451-4429*

MADISONVILLE

The "horse capital of Texas," Madison is situated on one of the routes of the El Camino Real, on the site of the lost Spanish settlement of Bucareli. It is the home of the Sidewalk Cattleman's Association. You'll find Madisonville about 70 miles north of Houston and a couple miles west of I-45.

THE LOG CABIN

2448 Cannon Lane, Madisonville, TX 77864   409-348-5490
George & Liz Delfeld, Innkeepers   FAX 409-348-5490
EMAIL ranch102@lcc.net   WEBSITE www.bbhost.com/thelogcabin

LOCATION	Approximately 4 miles south of Madisonville off Highway 75. Turn right on County Road 110 (Peedee Lane), go 0.25 mile, and turn right again, on County Road 111 (Cannon Lane). Go 1.5 miles down the dirt road.
DESCRIPTION	A 1982 log cabin with country decor.
RATES	Year-round rate is $95. There is no minimum stay and cancellation requires seven days' notice.
CREDIT CARDS	No
BREAKFAST	Full country breakfast includes either eggs, waffles, pancakes, French toast, or breakfast tacos; served with sausage, bacon, coffee, and orange juice. Picnic lunches are available by request.
AMENITIES	Ben Franklin fireplace, air conditioning and heating, candles, bath salts and bubbles, library, videos, robes, four lakes, fishing, paddle boat, hiking, biking, bird-watching, front porch.
RESTRICTIONS	No smoking. Blackie, Midnight, and Trouble are the resident cats; Blue, Sugar, and Charlie are the dogs; Jeff and Cinnamon are the horses. There is also a herd of cattle on the property. "Some petting is permitted (depending upon the cattle). Very gentle, will not chase you around the fields no matter what color you wear."

MARATHON

CAPTAIN SHEPARD'S INN

PO Box 46, Marathon, TX 79842   800-884-4243
Bill Stevens, Manager
WEBSITE www.gagehotel.com

MARBLE FALLS

Situated on the Blue Bonnet Trail in west Texas lake country, Marble Falls plays host to the annual Hill Country Music Awards. Barbecue and chili cookoffs are a common occurence during spring and summer. Marble Falls is less than an hour northwest of Austin on Highway 281.

COW CREEK BED & BREAKFAST

24607 FM 1431, Marble Falls, TX 78654   512-267-3652
Dusty Hall, Innkeeper   FAX 512-336-1629
EMAIL dustyhall@aol.com   WEBSITE www.touringtexas.com/cowcreek

LOCATION	Five-and-a-half miles west of Lago Vista and 21 miles east of Marble Falls on FM 1431, across the highway from Balcones Canyonland National Wildlife Refuge.
OPEN	All year
DESCRIPTION	A 1993 two-story traditional Texas lodge with porches surrounding both floors that overlook Lake Travis and the Texas Hill Country. The lodge features a mix of traditional Texas and oriental decor.
NO. OF ROOMS	Six rooms with private bathrooms. Try the Hopalong Cassidy Room.
RATES	Year-round rates are $65-115 for a single or double. There is a two-night minimum stay during holidays. Ask about a cancellation policy.
CREDIT CARDS	American Express, Diners Club, MasterCard, Visa
BREAKFAST	Full breakfast is served in the dining room and varies daily but will likely consist of breakfast tacos or croissants with ham and turkey, plus cereal, fresh fruit, and pastries.
AMENITIES	Paddle boats and canoe, facilities for meetings and family reunions.
RESTRICTIONS	No smoking, no pets. There are two goats and a cat named Tiger on the property.

LIBERTY HALL GUEST HAUS

119 Avenue G, No. 103, Marble Falls, TX 78654   830-693-4518
WEBSITE www.marblefallstexas.com/liberty.htm

MARFA

THE ARCON INN

215 North Austin, Marfa, TX 79843

915-729-4826
FAX 915-729-3391

MARLIN

HIGHLANDS MANSION BED & BREAKFAST

1413 McClanahan Road, Marlin, TX 76661
WEBSITE members.aol.com/highlndbnb/
WEBSITE www.bbonline.com/tx/highlands/

254-803-2813
FAX 254-803-2813

MARSHALL

About 130 miles east of Dallas and 30 miles west of the Louisiana border on I-20, Marshall celebrates Stagecoach Days in May, the Fireant Festival in October, and the Wonderland of Lights Christmas Festival. Lake o' the Pines and Caddo Lake are close at hand. Check out the Michelson Art Museum, Marshall's historic courthouse, the Starr home, and the T&P Depot.

HEART'S HILL BED & BREAKFAST

512 East Austin Street, Marshall, TX 75670
WEBSITE www.heartshill.com

903-935-6628

HISTORY HOUSE FOR GUESTS

308 West Houston, Marshall, TX 75670
Anne Dennis, Innkeeper

903-938-9171

Rosemont Cottage

407 West Travis, Marshall, TX 75670   903-935-3044
WEBSITE *starrfam@shreve.net*   FAX 903-938-6039

LOCATION	From Highway 59 south, turn west onto Travis Street and go 2 miles. The B&B is on the right, at the Starr Family Home State Historical Park.
OPEN	All year
DESCRIPTION	An 1838 Italianate home furnished with period antiques and lace curtains, with beveled windows and wood paneling; listed on the State and National Historic Registers.
NO. OF ROOMS	One room with a private bathroom.
RATES	Year-round rate is $85 for a single or double. There is no minimum stay.
CREDIT CARDS	No
BREAKFAST	Continental breakfast is served in the dining room and includes juice, milk, cereal, fruit, coffee, pastries, and doughnuts. Dinner and full breakfasts are also available with advance notice.
AMENITIES	Tour Maplecroft Mansion, built by James Franklin Starr in 1870; front porch has a pair of comfortable rocking chairs; king-size bed.
RESTRICTIONS	No smoking, no pets.

The Solomon House

207 North Grove, Marshall, TX 75670   903-927-1368
David & Shannon Howard, Innkeepers   888-900-1894
EMAIL *solomon@etbu.edu*
WEBSITE *www.texassleepaways.com/solomonhouse/*

LOCATION	From I-20, exit north onto Highway 59. Go 4 miles to Highway 80 and turn left. Drive 0.5 mile and turn left onto North Grove. The Solomon House is two blocks south of Highway 80 on the corner of North Grove and Rusk Street.
OPEN	All year
DESCRIPTION	An 1894 two-story colonial inn with an inviting brick porch, pocket doors, a handcarved staircase, dental molding, and columns, with elegant colonial and Victorian decor.
NO. OF ROOMS	One room with a private bathroom and two rooms share a bathroom. Try Antoinette's Room.

RATES	Year-round rates are $100 for a single or double with a private bathroom, $90 for a single or double with a shared bathroom, and $175 for a suite. There is no minimum stay and cancellation requires two weeks' notice.
CREDIT CARDS	American Express, Discover, MasterCard, Visa
BREAKFAST	Full breakfast is served by candlelight in the dining room and includes a lovely fruit parfait, an elegant frittata with cheese, an oversized biscuit, sausage, muffins, juice and plenty of coffee or hot tea. With advance notice catered meals can be served in guestrooms or in the dining room.
RESTRICTIONS	No smoking. Madeline is the resident cat.

THREE OAKS BED & BREAKFAST

609 North Washington Avenue, Marshall, TX 75670   903-935-6777
WEBSITE *www.bbonline.com/tx/threeoaks/index.html*

WISTERIA GARDEN BED & BREAKFAST

215 East Rusk, Marshall, TX 75670   903-938-7611
WEBSITE *www.prysm.net/~wisteria*
WEBSITE *www.shreve.net/~wisteria/reservation.htm*

MARTINDALE

FORGET-ME-NOT RIVER INN

310 Main Street, Martindale, TX 78655   512-357-6385
Mamie & Edvin Rohlack, Resident Owners

MASON

Mason is situated in the upper western reaches of the Texas Hill Country, 110 miles west of Austin via Highways 71 and 29. Check out old Fort Mason, the 1880s-era town square, and the famous London Dance Hall. The bluebonnets and wildflowers are spectacular in April and May. Enchanted Rock State Natural Area is a short drive to the south.

BRIDGES HOUSE

305 Broad Street, Mason, TX 76856   *915-347-6440*
Jamie & Mary Hemphill, Innkeepers   *800-776-3519*
                                                     FAX 915-347-6711

LOCATION	From Courthouse Square, turn north on Broad Street and go 2 blocks.
OPEN	All year
DESCRIPTION	An 1885 German sandstone host home with very thick walls, 12-foot ceilings, and decorated with antiques and country accessories. Listed on the National Historic Register.
NO. OF ROOMS	Two rooms share a private bathroom. "We will not rent two rooms to strangers. They must know each other to share the bath."
RATES	Year-round rates are $60 for a single or double. Both rooms are rented to families or groups for $100. There is no minimum stay. Ask about a cancellation policy.
CREDIT CARDS	No
BREAKFAST	Continental breakfast is served.
RESTRICTIONS	No smoking, no pets, no parties unless cleared with the hosts.

CARRIAGE HOUSE BED & BREAKFAST

1127 Westmoreland, Mason, TX 76856   *915-347-6829*

THE HASSE HOUSE AND RANCH

PO Box 58, Mason, TX 76856   915-347-6463
Laverne Lee, Resident Owner

LOCATION	In the town of Art, 6 miles east of Mason on Highway 29, directly across from the church.
OPEN	All year
DESCRIPTION	An 1883 two-story early German pioneer house, constructed of native stone and built by the owner's great grandparents. Listed on the National Historic Register. The interior is furnished with family antiques. Operated as a guesthouse and rented to only one group at a time.
NO. OF ROOMS	Two rooms with private bathrooms.
RATES	Year-round rates for the guesthouse are $90 for a double and $180 for four. There is a two-night minimum stay required on major holidays.
CREDIT CARDS	MasterCard, Visa
BREAKFAST	Continental plus is left in the kitchen and includes sweet rolls, homemade bread, jellies, cereal, milk, coffee, teas, fresh fruit, fruit juices, granola bars, and raisins.
AMENITIES	Privacy, central air conditioning and heat, washer and dryer, fully equipped kitchen, patio, porch swing, 2-mile nature path and hiking trails on a 320-acre ranch, wildflowers including bluebonnets in the spring, bird-watching, and plentiful wildlife.
RESTRICTIONS	No pets. The working ranch has cattle, deer, wild turkeys, quail, and rabbits.

MASON SQUARE BED & BREAKFAST

122 Fort McKavitt, Mason, TX   915-347-6398
Monica & Brent Hinckley, Resident Owners   800-369-0405

OLD LIBERTY BED & BREAKFAST

602 South San Antonio Highway, Mason, TX 76856   915-347-6685

OMA'S AND OPA'S BED & BREAKFAST

617 El Paso Street, Mason, TX 76856   915-347-6477
                                                       800-508-5101

MCGREGOR

Fifteen miles west of Waco on Highway 84, McGregor celebrates the annual
Founders Day Festival in September. Mother Neff State Park and Belton Lake
are just to the south.

LIGHTHOUSE BED & BREAKFAST

421 South Harrison Street, McGregor, TX 76657   254-840-2683
Jerry & Jan Walters, Innkeepers   800-840-2683
EMAIL lighthousebedandbreakfast@juno.com   FAX 254-840-2683
WEBSITE www.bbonline.com/tx/lighthouse

LOCATION	Fourteen miles west of Waco. Take Highway 84 west to Highway 317 in McGregor and turn south. Drive 0.5 mile through the center of town to 5th Street, turn west, and drive 0.5 mile to Harrison Street.
OPEN	All year
DESCRIPTION	An 1894 three-story Queen Anne Victorian inn with a wraparound front porch, decorated with Victorian period pieces and other antiques.
NO. OF ROOMS	Seven rooms with private bathrooms. Try the Library Suite.
RATES	Year-round rates are $75-85 for a single or double and $85 for a suite. There is a minimum stay during some weekends and cancellation requires 14 days' notice.
CREDIT CARDS	American Express, Discover, MasterCard, Visa
BREAKFAST	Full breakfast is served in the dining room and includes sausage, homemade bread, fruit, cinnamon rolls or other sweet bread, orange juice, and other beverages.
AMENITIES	Afternoon tea and/or dessert, robes in most rooms, several fireplaces, meeting facilities, air conditioning, ceiling fans, library, transportation to and from local train depot or airport.
RESTRICTIONS	No smoking, no pets, limited facilities for children.
MEMBER	International Inns and Bed & Breakfast Exchange

MEMPHIS

MEMPHIS HOTEL BED & BREAKFAST

108 North 5th Street, Memphis, TX 79245   806-259-2198
Wanda Hall, Resident Owner   800-259-2234

MIAMA

MANOR HOUSE BED & BREAKFAST

112 Commercial Street, Miami, TX 79059   806-868-4771
EMAIL weswel@nts-online.net

MINEOLA

A quiet community surrounded by blueberry and Christmas tree farms, Mineola offers easy access to three state parks and several lakes with great bass fishing. Local events are headlined by the May Days Bean Festival, the Ironhorse Festival, and the Christmas Wonderland of Lights. Mineola sits at the intersection of Highways 69 and 80.

FALL FARM

Route 3, Box 289-D, Mineola, TX 75773   903-768-2449
Carol Fall, Resident Owner

THE LOTT HOME BED & BREAKFAST COTTAGES

311 East Kilpatrick, Mineola, TX 75773   903-569-0341
Sharon & Mark Chamblee, Innkeepers   888-232-5688
EMAIL lotthomecottages@tyler.net   903-569-9805

The Lott Home Bed & Breakfast Cottages, Mineola

LOCATION	One block north of Highway 80 and 2 blocks east of Highway 69.
OPEN	All year
DESCRIPTION	Two 1918 two-story prairie-style cottages listed on the National and State Historic Registers.
NO. OF ROOMS	Two rooms with private bathrooms.
RATES	Year-round rate is $95 for a single or double. There is no minimum stay.
CREDIT CARDS	Discover, MasterCard, Visa
BREAKFAST	Full breakfast is served in the dining room.
AMENITIES	Outdoor fireplace and patio, gardens, complimentary beverages in rooms, transportation to and from the train station.
RESTRICTIONS	No smoking, no pets, no children. Cody is the resident German shepherd, and Sebastian is the resident cat.
REVIEWED	*The Annual Directory of Southern Bed & Breakfasts, The Annual Directory of Western Bed & Breakfasts*

MUNZESHEIMER MANOR

202 North Newsom, Mineola, TX 75773　　　　　　　903-569-6634
Bob & Sherry Murray, Resident Owners
WEBSITE *www.munzesheimer.com*

KUDOS/COMMENTS　"Attractive and very interesting, great food, and the owners are
　　　　　　　　　wonder hosts."

NOBLE MANOR

411 East Kilpatrick Street, Mineola, TX 75773　　　　　903-569-5720
Rick & Shirley Gordon, Innkeepers　　　　　　FAX 903-569-0472
WEBSITE *www.virtualcities.com*

LOCATION	Approximately 80 miles from both Dallas and Shreveport at the intersection of Highways 80 and 69.
OPEN	All year
DESCRIPTION	A 1913 three-story Greek revival inn with restored hardwood floors, needlepoint rugs, vintage chandeliers, and furnished in casual elegance with antiques and traditional decor.
NO. OF ROOMS	Nine rooms with private bathrooms.
RATES	Year-round rates are $80-125 for a single or double, $95-115 for a suite, and $125 for the private cottage. There is no minimum stay. Ask about a cancellation policy.
CREDIT CARDS	American Express, MasterCard, Visa

Noble Manor, Mineola

BREAKFAST	Full gourmet breakfast is served in the dining room.
AMENITIES	Coffee-makers in all rooms, central heat and air conditioning, meeting room with kitchen and bathroom, whirlpool tubs, fireplaces, hot tub with private cottage, library, bicycles.
RESTRICTIONS	No smoking, no pets, children over 12 are welcome. There are two outdoor cats.
REVIEWED	*Great Stays of Texas, Quick Escapes from Dallas/Fort Worth*
MEMBER	Professional Association of Innkeepers International

MINERAL WELLS

SILK STOCKING ROW BED & BREAKFAST

415 Northwest 4th Street, Mineral Wells, TX 76067   *940-325-4101*
EMAIL silkrowbb@aol.com
WEBSITE www.bestinns.net/usa/tx/silkstocking.html

MONTGOMERY

The third oldest town in Texas, Montgomery is within 10 minutes of Lake Conroe and San Jacinto–Sam Houston National Forest, about 60 miles north of Houston, and a dozen miles west of Conroe on Highway 105.

BED & BREAKFAST OF MONTGOMERY

709 College, Montgomery, TX 77356   *409-597-3900*
Dewona & Ray Johnson, Innkeepers   *FAX 409-582-1090*
EMAIL bbmontgytx@aol.com
WEBSITE members.aol.com/bbmontgytx/index.htm

LOCATION	From I-45, exit onto Highway 105 west and travel 15 miles to Montgomery. Take a right on FM 149, drive two blocks to College, and turn left.
OPEN	All year
DESCRIPTION	An 1852 Victorian inn decorated with antique furnishings, situated in a country setting. There are several porches offering views of rolling hills.

Bed & Breakfast of Montgomery, Montgomery

NO. OF ROOMS	Two rooms with private bathrooms. Try the Victorian Room.
RATES	Year-round rates are $85 for a single or double. There is no minimum stay and cancellation requires 14 days' notice.
CREDIT CARDS	No
BREAKFAST	Full breakfast is served in the dining room and includes a hot entrée, fruit parfait, muffins, and beverages.
AMENITIES	Air conditioning, cable TV, phone in common area, bicycles, cold beverages, snacks, robes, piano in parlor.
RESTRICTIONS	No smoking, no pets, no children

MT. VERNON

THE VERANDA AT HOPEWELL

Route 1, Box 98, Mt. Vernon, TX 75457
EMAIL robw@mt-vernon.com
WEBSITE www.ourveranda.com

903-588-2402
888-257-0180

MUENSTER

A delightful German community, Muenster celebrates its heritage in high style every April with Germanfest. This little town is about 75 miles north of Fort Worth, a dozen miles west of I-35 on Highway 82.

FISCHERHAUS BED & BREAKFAST

222 North Oak, Muenster, TX 76252   940-759-4211
Louise Fisher, Innkeeper

LOCATION	One block off the Main Street.
OPEN	All year
DESCRIPTION	A restored 1890s cottage featuring "German sturdiness and plainness," with a bit of comfy Victorian decor. The building was originally a shoe and harness shop.
NO. OF ROOMS	Two rooms share one bathroom. The cottage includes a kitchen and living room.
RATES	Year-round rates are $60 for a double and $75 for four. Ask about cancellation information.
CREDIT CARDS	Discover, MasterCard, Visa
BREAKFAST	Continental breakfast is left in the cottage before guests arrive and includes orange juice, sweet rolls, and coffee.
RESTRICTIONS	No smoking

NACOGDOCHES

One of the oldest towns in Texas, about 65 miles south of Longview via Highway 259, Nacogdoches' charming cobbled streets and Millard's Crossing historic village are quintessential small-town East Texas. The official "Blueberry Capital of Texas" celebrates its distinction every June with a Blueberry Festival. Nacogdoches is home to Stephen F. Austin State University and hosts the Heritage Festival in June, the Piney Woods Fair in October, the Christmas in Texas Festival in early December, and Trade Days during the third weekend of each month. Sample the bass fishing at Lake Nacogdoches.

ANDERSON POINT

29 East Lake Estates, Nacogdoches, TX 75964   409-569-7445
Rachel Anderson, Resident Owner

LOCATION	Take FM 225 to East Lake Road and drive north for 5 miles to Anderson Point.

OPEN	All year
DESCRIPTION	A 1984 two-story French-style host home on a lake with views of the water from every room. Guest quarters are the entire downstairs of the house.
NO. OF ROOMS	Two rooms share one bathroom.
RATES	Year-round rates for a single or double are $65-75. Cancellations requires 72 hours' notice.
CREDIT CARDS	MasterCard, Visa
BREAKFAST	Full breakfast is served in the dining room and includes an entrée such as French toast or a breakfast casserole, juice, coffee, and sweet breads.
AMENITIES	Fishing off the pier, swimming, hiking, grill and picnic table, use of small refrigerator and sink.
RESTRICTIONS	No smoking inside, no alcohol

HARDEMAN GUEST HOUSE

316 North Church Street, Nacogdoches, TX 75961   409-569-1947
Lea Smith, Resident Owner   *FAX 409-569-1947*

LOCATION	Three blocks north of the downtown square and 3 blocks east of Highway 59 north (North Street).
OPEN	All year
DESCRIPTION	A two-story 1892/1912 Greek revival home with a wraparound porch and furnished with antiques.
NO. OF ROOMS	Four rooms with private bathrooms.
RATES	Year-round rates for a single or double are $65-80, $10 for each extra person. There is no minimum stay required. Cancellation requires 72 hours' notice.
CREDIT CARDS	MasterCard, Visa
BREAKFAST	Full breakfast is served in the dining room on fine china with silver and crystal and usually includes eggs, sausage or bacon, hot homemade breads, fruit, coffee, tea, juice, and milk.
AMENITIES	Early morning coffee and tea, work space and fax available for business travelers, beverages available on request.
RESTRICTIONS	No smoking. Lea is pet friendly—"Anything but a snake or a monkey is welcome."
REVIEWED	*Texas Bed & Breakfast Cookbook, Guide to Texas Bed & Breakfasts*

Llano Grande Plantation Bed & Breakfast, Nacogdoches

KUDOS/COMMENTS "Located in the heart of Nacogdoches. The proprietor is an excellent cook."

LITTLE HOUSE B&B

110 North Sanders, Nacogdoches, TX 75961   409-564-2735
Gene & Judy Hale, Resident Owners

LLANO GRANDE PLANTATION BED & BREAKFAST

Route 4, Box 9400, Nacogdoches, TX 75964   409-569-1249
Charles & Ann Phillips, Resident Owners
WEBSITE *www.llanogrande.com*

Mound Street Bed & Breakfast

408 North Mound Street, Nacogdoches, TX 75961   *409-569-2211*
Mary Elizabeth & Chappell Jordan, Innkeepers

LOCATION	From Business Highway 59, go east on Highway 21 through historic downtown Nacogdoches and take a left on Mound Street.
OPEN	All year
DESCRIPTION	An 1899 two-story Victorian inn, a Nacogdoches landmark, decorated with Victorian furnishings and featuring columns and pedestals, rambling galleries, and sun porches. Listed on the National Historic Register.
NO. OF ROOMS	Two rooms with private bathrooms and two rooms share one bathroom.
RATES	Year-round rates are $80-95 for a single or double with a private bathroom, $70 for a single or double with a shared bathroom, and $90 for the guesthouse. There is no minimum stay and cancellation requires 72 hours' notice.
CREDIT CARDS	MasterCard, Visa
BREAKFAST	A bountiful home-baked breakfast is served in the dining room.
RESTRICTIONS	No smoking, no pets, no children. Tansy is the resident pug dog and J. B. is the cat.
REVIEWED	*Texas Bed & Breakfast*

Mound Street Bed & Breakfast, Nacogdoches

PINE CREEK LODGE

Route 3, Box 1238, Nacogdoches, TX 75964   409-560-6282
Elmer & Edna Pitts, Resident Owners
WEBSITE *www.virtualcities.com/ons/tx/k/txk2601.htm*

STAG LEAP RETREAT

Farm Road 2782, Nacogdoches, TX 75964   409-560-0766
Wayne & Mattie Collins, Innkeepers
Some Spanish spoken
EMAIL *stagleap@lcc.net*
WEBSITE *www.stagleap.com*

LOCATION	From Nacogdoches, take Highway 7 west for 7.2 miles, turn right onto FM 2782, and drive 2 miles to the gate. From Tyler, take Highway 69 to the Highway 7 exit, turn left, drive about 8 miles to FM 2782, turn left, and drive 2 miles to the gate.
OPEN	All year
DESCRIPTION	Three separate cottages with English country decor, situated on a 200-acre woodland.
NO. OF ROOMS	A log cabin and cottages. Five rooms with private bathrooms.
RATES	Year-round rates are $50-120 for a single or double. There is no minimum stay. Ask about a cancellation policy.
CREDIT CARDS	No
BREAKFAST	Breakfast pantries in the cottages are stocked with sausage, bacon, biscuits, jelly, coffee, milk, juice, cereal, muffins or streudel. Special meals are available with advance reservations.
AMENITIES	Air conditioning, stereo, TV/VCR, charcoal/gas grills, miles of lush nature trails winding through the 200-acre property, golf cart, library, movies, snacks (peanuts, popcorn, hot chocolate and cider, teas, exotic coffees), scavenger hunts, hayrides, bonfires, weiner roasts, horseshoes, archery, creek wading. All cottages have full kitchens, decks, and grills.
RESTRICTIONS	No smoking, no pets inside. Scooter and Girl are the resident beagles; Smokey and Whiskers are the cats.
MEMBER	Texas Hotel & Motel Association

THE STEPAN INN

418 North Mound Street, Nacogdoches, TX 75961   409-560-9511
Sherri & Rod Stepan, Innkeepers   888-569-2282
EMAIL sdstepan@hotmail.com   FAX 409-560-1320
WEBSITE www.avccomm.com/inn/index.html

LOCATION	When entering Nacogdoches from the north or south, drive to Main Street (Highway 21) and head east 4 blocks to Mound Street. Turn left (north) and drive 4 more blocks to the inn.
OPEN	All year
DESCRIPTION	A 1900 two-story Greek revival with period decor and modern conveniences.
NO. OF ROOMS	Four two- and three-room suites with private bathrooms.
RATES	Year-round rates are $65 and up for a suite. Corporate rates are available. There is a minimum stay during graduation and cancellation requires 48 hours' notice.
CREDIT CARDS	American Express, Discover, MasterCard, Visa
BREAKFAST	Continental breakfast is served in the guestrooms and includes fresh fruits, breads, cereals, coffee, and juice.
AMENITIES	Each suite has a private entrance, bath with clawfoot tub and shower, kitchen with refrigerator, microwave, and coffee-maker; at least one TV, in-room telephone, business services (fax, copier, et cetera) available on site; located 4 blocks from downtown and 6 blocks from Stephen F. Austin University.
RESTRICTIONS	No smoking, no pets
MEMBER	Nacogdoches Bed & Breakfast Association

NAVASOTA

About 75 miles northwest of Houston on Highway 6, Navasota sits on the doorstep of Washington on the Brazos State Park. Come celebrate Nostalgia Day in early May.

THE CASTLE INN

1403 East Washington Avenue, Navasota, TX 77868   *409-825-8051*
Joyce & Gene Daniel, Resident Owners   *800-661-4346*
EMAIL *castle@myriad.net*

LOCATION	Twenty miles south of Bryan College Station. Take Highway 6 south to Navasota and take the third Navasota exit, Highway 105. Turn right and proceed 0.4 mile. The house is set back off the road.
OPEN	All year
DESCRIPTION	An 1893 three-story Victorian inn listed on the State Historic Register. The mansion was built as a wedding present for Ward Tempelman's bride and has beveled glass windows, high ceilings, and carved mantles.
NO. OF ROOMS	Four rooms with private bathrooms.
RATES	Year-round rates for a double are $100-125. There is no minimum stay. Ask about a cancellation policy.
CREDIT CARDS	American Express, Discover, MasterCard, Visa
BREAKFAST	Full gourmet breakfast is served in the dining room and includes three courses such as melon and prosciutto, followed by omelets, potatoes and Canadian bacon, and crepes.
AMENITIES	Complimentary bottle of champagne for anniversaries or wedding parties, chocolates, bottled water in rooms, bathrobes, signature soaps.
RESTRICTIONS	No smoking, no pets, children over 12 are welcome.
REVIEWED	*Best Places to Stay in the Southwest; The Official Guide to American Historic Inns; Country Inns, Lodges & Historic Hotels; Old House Lover's Guide to Inns & B&Bs*
MEMBER	Historic Accommodations of Texas

NEW BRAUNFELS

This historic German settlement is 35 miles northeast of San Antonio and is famous for sausages, bread, and Gemütlichkeit. For ten days in November, Wurstfest celebrates the "best of the wurst." Visit the Schlitterbahn Water Park, the Hummel and Sophienburg Museums, and the Gruene Historic District. Nearby Landa Park boasts the largest natural spring in Texas. The Guadalupe and Comal Rivers are good for tubing and rafting.

ANTOSH HOF

408 Bear Creek Drive, New Braunfels, TX 78132   *830-620-0810*

CASTLE AVALON

PO Box 310418, New Braunfels, TX 78132   *830-885-4780*
WEBSITE www.castleavalon.com

FAUST HOTEL

240 South Seguin, New Braunfels, TX 78130   *830-625-7791*
WEBSITE www.nbtexas.com/faust

GRUENE COUNTRY HOMESTEAD BED & BREAKFAST

832 Gruene Road, New Braunfels, TX 78130   *830-606-0216*
Billie & Ed Miles, Resident Owners   *800-238-5534*
Spanish spoken   *FAX 830-625-6390*
EMAIL homestead@compuvision.net
WEBSITE www.io.com/gruenehomesteadinn

LOCATION	From I-35, take exit 189 to Loop 337. Turn right on Common (Rudy's is on the right), go to the four-way stop, and turn left onto Gruene Road. The inn is 0.25 mile down on the right.
OPEN	All year

NEW BRAUNFELS   241

Gruene Country Homestead Bed & Breakfast, New Braunfels

DESCRIPTION	Several homes built between the 1860s and early 1900s, decorated with country elegance, and set on 8 acres of Texas farmland. The innkeepers have relocated and restored old homes from the area.
NO. OF ROOMS	Eighteen rooms with private bathrooms.
RATES	Year-round rates are $95-135 for a single or double. There is a two-night minimum stay on weekends, three nights during holiday weekends. Cancellation requires 14 days' notice with a $10 fee.
CREDIT CARDS	Discover, MasterCard, Visa
BREAKFAST	Coffee and muffins are served.
AMENITIES	Pool, Jacuzzi, full-service restaurant and bar on the main property, coffee-makers, king- or queen-size beds, cable TV, porches, private sitting areas.
RESTRICTIONS	No smoking, no pets, no children. Sneaky Pie is the resident cat.
REVIEWED	*The Great Stays of Texas*
MEMBER	Historic Accommodations of Texas, Professional Association of Innkeepers International, New Braunfels Lodging Association
AWARDS	1998, Top 10 B&Bs and Historic Inns, *Texas Highways* magazine; March 1999, One of the Top 2 Places in New Braunfels, *Time* magazine
KUDOS/COMMENTS	"New old-German fachwerk walls. Very clean and very talented hosts, the art is in the walls."

GRUENE MANSION INN REST

1275 Gruene Road, New Braunfels, TX 78130   830-629-2641
WEBSITE www.gruene.net/gruenemansion

HISTORIC KUEBLER–WALDRIP HAUS & DANVILLE SCHOOL BED & BREAKFAST

1620 Hueco Springs Loop Road, New Braunfels, TX 78132   830-625-8372
Margy & Darrell Waldrip, Resident Owners   800-299-8372
Spanish spoken   FAX 830-625-8372

LOCATION	Follow Loop 337 to River Road. Turn northwest at the signal light onto River Road. Go 1.8 miles to the fork in the road and take the left fork. Go 0.25 mile to the first mailbox.
OPEN	All year
DESCRIPTION	Kuebler-Waldrip Haus is an 1847 two-story German pioneer home with hand-hewn limestone and exposed timbers. The Danville School is a former one-room rural schoolhouse built in 1863. The homes are set on 43 acres and each is decorated with a mix of antiques and Southwest furnishings.
NO. OF ROOMS	Ten rooms with private bathrooms.
RATES	Year-round rates for a double are $99-169. There is a two-night minimum stay on weekends. Ask about discounts and a cancellation policy.
CREDIT CARDS	American Express, Discover, MasterCard, Visa
BREAKFAST	Full breakfast is served in the dining room and includes juice, fresh fruit, coffee, tea, milk, meat, brunch eggs and green chilies, pancakes, homemade breads and coffeecakes. Special meals available by arrangement.
AMENITIES	Private decks, porches, near popular bicycling road by river, air conditioning, fireplaces in common areas, three baths have Jacuzzis, kitchen, meeting facilities, fax, copy machine, overhead projector, handicapped accessible.
RESTRICTIONS	No smoking
MEMBER	New Braunfels Bed & Breakfast Association, Historic Accommodations of Texas, Texas Hotel & Motel Association
KUDOS/COMMENTS	"A real taste of Texas in the Hill Country, ranch feel with tasteful modern appointments."

HUNTER ROAD STAGECOACH INN
BED & BREAKFAST

5441 FM 1102, New Braunfels, TX 78132   *830-620-0257*
WEBSITE texasbedandbreakfast.com/stagecoachinn.htm

KARBACH HAUS BED & BREAKFAST HOME

487 West San Antonio Street, New Braunfels, TX 78130   *830-625-2131*
Captain Ben Jack Kinney &   *800-972-5941*
Kathy Karbach Kinney, Resident Owners   *FAX 830-629-0303*
Spanish and German spoken
EMAIL khausbnb@aol.com
WEBSITE www.texasbedandbreakfast.com/karbach.htm

LOCATION	From the Main Plaza, take West San Antonio Street west for 4 blocks. The Karbach Haus is between Academy and Clemens Streets on the south side of the street.
OPEN	All year
DESCRIPTION	A 1906 two-story plains-style inn with a green metal roof, 13 gables, cement pillars, and a wraparound front porch, decorated with traditional furnishings, many antiques, and family heirlooms. The house is situated on an acre estate that includes a separate carriage house.
NO. OF ROOMS	Six rooms with private bathrooms. Try the Hayloft.
RATES	March through September, Christmas, and Wurstfest week in the fall, rates are $110-200 for a single or double. October through February, rates are $105-160 for a single or double. There is a two-night minimum stay during weekends and holidays. Ask about a cancellation policy.
CREDIT CARDS	Discover, MasterCard, Visa
BREAKFAST	Full breakfast is served in the dining room or sun parlor and includes gourmet coffee or tea, fruit juices, fresh seasonal fruit salad, homemade breads or muffins, fruit sauce, cheese board, an egg casserole, meat selection, and something sweet such as pecan waffles, German pancakes, or French toast.
AMENITIES	Two rooms with Jacuzzis, in-room cable TV/VCRs, video library, robes, queen- or king-size beds, down quilts, designer linens, chocolates by the beds, central heat and air conditioning, ceiling fans, grand piano, playing cards, dominoes, board games, heated pool, whirlpool spa in landscaped gardens, conference/party room, luxury apartment in separate carriage house.

Karbach Haus Bed & Breakfast Home, New Braunfels

RESTRICTIONS	No smoking, no pets, no children
REVIEWED	*The Great Stays of Texas; Texas Bed & Breakfast Cookbook; The Best Texas Bed & Breakfasts; The Complete Guide to Bed & Breakfasts, Inns and Guest Houses in the United States, Canada and Worldwide; The Official Guide to American Historic Inns*
MEMBER	Historic Accommodations of Texas, Professional Association of Innkeepers International, Texas Hotel & Motel Association, New Braunfels Bed & Breakfast Association
KUDOS/COMMENTS	"Beautifully accommodated historic residence in the center of town is rich in history, comfort, and excellent hosting."

LAMB'S REST INN

1385 Edwards Boulevard, New Braunfels, TX 78132   830-609-3932
WEBSITE www.bbhost.com/lambsrestbb/

OAK HILL ESTATE

1355 River Road, New Braunfels, TX 78132   830-625-3170

KUDOS/COMMENTS	"Beautiful, very large home on manicured estate, hosted by a very pleasant lady." "Luxury accommodations, large guestrooms, friendly hosts."

Prince Solms Inn, New Braunfels

PRINCE SOLMS INN

295 East San Antonio Street, New Braunfels, TX 78130   830-625-9169
Robert J. & Patsy Brent, Innkeepers   800-625-9169
WEBSITE *www.hat.org*   FAX 830-625-9169

LOCATION	Take exit 187 (Lake McQueeny) off I-35, turn right if traveling south, left if traveling north, drive 1 mile to the town square, and turn right.
OPEN	All year
DESCRIPTION	An 1898 two-story European inn furnished with period antiques.
NO. OF ROOMS	Ten rooms with private bathrooms. Try Sophie's Suite.
RATES	Year-round rates are $89-129 for a single or double, $139-159 for a suite, and $229 for the guesthouse. There is a minimum stay during major holiday weekends and special events. Cancellation requires seven days' notice.
CREDIT CARDS	American Express, Discover, MasterCard, Visa
BREAKFAST	Full breakfast includes egg dishes, pancakes, French toast, sausage, fresh fruit, homemade breads, juice, coffee, tea. Dinner is also available.

AMENITIES	In-room phones, TVs in suites, air conditioning.
RESTRICTIONS	No smoking, no pets, children over 12 are welcome.
REVIEWED	*Texas Highways* magazine, *Day Trips from San Antonio and Austin*
MEMBER	Historic Hospitality Accommodations of Texas, Professional Association of Innkeepers International, New Braunfels Bed & Breakfast Association
RATED	Mobil 3 Stars
KUDOS/COMMENTS	"Great historic property. World-class restaurant."

RIVER HAUS

817 East Zipp Road, New Braunfels, TX 78130　　　830-625-6411
Dick & Arlene Buhl, Resident Owners
WEBSITE itn.bbchannel.com/bbc/p211971.asp

RIVERSIDE HAVEN BED & BREAKFAST

1491 Edwards Boulevard, New Braunfels, TX 78132　　　830-625-5823
French, Spanish, German, and Portuguese spoken

LOCATION	From Gruene, 0.5 mile up the Guadalupe River. Take Gruene Road past the river, turn right on Ervenberg, then turn right on Edwards.
OPEN	March through December
DESCRIPTION	A 1962 three-story A-frame, chalet-style host home with country decor, situated on 1 acre of riverfront property.
NO. OF ROOMS	Four rooms with private bathrooms.
RATES	Please inquire about current rates and cancellation information.
CREDIT CARDS	No
BREAKFAST	Full breakfast is served.
AMENITIES	Swimming, fishing, and bird-watching.
RESTRICTIONS	No smoking, no pets, children over 10 are welcome.

TEXAS SUNCATCHERS INN

1316 West Coll Street, New Braunfels, TX 830-609-1062
Kimberly Harrison, Innkeeper FAX 830-609-1062
EMAIL Txsuncatch@aol.com
WEBSITE www.bbonline.com/tx/suncatchers

LOCATION	From I-35, take exit 186. Travel north on Walnut Street for 2 blocks to Coll Street. Turn left and go 3 blocks (through the intersection of Coll and Chestnut). The inn is on your right.
OPEN	All year
DESCRIPTION	A 1939 ranch-style cottage with comfortable Texas country decor.
NO. OF ROOMS	Three rooms with private bathrooms.
RATES	Year-round rates are $85-150 for a single or double and $125-150 for a suite. There is a minimum stay during weekends and holidays, and cancellation requires 10 days' notice.
CREDIT CARDS	American Express, Discover, MasterCard, Visa
BREAKFAST	Continental plus is served in the dining room and includes gourmet coffee and teas, fresh fruit, yogurt, home-baked breads and muffins, "and something extra."
AMENITIES	Pool, hot tub, indoor/outdoor fireplaces, large patio and garden area great for gatherings.
RESTRICTIONS	No smoking, no pets. Sidney is the resident parrot.
MEMBER	New Braunfels Bed & Breakfast Association

WHITE HOUSE BED & BREAKFAST

217 Mittman Circle, New Braunfels, TX 78132 830-629-9354
Jerry & Beverly White, Innkeepers FAX 830-629-9354
Texan spoken
EMAIL jerry.38217@juno.com
WEBSITE www.texasbedandbreakfast.com/whitehouse.html

LOCATION	Take exit 189 off I-35 and go west on Highway 46 about 6 miles to FM 1863. Turn left, drive 1 mile, and turn right onto Cedar Grove.
OPEN	All year except Thanksgiving and Christmas
DESCRIPTION	A 1974 Spanish-style white-brick ranch home with country and contemporary decor, situated in the Texas Hill Country on an acre with a pond. A newly built cottage sits beside the pond.

NO. OF ROOMS	Three rooms with private bathrooms and two rooms share one bathroom. Try the Rey Room.
RATES	Year-round rates are $60-70 for a single or double with a private bathroom, $45-50 for a single or double with a shared bathroom, and $95 for the cottage. There is a minimum stay on weekends from May through August and cancellation requires 48 hours' notice.
CREDIT CARDS	No
BREAKFAST	Full breakfast is served in the enclosed garden room and includes egg casseroles, French toast, waffles, or pancakes, muffins, fresh fruit, coffee, and tea.
AMENITIES	Large library and meeting room, fishing in large pond.
RESTRICTIONS	No smoking, no pets, and no grouchy guests. Visitors may be greeted by Cleo, the black Labrador, and Pepper, the schnauzer. Look for wild deer.
REVIEWED	*Bed & Breakfast USA*
MEMBER	New Braunfels Bed & Breakfast Association, New Braunfels Chamber of Commerce

ODESSA

K-BAR RANCH HUNTING LODGE

15448 South Jasper Avenue, # A, Odessa, TX 79763   915-580-5880

MELLIE VAN HORN'S INN & RESTAURANT

903 North Sam Houston Avenue, Odessa, TX 79761   915-337-3000

OLTON

About 30 miles west of Plainview and 50 miles northwest of Lubbock, Olton is a tiny west Texas plains town. Olton hosts the annual Sandhills Celebration.

THE WILD PLUM

708 Main Street, Olton, TX 79064   *806-285-3014*
EMAIL *wildplum@fivearea.com*

LOCATION	From Lubbock, take Highway 84 north to Anton and go north 28 miles on FM 168. From Plainview, take Highway 70 west for 23 miles and turn south at the intersection with FM 168. The B&B is 7 blocks south of Highway 70 on the west side of the street.
OPEN	No
DESCRIPTION	A renovated 1937 two-story Victorian inn, originally a mercantile building, decorated in Victorian style.
NO. OF ROOMS	Seven rooms with private bathrooms.
RATES	Rates are $50-55 for a single or double. There is no minimum stay and cancellation requires seven days' notice.
CREDIT CARDS	No
BREAKFAST	Full breakfast is served in the dining room and may consist of a breakfast casserole, waffles, pancakes, French toast, or biscuits and gravy. Dinner is available by reservation only.
RESTRICTIONS	No smoking

PAIGE

Paige is a very quiet rural town about 35 miles east of Austin on Highway 290. Buescher and Bastrop State Parks are nearby.

THE CEDAR LODGE BED & BREAKFAST

1128 League Line Road, Paige, TX 78659   *512-253-6575*
Dan & Carol Elkins, Resident Owners

LOCATION	From Highway 290 (Austin to Gedding), take Highway 2104 for 5.5 miles, turn south onto Highway 2239, and go about 400 yards.
OPEN	All year

DESCRIPTION	A 1968 log cabin decorated with modern rustic furnishings, situated in a ranch setting.
NO. OF ROOMS	Four rooms in the cabin with shared bathrooms.
RATES	Year-round rates are $85 for a double. There is no minimum stay and cancellation requires one weeks' notice.
CREDIT CARDS	No
BREAKFAST	Full breakfast is stocked in the kitchen for guests to prepare.
AMENITIES	Swimming pool, tennis court, boats, fishing, hiking in the woods, picnic area, hay rides, facilities for family reunions and vacations.
RESTRICTIONS	Smoking outside only, no pets, no alcohol. Children are welcome.

PALACIOS

About halfway between Houston and Corpus Christi, this remote small town features wonderful bay views and no commercial clutter. Tres Palacios Bay hosts sailing regattas throughout the summer. The bird-watching couldn't be better, with 11 local sites on the Great Texas Birding Trail. Check out the July Fourth Bayfront Festival, the Blessing of the Fleet, and the annual Friends of the Library Dance on the pavilion.

LE JARDIN DE LA MER (GARDEN BY THE SEA)

304 5th Street, Palacios, TX 77465
Donnie & Winfrey Horton, Innkeepers
EMAIL dsm@wcnet.net
WEBSITE www.bbhost.com/lejardindelamer

361-972-5039
800-895-8934
FAX 361-972-5039

LOCATION	Two hours south of Houston, take Highway 59 south to Highway 71 south to Highway 35 south. Take the downtown route to Highway 458 (Main) and turn north on 5th. The B&B is on the corner of Main and 5th in the same building as D's Market Place.
OPEN	All year
DESCRIPTION	A 1910 brick commercial building decorated in the style of the New Orleans French Quarter featuring painted wood furniture, 13-foot ceilings, and black wrought-iron canopy beds, with a fenced garden area.
NO. OF ROOMS	Three rooms with private bathrooms.
RATES	Year-round rates are $75-85 for a single or double. There is no minimum stay and cancellation requires seven days' notice.
CREDIT CARDS	American Express, Discover, MasterCard, Visa

BREAKFAST	Full three- to four-course breakfast is served in the dining room and includes sweet potato pancakes (a specialty), soufflés, sweetbreads, seasonal fruit, and juices.
AMENITIES	Dessert served on night of check-in, robes, early morning coffee, bicycles with helmets, TV/VCR in rooms, videos, telephones, facility available for small conferences or meetings, garden, games, guests have access to microwave, refrigerator, and ice-maker.
RESTRICTIONS	No smoking, no pets
REVIEWED	*Romantic Texas*
MEMBER	Historical and Hospitality Accommodations of Texas
AWARDS	1998, Renovation and Preservation Award, Palacios Area Historical Society

MAIN BED & BREAKFAST

208 Main Street, Palacios, TX 77465   *512-972-3408*

MOONLIGHT BAY BED & BREAKFAST

506 South Bay Boulevard, Palacios, TX 77465   *361-972-2232*
Gaye & Earl Hudson, Innkeepers   *877-461-7070*
Thai and Spanish spoken   *FAX 361-972-2008*
EMAIL grogers@wcnet.net
WEBSITE www.bbhost.com/moonlightbaybb

LOCATION	From Houston, take Highway 59 south to El Campo. Take Highway 71 to Highway 35 and turn right to Palacios. Follow Business Highway 35 to the first red light (Main and 4th). Turn left, go 2 blocks, turn right onto South Bay Boulevard, and drive 1 block.
OPEN	All year
DESCRIPTION	A 1910 three-story Craftsman bungalow decorated with casual elegance, with spectacular views from bayfront verandas and wraparound front porch. Listed on the State Historic Register.
NO. OF ROOMS	Seven rooms with private bathrooms. Try the room called A Gift from the Sea.
RATES	Year-round rates are $65-140 for a single or double and $150 for a suite. There is no minimum stay and cancellation requires seven days' notice.
CREDIT CARDS	American Express, Diners Club, Discover, MasterCard, Visa

BREAKFAST	Full breakfast is served in the formal dining room and includes fresh-ground crème brûlée coffee, juice, homemade breads and muffins, fresh fruit with edible flowers, bacon, sausage, and an entrée. Dinner is also available.
AMENITIES	Piano library, grand piano, and piano on upstairs veranda, international liqueur collection, fresh flowers, robes and slippers, some in-room refrigerators, coffee and tea service, afternoon tea and piano performance by owner on Friday and Saturday afternoons, a 3.5-mile lighted walkway along the bayfront, rockers for dreaming.
RESTRICTIONS	No smoking, no pets, no children. Bronte is the resident pooch; Pepper and Turbo are the cats. They are all outdoor animals.
REVIEWED	*The Texas Monthly—Texas Bed & Breakfast, Romantic Texas*
MEMBER	Historic and Hospitality Accommodations of Texas, Texas Hotel & Motel Association, Gulf Coast Bed & Breakfast Association
AWARDS	1999, Business of the Year Award, Palacios Chamber of Commerce
KUDOS/COMMENTS	"Very comfortable, cool, decorated with taste and the breakfast was good. The hostess was very congenial." "Romantic." "Perfect hostess."

PAPER MOON BED & BREAKFAST

508 South Bay Boulevard, Palacios, TX 77465   512-972-2232
WEBSITE www.bbhost.com:8008/moonlightbaybb

KUDOS/COMMENTS   "Epitomizes romance."

PALESTINE

Forty-six miles south of Tyler on Highway 155, Palestine boasts plenty of old-fashioned charm and lots of dogwood trees. Celebrate the Texas Dogwood Trails Festival the last two weekends in March and the Hot Pepper Festival in October. Take a ride on an antique steam engine along the Texas State Railroad.

ASH-BOWERS MANSION

301 South Magnolia, Palestine, TX 75801   903-729-1935
Jim & Lee Jarrett, Resident Owners

Bailey Bunkhouse

Route 7, Box 7618, Palestine, TX 75801   903-549-2028
Bailey brothers, Resident Owners   903-549-2059

LOCATION	From Loop 256 in Palestine, go north on Highway 155 for 6.5 miles. Turn left on FM 321 and go 2 miles. Take a right on County Road 441 at the Lawrence Cemetery sign. Go 0.2 mile, and the B&B is the first gate on the right.
OPEN	All year
DESCRIPTION	A 1975 private two-story Dutch-style barn filled with antiques, collectibles, primitives, gifts, and great junk, situated on 30 wooded acres.
NO. OF ROOMS	Two rooms and loft share one bathroom.
RATES	Year-round rate is $60 per couple and $10 for each child under 15. Extra adults are $30 each. There is no minimum stay and cancellation requires one week's notice.
CREDIT CARDS	No
BREAKFAST	Continental breakfast of juice, rolls, and coffee is left in the bunkhouse. Other meals are available on request.
AMENITIES	Air conditioning, kitchen, heaters, fireplace, fishing (guests supply their own equipment), TV, outdoor games, facilities for weddings and reunions.
RESTRICTIONS	No smoking inside. There are two cats, Orphie and Penny, and a Border collie named Scooter that live in the owners' residence.
REVIEWED	A Lady's Day Out

Hassell House Bed & Breakfast

Palestine, TX 75801   903-731-9150
WEBSITE www.flash.net/~haselhse/index.htm

Wiffletree Inn

1001 North Sycamore, Palestine, TX 75801   903-723-6793
WEBSITE ivillage.bbchannel.com/bbc/p150113.asp   800-354-2018

PITTSBURG

Pittsburg is situated near three beautiful lakes in northeastern Texas. It is home to the Ezekiel Airship (built in 1904), two museums, and several antique shops. Thirty-eight miles northwest of Longview on Highway 271.

CARSON HOUSE INN

302 Mount Pleasant Street, Pittsburg, TX 75686   *903-856-2468*
EMAIL carsonig@1starnet.com   *888-302-1878*
WEBSITE www.carsonhouse.qpg.com/   *FAX 903-856-0709*

LOCATION	Follow I-30 to Highway 271 south and go 10 miles to Pittsburg. Turn left on Business Loop 238, go 1 mile; the B&B is on the left.
OPEN	All year
DESCRIPTION	A restored 1878 two-story Victorian Gothic inn with curly pine interior, situated on a wooded acre with a grape arbor and waterfall. A gourmet restaurant with candlelight dining is located on the first floor. The Carson House Inn is the oldest continuously occupied home in Pittsburg.
NO. OF ROOMS	Five rooms with private bathrooms. There is also a railcar guesthouse with a kitchenette.
RATES	Year-round rates are $49-69. Corporate and weekly rates are available. There is no minimum stay and cancellation requires 10 days' notice.
CREDIT CARDS	American Express, Discover, MasterCard, Visa
BREAKFAST	Full breakfast is served in the dining room. Lunch, dinner, and catering are also available.
AMENITIES	Bath house with spa, gourmet restaurant, complimentary beverages, outdoor dining courtyard, waterfall with fish pond, meeting facilities, central heat and air conditioning, handicapped accessible.
RESTRICTIONS	No smoking, no pets
REVIEWED	*Texas Highways, Southern Living*
MEMBER	Texas Hotel & Motel Association

HOLMAN HOUSE BED & BREAKFAST

218 North Texas Street, Pittsburg, TX 75686   903-856-7552
EMAIL *holmanhous@aol.com*

PLAINVIEW

A TOUCH OF HOME

815 Columbia, Plainview, TX 79072   806-296-2505

PLANO

CARPENTER HOUSE

1211 East 16th Street, Plano, TX 75074   972-424-1889

PLEASANTON

OAKS AND FOLKS INN

PO Box 558, Pleasanton, TX 78064   210-569-2530

PORT ARANSAS

HARBOR VIEW BED & BREAKFAST

340 West Cotter Avenue, Port Aransas, TX 78373   512-749-4294
WEBSITE *www.islacc.com*

Harbor View Bed & Breakfast

506 East Avenue G, Port Aransas, TX 78373   512-749-5621

Port Isabel

Queen Isabel Inn

300 Garcia Street, Port Isabel, TX 78578   830-943-1468
Pat Younger, Resident Owner   800-943-1468

Post

Hotel Garza

302 East Main, Post, TX 79356   806-495-3962
Janice & Jim Plummer, Resident Owners
WEBSITE www.bbhost.com/hotelgarza

POTTSBORO

Lake Texoma covers 90,000 acres and is managed by the Corp of Engineers. Its tremendous size, forested hills, and sandy beaches make it the Pottsboro area's key tourist attraction. In winter bald eagles roost along the shoreline. Eisenhower's birthplace is just down the road at Denison. Pottsboro is about 60 miles north of Dallas

CAPTAIN CAL'S LAKESIDE LODGE

181 1st Street, Pottsboro, TX 75076   903-786-3499
Cal & Dinah Callander, Innkeepers   888-8TEXOMA
EMAIL *captcal@airmail.net*
WEBSITE *captcal.freeservers.com/home.html*

LOCATION	From Highway 120 in Pottsboro, go 5.6 miles to Highport Road, turn west, and drive 0.7 mile to the Henderson Camp store. Veer to the right and continue on a paved road around the circle to the lodge.
OPEN	All year
DESCRIPTION	A 1998 contemporary cottage furnished in a traditional fishing/navy theme, with lake views, a large covered porch, a boat dock, and direct access to Lake Texoma.
NO. OF ROOMS	The private cottage has three rooms that share a bathroom.
RATES	Year-round rates are $150 for a single or double and $750 for a weekly rental. There is a minimum stay from July through September and cancellation requires three weeks' notice.
CREDIT CARDS	MasterCard, Visa
BREAKFAST	Homemade breakfast burritos are served. Fish frys are arranged with advance notice.
AMENITIES	Boathouse with boatslip; fishing and swimming from private dock; very secluded and quiet; central heat and air conditioning; kitchen amenities include electric range, coffee-maker, microwave, full-size refrigerator, pots, pans, dishes, and silverware; antique brass bed in master bedroom; full-size washer and dryer; gas grill on porch.
RESTRICTIONS	No pets. Jessie is the resident pooch. "Jessie is a very loving dog and adores children. She loves to play."

YACHT-O-FUN

PO Box 1480, Pottsboro, TX 75076   903-786-8188
WEBSITE *gtesupersite.com/yacht-o-fun/*

QUITAQUE

QUITAQUE QUAIL LODGE

PO Box 36, Quitaque, TX 79255

806-455-1261
800-299-1261

RANGER

Site of the original Texas Rangers' camp, the town honors its heritage with the Roaring Ranger Days Festival at the end of September and beginning of October. Check out the McClesky Oil Well, the historic, renovated well that started the oil boom in Ranger and overnight turned this quiet little burg into a bustling boomtown. You'll find Ranger about 80 miles west of Forth Worth off I-20.

CREAGER HOUSE BED & BREAKFAST

441 West Main Street, Ranger, TX 76470
Spanish and Portuguese spoken
EMAIL jmtilley@eastland.net

254-647-1441
800-250-3672

LOCATION	From Fort Worth, take I-20 west for about 90 miles to Ranger exit 354. Drive 3.3 miles to the light, take a right, and drive 4 blocks.
OPEN	All year
DESCRIPTION	A 1935 two-story Dutch colonial inn decorated with some antiques.
NO. OF ROOMS	One room with a private bathroom and four rooms share two bathrooms. Try the Rose Room.
RATES	Year-round rates are $60-90 for a single or double with a private bathroom, $50-60 for a single or double with a shared bathroom, and $90 for a suite. There is no minimum stay and cancellation requires 24 hours' notice.
CREDIT CARDS	American Express, Discover, MasterCard, Visa
BREAKFAST	Full breakfast is served in the dining room and includes waffles, homemade sweet rolls, or pancakes; ham, bacon, or sausage; eggs; fruit; juice, coffee, and tea. Lunch and dinner are also available for an additional charge.
AMENITIES	One handicapped accessible room, hot tub, large sitting porch, complete wedding and catering services, heating and air conditioning, homemade goodies and fruit in rooms upon arrival.
RESTRICTIONS	No smoking, no pets

RAYMONDVILLE

Close to South Padre Island and about 50 miles north of Matamoros, Mexico, on Highway 77, Raymondville is prime bird-watching territory. Nearby events and attractions include Mission's Butterfly Festival in October, Harlingen's Rio Grande Valley Birding Festival in November, the Laguna Atascosa and Santa Ann National Wildlife Refuges, and Benson State Park.

THE INN AT EL CANELO

El Canelo Ranch, Raymondville, TX 78580   956-689-5042
Spanish spoken

LOCATION	Ten miles north of Raymondville on Highway 77, turn left across the railroad tracks and drive 3 miles. Turn right at the El Canelo Ranch sign and go 2.5 miles to the inn.
OPEN	All year
DESCRIPTION	A 1983 two-story ranch-style country inn decorated with antiques and located in the remote Texas mesquite bush.
NO. OF ROOMS	Five rooms with private bathrooms.
RATES	Please inquire about current rates and cancellation information.
CREDIT CARDS	No
BREAKFAST	Full breakfast is served in the dining room.
AMENITIES	Complimentary beverages, bird-watching, air conditioning.
RESTRICTIONS	No smoking. Please ask about pets and children.
REVIEWED	*The Birder's Guide to Bed & Breakfasts*
KUDOS/COMMENTS	"Great getaway on a working ranch, gourmet meals, friendly innkeepers."

RIO MEDINA

THE HABY SETTLEMENT INN

3980 FM 471 North, Rio Medina, TX 78066   830-538-2441
Paul & Bonnie Jaks, Owners

ROCKDALE

RAINBOW COURTS BED & BREAKFAST

915 East Cameron Avenue, Rockdale, TX 76567   *512-446-2361*

ROCKPORT

Just north of Corpus Christi on the morsel of land that splits Aransas and Copano Bays, Rockport celebrates Oysterfest in March, the Rockport Art Fest in July, Columbus Weekend Seafair, the Texas Maritime Wine Festival, the Coastal Celebration of Lights, and Zachary Taylor Days. The Texas Maritime Museum is worth a visit. The bay offers fishing, shrimping, and bird-watching.

ANTHONY'S BY THE SEA

732 South Pearl Street, Rockport, TX 78382   *361-729-6100*
Anthony & Dennis, Resident Owners   *800-460-2557*
Spanish spoken   *FAX 361-729-2450*
WEBSITE www.rockport-fulton.org

LOCATION	Call for directions.
OPEN	All year
DESCRIPTION	A large 1953 brick ranch-style home, with two separate guesthouses.
NO. OF ROOMS	Two rooms with private bathrooms and a two-room suite with a private bathroom.
RATES	Please inquire about current rates and cancellation information.
CREDIT CARDS	MasterCard, Visa
BREAKFAST	Full breakfast is served in the dining room or on the patio and includes a choice of three entrées.
AMENITIES	Pool, hot tub, barbecue, and fountain.
RESTRICTIONS	Smoking areas and smoking rooms available. Pets and children are welcome.
REVIEWED	*Inn Places, Bed & Breakfast Texas Style*

Blue Heron Inn, Rockport

BLUE HERON INN

801 Patton Street, Rockport, TX 78382   512-729-7526
Gary & Nancy Cooper, Resident Owners

LOCATION	Located in the center of Rockport on Highway 35, 30 minutes north of Corpus Christi on the Gulf Coast. The inn is across the street from Rockport Beach.
OPEN	All year
DESCRIPTION	An 1890 two-and-a-half-story federal-style inn with water views from the guest rooms. The interior decor is "casual elegant" and features oriental art as well as the works of local artists.
NO. OF ROOMS	Two rooms with private bathrooms and two rooms share one bathroom. Try the Bay Room.
RATES	Year-round rates are $105 for a single or double with a private bathroom and $95 for a single or double with a shared bathroom. There is a minimum stay during holidays and special events, and cancellation requires 48 hours' notice.
CREDIT CARDS	American Express, MasterCard, Visa
BREAKFAST	Full breakfast is served in the garden room and includes fresh fruit, a creative main entrée, homemade bread, homemade jellies and jams.

AMENITIES	Cable TV, refrigerator, complimentary soft drinks, wine, homemade treats in the afternoon, beach towels, rose and herb garden around large patio.
RESTRICTIONS	No smoking, no pets, children over 12 are welcome.
REVIEWED	*The Birder's Guide to Bed & Breakfasts*
MEMBER	Texas Hotel & Motel Association, Gulf Coast Bed & Breakfast Association
KUDOS/COMMENTS	"Very nice."

CAYMAN HOUSE

5030 North Highway 35, Rockport, TX 78382   361-790-8884
Donna Knox & Michael Marsden, Innkeepers   888-660-2473
Minimal French and Spanish spoken   FAX 361-790-8884
EMAIL *birders@trip.net*   WEBSITE *www.cybernet-ics.com/birders*

LOCATION	On Highway 35 north, on the east side of the highway, 0.4 mile north of the Aransas County Airport, 0.9 mile south of Copano Bay Causeway.
OPEN	All year
DESCRIPTION	A 1970s-era modern inn on a wooded acreage about 120 yards from the bay. "We see over 140 species of birds on our grounds each year. We specialize in accommodations for birders."
NO. OF ROOMS	Three rooms with private bathrooms.
RATES	Year-round rates are $70-80 for a single or double. There is a two-night minimum stay during some holiday weekends and cancellation requires three days' notice.

Cayman House, Rockport

CREDIT CARDS	No
BREAKFAST	Full breakfast is served in the sitting room and includes fresh fruit and juices, a hot entrée, homemade nut breads and jams, a choice of teas, and a blend of fresh-ground coffee. Packed lunches are also available.
AMENITIES	Air conditioning and cable TV in all rooms; refreshments (including wine or beer) in the evenings served in the central sitting room, space for parking boats. Amenities for birders include bird-feeding stations, early breakfasts, extensive birding library, discounts on birding tours, expert assistance with locating and identifying birds.
RESTRICTIONS	No smoking, generally no pets. Tinka is the resident cat.
REVIEWED	*The Texas Handbook*

CHANDLER HOUSE BED & BREAKFAST

801 South Church Street, Rockport, TX 78382   *361-729-2285*
Michelle Barnes & Mary Burney, Innkeepers   *800-843-1808*
EMAIL *michelle@2fords.net*   *FAX 361-729-2997*
WEBSITE *www.chandlerhouse.com*

LOCATION	Three hours south of San Antonio and three blocks south of downtown Rockport on Loop 70.
OPEN	Closed during the last two weeks of December
DESCRIPTION	An 1874 two-story Victorian with original long-leaf pine walls and situated on the Texas Gulf Coast.
NO. OF ROOMS	Three rooms with private bathrooms.
RATES	Year-round rates are $100-115 for a single or double. There is a two-night minimum stay on holidays and cancellation requires 48 hours' notice.
CREDIT CARDS	American Express, Discover, MasterCard, Visa
BREAKFAST	Full breakfast is served in the dining room and includes coffee, blended juices, fresh seasonal fruit, Belgian waffles, French toast, eggs Benedict, and homemade muffins, rolls, and breads. Lunch is served in the tearoom.
AMENITIES	Turndown service with chocolates; champagne and flowers for special occasions; glycerine soaps; and robes.
RESTRICTIONS	No smoking, no pets, children over 12 are welcome.
MEMBER	Professional Association of Innkeepers International, Texas Hotel & Motel Association

Hummingbird Lodge & Education Center

5652 FM 1781, Rockport, TX 78382   512-729-7555

Rocksprings

Guest House Bed & Breakfast

Rocksprings, TX 78880   830-683-6303

Wildflower Cottage

411 Wells Street, Rocksprings, TX 78880   830-683-3130

Rockwall

On Lake Lavon, about 15 miles east of Dallas off I-35, Rockwall features Goliad boutique shops, a town square with antique shops, and Buffalo Creek and The Shores golf courses. Enjoy a dinner cruise aboard the paddleboat Texas Queen.

Barton on Boydstun

505 East Boydstun, Rockwall, TX 75087   972-771-4350
Edie & Lindy Barton, Innkeepers
EMAIL *ebarton@bartononboydstun.com*
WEBSITE *www.bartononboydstun.com*

LOCATION	Head east from Dallas on I-30 to exit 250. Turn left, go 1.4 miles to Boydstun (the third traffic signal), and turn left. Drive 3 blocks. The B&B is on the left.
OPEN	All year
DESCRIPTION	A 1996 cottage with elegant decor, original art, and a bronze sculpture garden.

NO. OF ROOMS	Three rooms with private bathrooms. Try the Four Winds Room.
RATES	Year-round rates are $110-125 for a single or double. There is no minimum stay and cancellation requires five days' notice, three weeks during holiday weekends.
CREDIT CARDS	American Express, MasterCard, Visa
BREAKFAST	Full breakfast is served in guestrooms and includes fresh seasonal fruit, juices, coffee or tea, ham and cheese quiche, and banana or cranberry bread.
AMENITIES	Private entrance and porch, ten-foot ceilings, individual temperature control, original art in rooms, windows overlook bronze sculpture garden, winding pathway to Bois d'arc Chapel, fine art gallery on property available for receptions, handicapped accessible.
RESTRICTIONS	No smoking, no pets, no children
REVIEWED	*San Antonio Express Travel Guide, The Texas Monthly: Texas Bed & Breakfast, Texas Bed & Breakfast Cookbook*
MEMBER	Bed & Breakfast Texas Style

STAFFORD HOUSE

406 Star Street, Rockwall, TX 75087 972-771-2911
WEBSITE *www.freeyellow.com/members/gbl/page2.html* 888-207-7716
FAX 972-722-3013

ROPESVILLE

About 15 miles southwest of Lubbock on Highway 62/82, Ropesville is a quiet, peaceful west Texas community. Come for the calm of it.

MCNABB'S GREEN ACRES

Route 1, Box 14, Ropesville, TX 79358 806-562-4411
Sandra & Ronnie McNabb, Resident Owners

LOCATION	Four miles east of Ropesville on FM 41. Go east at the blinking light on Highway 62/82.
OPEN	All year

DESCRIPTION	An early 1930s one-and-a-half-story Cape Cod–style home, decorated with antiques, situated on an organic vegetable farm.
NO. OF ROOMS	Two rooms with private bathrooms and two rooms share one bathroom.
RATES	Please inquire about current rates and cancellation information.
CREDIT CARDS	No
BREAKFAST	Full breakfast is served in the dining room or on the patio.
AMENITIES	Central heat and air conditioning, ceiling fans, fireplace, koi pond, greenhouse.
RESTRICTIONS	No smoking. Children of all ages are welcome.

ROUND ROCK

ST. CHARLES BED & BREAKFAST

8 Chisholm Trail, Round Rock, TX 78681   512-244-6850
Lenore Hair, Resident Owner

ROUND TOP

Don't miss "The Bard in a Barn" at the Winedale Shakespeare Festival from mid-July through August. Festival Hill Concerts run from Memorial Day weekend through July 15. Check out Fall and Spring Gardening Symposiums, wildflower trails, and Henkel Square, which features German farm buildings carefully restored and furnished as they were in the 19th century. Emma Lee Turney's Antique Weekends are held twice yearly, during April and October.

BRIARFIELD AT ROUND TOP BED & BREAKFAST

219 FM 954, Round Top, TX 78954   409-249-3973
Mary Stanhope & Roland Nester, Innkeepers   800-472-1134
EMAIL *stanhope@cvtv.net*   FAX 409-249-3961
WEBSITE *www.briarfieldatroundtop.com*

Briarfield at Round Top Bed & Breakfast, Round Top

LOCATION	From Round Top, take Highway 237 south for 3 miles, turn east on FM 954, and go 0.1 mile.
OPEN	All year
DESCRIPTION	Two Texas country homes built in 1883 and 1889, with painted hardwood floors and decorated with antiques and cedar furniture.
NO. OF ROOMS	Seven rooms with private bathrooms. Try the Mitchell Room.
RATES	Year-round rates are $85-105 for a single or double. There is a minimum stay during special events and cancellation requires two weeks' notice for a full refund.
CREDIT CARDS	MasterCard, Visa
BREAKFAST	Full breakfast is served in the dining room and includes an egg casserole, pigs-in-a-blanket, homemade biscuits, muffins, orange juice, and coffee. A breakfast basket may be delivered to your room. Lunch is available for groups.
AMENITIES	Greenhouse, gardens, rocking chairs, central air conditioning and heat, wheelchair accessible, meeting room with kitchen, ice cream sundaes, popcorn, soft drinks, TV/VCR and videos, boardgames, walking paths, four porches.
RESTRICTIONS	No smoking, no pets, children over five are welcome.
MEMBER	Texas Hotel & Motel Association

HEART OF MY HEART RANCH
BED & BREAKFAST

403 Florida Chapel Road, Round Top, TX 78954   409-249-3171
Frances & Bill Harris, Resident Owners   800-327-1242
EMAIL heart17@cvtv.net   FAX 409-249-3171
WEBSITE www.heartofmyheartranch.com

LOCATION	Heading toward LaGrange, the B&B is 1.5 miles from the blinking light on Highway 237. Turn left at Florida Chapel Road and look for a red gate.
OPEN	All year
DESCRIPTION	A 1985 two-story Victorian-style main house, and two early 1800s log houses, with a small fishing lake.
NO. OF ROOMS	Thirteen rooms with private bathrooms; two cottages each with two rooms and one bathroom; and two suites with two rooms and one bathroom.
RATES	Year-round rates for a single or double are $135-225. There is a two-night minimum stay required on weekends and cancellation requires two weeks' notice for a 50 percent refund of deposit.
CREDIT CARDS	American Express, Discover, MasterCard, Visa
BREAKFAST	Full breakfast is served buffet style in the dining room or on the porch and includes items such as fresh-baked breads, casseroles, meats, side dishes, waffles, homemade granola, yogurt, fresh fruit, juice, coffees, and teas. Picnic baskets and special meals are available by arrangement.
AMENITIES	Lake, boats, fishing, hot tub, swimming pool, robes, fresh flowers, lemonade and cookies, wine, TV/VCR in each room, video library, hiking trails, bicycles, conference room and kitchen for guest use.
RESTRICTIONS	No smoking, no pets. The farm animals include two black Labs, a mutt, one cat, one pony, a horse, and six miniature donkeys. "Our animals are an important part of our staff."
REVIEWED	*Innkeepers Register, Texas Bed & Breakfast, Day Trips From Houston, A Lady's Day Out*
MEMBER	Professional Association of Innkeepers International, American Association of Independent Innkeepers, Texas Hotel & Motel Association
RATED	AAA 3 Diamonds, Mobil 3 Stars
KUDOS/COMMENTS	"Wonderful facility in the country for small weddings, family reunions, weekend getaways. Very gracious, friendly hosts with excellent food. Wide choice of accommodations."

MAD HATTER INN

301 West Mill Street, Round Top, TX 78954   409-249-3331
Kathleen & Kirk Whetley, Resident Owners

OUTPOST AT CEDAR CREEK

5808 Wagner Road, Round Top, TX 78954   409-836-4975

ROUND TOP INN

PO Box 212, Round Top, TX 78954   409-249-5294
Frank & Kathy Johnston, Resident Owners   888-356-8946
Spanish spoken   FAX 409-249-5506
EMAIL frank@cvtv.net   WEBSITE www.roundtopinn.com

LOCATION	Three blocks south of the town square, on Highway 237.
OPEN	All year
DESCRIPTION	The inn consists of nine historic buildings constructed from 1840 to 1890, and includes several guesthouses and a conference center. The guesthouses are situated under huge live oaks on a hill with a view. All buildings are connected by stone walkways and gardens. Fully restored but kept original wherever possible, with pine floors and wood walls. Listed on the State Historic Register.
NO. OF ROOMS	Five rooms have private bathrooms.
RATES	Year-round rates are $95-120. There is a two-night minimum stay on weekends and cancellation requires 14 days' notice.
CREDIT CARDS	MasterCard, Visa
BREAKFAST	Full country breakfast is served in the dining room and includes breakfast casserole, meats, fresh fruit, pastries, granola, orange juice, coffee, and tea.
AMENITIES	Conference room, bottled mineral water, big-screen TV, porch rockers, in-room coffee service, fresh flowers, display gardens, three shops on the property (pottery and wrought-iron shop, herbs and garden shop, and country gifts and small antiques shop), lemonade or hot cocoa, central heat and air conditioning, library.
RESTRICTIONS	No smoking, no pets, children over 11 are welcome.
MEMBER	Texas Hotel & Motel Association

The Settlement at Round Top, Round Top

THE SETTLEMENT AT ROUND TOP

2218 Hartfield Road, Round Top, TX 78594   *409-249-5015*
Karen & Larry Beevers, Innkeepers   *888-ROUNDTOP*
EMAIL *stay@thesettlement.com*   *FAX 409-249-5587*
WEBSITE *www.thesettlement.com*

LOCATION	Take Highway 237 south of Round Top for 1.5 miles, turn west onto Hartfield Road, drive 0.5 mile, and the inn is on the right. Take the second entrance.
OPEN	All year
DESCRIPTION	Eight pioneer-era buildings including log cabins, cottages, and character buildings, constructed between 1823 and 1882, with decor that is true to the period.
NO. OF ROOMS	Ten rooms with private bathrooms. Try the Frontier East or West.
RATES	Year-round rates are $95-120 for a single or double, $150-200 for a suite, and $135-200 for a guesthouse. Special rates are in effect during major antique show events. There is a two-night minimum stay for selected rooms and suites during weekends, and other restrictions apply during special events. Cancellation requires 14 days' notice.
CREDIT CARDS	American Express, Discover, MasterCard, Visa
BREAKFAST	Full breakfast is served buffet style in a restored Civil War–era barn and includes a hot entrée, meat, breads, biscuits, sweet rolls, house-blend coffee, teas, milk, and juice. Lunch, dinner, and special meals are available with advance notice.

AMENITIES	Air conditioning and heat, porches with rockers, robes and coffee-makers in suites, fireplaces and private whirlpools in selected rooms, outdoor hot tub, original art and antiques throughout, fine linens, private-label soaps and shampoo, flowers in rooms in season, guest kitchenette, common room with VCR and games, library.
RESTRICTIONS	No smoking inside, no pets, no children. Toy, Babe, Daisy, Violet, Meggan, Amulet, and Sebastian are the resident miniature horses.
REVIEWED	*Innkeeper's Register, The Great Stays of Texas, Texas Bed & Breakfast, Romantic Texas, The Romantic Southwest, Country Living* magazine, *Country Home* magazine
MEMBER	Independent Innkeepers Association, Historic & Hospitality Accommodations of Texas, Professional Association of Innkeepers International

ROYSE CITY

Thirty miles east of Dallas on I-30, Royse City sits between Lakes Lavon and Tawakoni. Celebrate Founder's Day during the first Saturday in May and Fun Fest in October.

COUNTRY LANE BED & BREAKFAST

Route 2, Box 94B, Royse City, TX 75189   *972-636-2600*
James & Annie Cornelius, Resident Owners   *FAX 214-635-2300*
EMAIL *jaelius@flash.net*
WEBSITE *www.communitysystems.com/countrylane*

LOCATION	From Dallas, take I-30 to Royse City exit 77B. Turn right on FM 35, and go 0.5 mile to FM 2453. Turn right and continue 0.25 mile to the B&B.
OPEN	All year
DESCRIPTION	A 1992 two-story Texas-style country inn situated on 5 acres with a pond. The interior is decorated in movie themes, 1950s memorabilia, and country antiques.
NO. OF ROOMS	Four rooms with private bathrooms.
RATES	Year-round rates are $60-90 for a double. There is no minimum stay and cancellation requires seven days' notice.
CREDIT CARDS	American Express, Discover, MasterCard, Visa
BREAKFAST	Full breakfast is served in the dining room or the guestrooms and includes omelets or other entrées, bacon, fresh fruit, muffins, fresh-squeezed orange juice, and gourmet coffee. Dinner is available by request.

AMENITIES	Two fireplaces, 1960s-era jukebox, videos, books, games, golf course close by, fishing pond in front yard.
RESTRICTIONS	No smoking, no pets. There are a cat and dog in residence.
REVIEWED	*Bed & Breakfasts and Country Inns, The Official Guide to American Historic Inns*
MEMBER	East Texas Bed & Breakfast Association, Texas Hotel & Motel Association, Professional Association of Innkeepers International

RUSK

Ride the historic steam train on the Texas State Railroad. Enjoy Fair on the Square during Memorial Day Weekend and Indian Summer Fest the second weekend in October. In early December, take in the parade and Christmas lighting celebration. Rusk is about 40 miles south of Tyler on Highway 69.

BEAN'S CREEK RANCH BED & BREAKFAST

County Road 2103, Rusk, TX 75785   903-683-6235
Louis & Stephanie Caveness, Resident Owners   FAX 903-683-4481
EMAIL *lcaveness@aol.com*

LOCATION	From Rusk, take Highway 84 west for 4.8 miles to Oakland. Go left on County Road 2103 for 1.6 miles. Look for the entrance to the B&B, on the left.
OPEN	All year
DESCRIPTION	Two 1988 cottages with western decor situated beside a small spring lake on a 90-acre ranch in East Texas timber country.
NO. OF ROOMS	Two cottages with private bathrooms.
RATES	Year-round rates are $60-70 for a single or double.
CREDIT CARDS	No
BREAKFAST	Continental breakfast includes homemade breads and muffins, fruits, and juice.
AMENITIES	Swimming pool, fishing, hiking trails in the forest.
RESTRICTIONS	None. The property is host to Texas longhorn cattle, horses, and dogs.

Cherokee Rose, Rusk

CHEROKEE ROSE

Highway 84 West, Rusk, TX 75785
Suzanne McCarty, Innkeeper
EMAIL *smccarty@sosweb.net*

903-683-6322
FAX 903-683-6322

LOCATION	Located on the left side of Highway 84 west of Rusk, 0.5 mile west of the entrance to Texas State Railroad Park.
OPEN	All year
DESCRIPTION	A 1995 Texas "dog trot" country inn with wide porches, rocking chairs, and swings, situated on 11 acres with a one-acre lake.
NO. OF ROOMS	Three rooms with private bathrooms.
RATES	Year-round rates are $75 for a single or double and $110 for a suite. There is no minimum stay and cancellation requires 48 hours' notice.
CREDIT CARDS	No
BREAKFAST	Continental plus is served in the guestrooms and includes homemade muffins, sausage, biscuits, fruit, cereal, assorted juices, milk, coffee, and tea.
AMENITIES	Central air conditioning and heat with individual controls, handicapped accessible, storytelling, guests can feed the fish and chickens and gather eggs.

RESTRICTIONS No smoking, children of all ages are welcome. There are several chickens on the property.

REVIEWED *Texas Monthly, Texas—Off the Beaten Path*

DANIELS' DEPOT

Route 4, Box 148, Rusk, TX 75785   903-795-3460
C. B. & Margie Daniels, Resident Owners

SALADO

Clear, spring-fed Salado Creek runs through this pretty little village on the old Chisholm Trail route. Between Austin and Waco on I-35, Salado features an antique show and historic home tours in April, a Texas artists' show in May, an arts and crafts show in August, Christmas in October, the Scottish Clan Festival in November, and the Christmas Stroll.

BRAMBLEY HEDGE COUNTRY INN

1530 Holland Road, Salado, TX 76571   *254-947-1914*
Billie & Carol Anne Hanks, Innkeepers   *800-407-2310*
Spanish spoken   *FAX 254-947-1031*
WEBSITE *www.touringtexas.com/brambley*

LOCATION	From I-35 north, take exit 283, turn left, and go exactly 1 mile.
OPEN	All year
DESCRIPTION	A 1996 two-story European carriage house with European country decor, set on 54 wooded acres.
NO. OF ROOMS	Four rooms with private bathrooms and two rooms share one bathroom.
RATES	Year-round rates are $115-125 for a single or double with a private bathroom and $95 for a single or double with a shared bathroom. There is a minimum stay during holidays and special events, and cancellation requires seven days' notice.
CREDIT CARDS	American Express, MasterCard, Visa
BREAKFAST	Full breakfast is served in the dining room and includes muffins, croissants, yogurt, cereal, fruit, juice, coffee, milk, breakfast meats, and an entrée such as bananas Foster, French toast, or Mexican quiche.

AMENITIES	Fresh flowers, robes, afternoon tea or refreshments, central heat and air conditioning, wood-burning fireplace in common area, private decks outside each room.
RESTRICTIONS	No smoking, no pets, children are allowed in the cottage. Sandy and Lady are the resident pooches. Patches, Pepper, and Gumby are the cats.
REVIEWED	*Texas Highways, Recommended Country Inns—The Southwest*
MEMBER	Salado Bed & Breakfast Association

COUNTRY PLACE BED & BREAKFAST

2290 FM 2268, Salado, TX 76571   254-947-9683
Elinor & Bob Tope, Innkeepers   800-439-3828
EMAIL *innkeep@vvm.com*   FAX 254-947-3215
WEBSITE *www.touringtexas.com/country*

LOCATION	From I-35, take Salado exit 283 and drive 2.5 miles east on FM 2268. The inn is on the left.
OPEN	All year
DESCRIPTION	A 1980 Texas farmhouse with a wraparound porch and comfortable country decor.
NO. OF ROOMS	Four rooms with private bathrooms. Try the Tartan Room.

Country Place Bed & Breakfast, Salado

RATES	Year-round rates are $85-100 for a single or double. There is no minimum stay and cancellation requires seven days' notice.
CREDIT CARDS	American Express, MasterCard, Visa
BREAKFAST	Full breakfast is served in the dining room and includes eggs, bacon or sausage, casseroles, pancakes, French toast, biscuits, fruit, sweet breads or muffins.
AMENITIES	Central heat and air conditioning; complimentary beverages; 5 acres of grassland, trees, and wildflowers.
RESTRICTIONS	No smoking, no pets, children over 12 are welcome. The resident cat is Dammy.
REVIEWED	*Texas Bed & Breakfast Cookbook*
MEMBER	Texas Hotel & Motel Association

HALLEY HOUSE BED & BREAKFAST

North Main, Salado, TX 76571   254-947-1000
Larry & Cathy Sands, Resident Owners   FAX 817-947-5508

KUDOS/COMMENTS "Beautiful old home on Main Street, charming owners, meeting facility is fabulous."

THE INN AT SALADO

7 North Main Street, Salado TX 76571   254-947-0027
Suzanne & Robert Petro, Innkeepers   800-724-0027
EMAIL *rooms@inn-at-salado.com*   FAX 254-947-3144
WEBSITE *www.inn-at-salado.com*

LOCATION	Salado is halfway between Austin and Waco, just off I-35. Take exit 284 and go east on Thomas Arnold Road. Turn left on Main Street; the inn will be on your right.
OPEN	All year
DESCRIPTION	An 1872 two-story Greek revival inn located in the heart of Salado's historic district and listed on the National Historic Register. The inn sits on 2 acres of landscaped grounds and includes two exterior cottages.
NO. OF ROOMS	Nine rooms with private bathrooms.

The Inn at Salado, Salado

RATES	Year-round rates are $70-110 for a single or double. There is a minimum stay on special event weekends and some holidays, and cancellation requires three days' notice.
CREDIT CARDS	American Express, Discover, MasterCard, Visa
BREAKFAST	Full breakfast is served in the dining room and includes quiche, biscuits and gravy, fresh fruit, and Belgian waffles.
AMENITIES	Wedding chapel, meeting facility, catering, central air conditioning, several rooms with fireplaces or wood-burning stoves, clawfoot tubs.
RESTRICTIONS	No smoking, no pets, children are welcome in selected rooms.
MEMBER	Historical Accommodations of Texas
RATED	Excellent, Historical Accommodations of Texas

THE ROSE MANSION BED & BREAKFAST

1 Rose Way, Salado, TX 76571
George & Alice Kolb, Resident Owners
WEBSITE touringtexas.com/rose/

817-947-8200
800-948-1004
FAX 817-947-1003

KUDOS/COMMENTS "Wonderful cabin."

VICKREY HOUSE BED & BREAKFAST

402 North Main, Salado, TX 76571
WEBSITE touringtexas.com/vickrey

254-947-5774
FAX 254-947-0031

SAN ANGELO

HINKLE HAUS BED & BREAKFAST

19 South Park Street, San Angelo, TX 76901
WEBSITE www.hinklehaus.com

915-653-1931

SAN ANTONIO

At the southern edge of the Texas Hill Country, San Antonio boasts two of the state's most glorious tourist draws: the historic Alamo Mission and the beautiful Riverwalk. There is always a wealth of things to do in this fiesta town. Explore the Mexican market, La Villita, the Institute of Texan Cultures, the botanical garden and zoo, Sea World, Fiesta Texas Amusement Park, and the McNay and San Antonio Art Museums. Celebrate the weeklong Fiesta and King William Fair in April, the Folk Life Festival in August, and the River Parade in December.

AARON'S GARDEN BED & BREAKFAST

302 King William, San Antonio, TX 78204

210-226-1111

THE ACADEMY HOUSE OF MONTE VISTA, A VICTORIAN BED & BREAKFAST

2317 North Main Avenue, San Antonio, TX 78212
EMAIL academyh@netxpress.com
WEBSITE www.ahbnb.com

210-731-8393
888-731-8393
FAX 210-733-1661

ADAMS HOUSE BED & BREAKFAST INN

231 Adams Street, San Antonio, TX 78210   *210-224-4791*
Nora Peterson & Richard Green, Innkeepers   *800-666-4810*
EMAIL adams@san-antonio-texas.com
WEBSITE www.san-antonio-texas.com

LOCATION	Drive 0.7 mile south of the Alamo Mission on South Alamo Street to Adams Street. Turn left and drive 2 blocks on Adams to the corner of Adams and Stieren Streets.
OPEN	All year
DESCRIPTION	A 1902 two-story, all-brick antebellum mansion featuring extensive Texas long-leaf red-pine paneling and trim, 11-foot ceilings, antiques and fine reproductions, and Victorian decor. The inn is listed on the State Historic Register.
NO. OF ROOMS	Four rooms with private bathrooms.
RATES	September through June, rates are $99-149 for a single or double. July and August, rates are $79-119 for a single or double. There is a minimum stay during weekends and holidays, and cancellation requires seven days' notice, 14 days during holidays.
CREDIT CARDS	American Express, Discover, MasterCard, Visa
BREAKFAST	Full breakfast is served in the dining room and includes three to four courses, beginning with fresh fruit, followed by an egg dish, finishing with a sweet dish. Cereal, breads, and yogurt are always available. Special meals are available by prior arrangement.
AMENITIES	All rooms have air conditioning, overhead ceiling fans, cable TV with premium movie channels, telephones, queen-size beds, fresh-cut flowers, candies; the Verandah Room has a Jacuzzi for two; the Carriage House has a kitchenette with microwave oven, refrigerator, sink, and dishwasher; soft drinks are always available.
RESTRICTIONS	No smoking. Harold is the resident cat. "Harold does not come into the house at any time. He is strictly an outdoor cat."
REVIEWED	*Frommer's*
MEMBER	Professional Association of Innkeepers International, Texas Hotel & Motel Association, Texas Bed & Breakfast Association, San Antonio Bed & Breakfast Association
RATED	AAA 3 Diamond, Mobil 3 Star

ALONSO HOUSE BED & BREAKFAST

1115 South St. Marys Street, San Antonio, TX 78210   210-224-9057

ARBOR HOUSE INN & SUITES

540 South St. Mary's Street, San Antonio, TX 78205	*210-472-2005*
Dale Schuette & Reg Stark, Innkeepers	*888-272-6700*
EMAIL *arborhaus@aol.com*	*FAX 210-472-2007*
WEBSITE *www.arborhouse.com*	

LOCATION	Arbor House is located one-and-a-half blocks south of the Riverwalk, 2 blocks southwest of the convention center.
OPEN	All year
DESCRIPTION	A 1903 two-story Queen Anne–style inn, which composes the southern side of an entire block in downtown San Antonio. There are five buildings. Each private house has three suites, pine floors, lots of windows, and unique artwork. The inn is listed on both the State and National Historic Registers.
NO. OF ROOMS	Eighteen rooms with private bathrooms.
RATES	October through May, rates are $95-195 for a single or double. June through September, rates are $85-160 for a single or double. There is a minimum stay during holidays and weekends, and cancellation requires three days' notice.
CREDIT CARDS	American Express, Diners Club, Discover, MasterCard, Visa
BREAKFAST	Continental plus is served in the guestrooms and includes fresh fruit, juice, and pastries.
AMENITIES	Cable TV, phones with voice mail, robes in rooms, coffee-makers, some rooms have refrigerators and microwaves, garden tubs, antique footed tubs, some Jacuzzi tubs, some private balconies, meeting room that accommodates 35, board room for 10, one room handicapped accessible, parking.
RESTRICTIONS	No smoking. Martha is the resident cat. "Martha greets all guests and 'asks' for a head pat. She may share rooms, too, if guests desire."
MEMBER	San Antonio Bed & Breakfast Association
RATED	AAA 3 Diamonds

Beauregard House Bed & Breakfast

215 Beauregard, San Antonio, TX 78204   210-222-1198
Ann Trabal, Resident Owner   800-841-9377
WEBSITE *www.beauregardbandb.org*

LOCATION	From Highway 10, take the Durango exit and follow the sign to downtown. Go south on South Alamo and right on Durango.
OPEN	All year
DESCRIPTION	A 1920 two-story Victorian inn with traditional and antique furnishings, hardwood floors, carved front door with beveled glass, a spacious front porch with a swing, and a backyard deck.
NO. OF ROOMS	Four rooms with private bathrooms.
RATES	Year-round rates for a single or double are $99-119. Group rates and special packages are available. There is a two-night minimum stay on weekends and cancellation requires seven days' notice.
CREDIT CARDS	MasterCard, Visa
BREAKFAST	Full breakfast is served on crystal and china in the dining room and includes a fruit dish, sweet bread, a main course, juices, and gourmet coffee.
AMENITIES	Lemonade and cookies on arrival, refreshments always available, champagne and balloons for special occasions, complimentary trolley passes. Located 1 block from the downtown trolley system, and 1 block from the famous Riverwalk.
RESTRICTIONS	No smoking, no pets, children over 12 are welcome.
MEMBER	Bed & Breakfast Association of San Antonio
RATED	Mobil 3 Stars

Beckmann Inn and Carriage House

222 East Guenther Street, San Antonio, TX 78204   210-229-1449
Betty Jo & Don Schwartz, Innkeepers   800-945-1449
EMAIL *beckinn@swbell.net*   FAX 210-229-1061
WEBSITE *www.beckmanninn.com*

LOCATION	From I-37 south, exit at Durango and take a right. Go 3 stoplights, take a left on South St. Mary's Street, then an immediate right on King William Street. Go 5 blocks to the end and take a left onto Guenther Street. The B&B is on the left.

OPEN	All year
DESCRIPTION	An 1886 two-story Victorian inn with Greek revival influences, with a wraparound porch, bay window, sun porch, and a two-story carriage house framed by a picket fence, decorated with American Victorian furnishings. Listed on the National Historic Register.
NO. OF ROOMS	Five rooms with private bathrooms.
RATES	Year-round rates are $90-140 for a single or double. There is a minimum stay on weekends and during holidays and special events. Cancellation requires 10 days' notice, 20 to 30 days during holidays and special events.
CREDIT CARDS	American Express, Diners Club, Discover, MasterCard, Visa
BREAKFAST	Full gourmet breakfast is served in the dining room on china with crystal and silver and includes stuffed cinnamon French toast with apricot glaze and Canadian bacon; a breakfast dessert of strawberries, kiwis, and chocolate struesel coffecake; fresh-ground coffee; and special fruit juice.
AMENITIES	Air-conditioning, ceiling fans, fresh flowers, TVs, phones, guest refrigerators, robes, fireplaces, very ornately carved high-back Victorian beds, off-street parking, trolley access to all the Riverwalk activities, sun porch.
RESTRICTIONS	No smoking inside, no pets, children over 12 are welcome.
REVIEWED	*Innkeeper's Register; Fodor's The Southwest Best Bed & Breakfasts; Frommer's San Antonio and Austin; Recommended Country Inns— The Southwest; America's Favorite Small Hotels and Inns; Texas— Off The Beaten Path; The Texas Monthly Bed & Breakfast; The Alamo City Guide; San Antonio Smart Guide; 28 Great American Cities Bed & Breakfast Guide; The Complete Guide to Bed & Breakfasts, Inns and Guesthouses; The National Trust Guide to Historic Bed & Breakfasts; The Official Guide to American Historic Inns; The Complete Guide To American Bed and Breakfasts; Bed and Breakfast USA; The Official Bed & Breakfast Guide*
MEMBER	The Independent Innkeepers Association
RATED	AAA 3 Diamonds, Mobil 3 Stars
KUDOS/COMMENTS	"Victorian inn with elegant antiques, warm hospitality, and true professionalism in the owners."

BELLE OF MONTE VISTA

505 Belknap Place, San Antonio, TX 78212   *210-732-4006*

BONNER GARDEN BED & BREAKFAST

145 East Agarita, San Antonio, TX 78212　　　　　　　*210-733-4222*
Noel & Jan Stenoien, Innkeepers　　　　　　　　　　*800-396-4222*
EMAIL noels@onr.com　　　　　　　　　　　　*FAX 210-733-6129*
WEBSITE www.cruising-america.com

LOCATION	Two miles north of downtown at the corner of McCullough and East Agarita Streets. From the airport, take Highway 218 south for 4 miles to the Mulberry exit. Turn right and drive 0.5 mile to McCullough. Turn right, drive 0.1 mile to Agarita, turn left, then turn right into the first driveway.
OPEN	All year
DESCRIPTION	A 1910 two-story Italianate inn with Italian Renaissance decor. It is a replica of an Italian villa built in the early 1600s and is surrounded by gardens, with a rooftop patio overlooking downtown San Antonio. Listed on the National and State Historic Registers.
NO. OF ROOMS	Five rooms with private bathrooms.
RATES	Year-round rates for a single or double are $85-115. There is a minimum stay on weekends and cancellation requires 72 hours' notice.
CREDIT CARDS	American Express, Diners Club, Discover, MasterCard, Visa
BREAKFAST	Full breakfast is served in the dining room and includes juice, coffee, tea; an entrée such as scrambled eggs, stuffed French toast, pancakes, or waffles; ham, sausage, or bacon; fresh fruits; coffeecake, muffins, or nut breads.
AMENITIES	Large swimming pool, air conditioning, meeting facilities, fax, phones, complimentary beverages during the day, wine, bicycles, video library.
RESTRICTIONS	No smoking, no pets
REVIEWED	*Frommer's*
MEMBER	San Antonio Bed & Breakfast Association
RATED	AAA 3 Diamonds
AWARDS	1985, San Antonio Conservation Society Award
KUDOS/COMMENTS	"The home and grounds were beautiful and clean. The hostess was warm and friendly. Good breakfast."

Brackenridge House Bed & Breakfast Inn, San Antonio

BRACKENRIDGE HOUSE BED & BREAKFAST INN

230 Madison, San Antonio, TX 78204
Bennie & Sue Blansett, Innkeepers
EMAIL *benniesueb@aol.com*
WEBSITE *www.brackenridgehouse.com*

210-271-3442
800-221-1412
FAX *210-226-3139*

LOCATION	Heading south on Highway 37, take the Durango exit and turn right, then left onto South St. Mary's Street, and right on Madison. From Highway 37 north, take a left onto Durango and follow the above directions.
OPEN	All year
DESCRIPTION	A 1901 two-story Greek revival inn with country Victorian decor, antiques, breezy verandas, original pine floors, high ceilings, and double-hung windows.
NO. OF ROOMS	Five rooms with private bathrooms and two rooms share a bathroom. Try Benet's Suite.

RATES	September through December and February through June, rates are $89-150 for a single or double with a private bathroom, $99-175 for a suite, and $125-250 for the carriage house. July, August, and January, rates are $89-99 for a single or double with a private bathroom, $99-109 for a suite, and $125-175 for the carriage house. There is a minimum stay during weekends and holidays, and cancellation requires seven days' notice.
CREDIT CARDS	Diners Club, Discover, MasterCard, Visa
BREAKFAST	Full family-style breakfast is served in the dining room and includes fruit, a main course, and dessert. Coffee and pastries are available for early risers.
AMENITIES	Air conditioning, off-street parking, cable TV with HBO and Showtime, coffee-makers, mini-refrigerators, microwaves, complimentary beverages, hot tub in garden, trolley passes, robes.
RESTRICTIONS	No smoking, no pets in the main house, children over 12 are welcome in the main house. Pets and children are OK in the carriage house.
MEMBER	Historic and Hospitality Accommodations of Texas, San Antonio Bed & Breakfast Association, Professional Association of Innkeepers International
RATED	AAA 3 Diamonds, Mobil 2 Stars
AWARDS	1986, Restoration Award, San Antonio Conservation Society
KUDOS/COMMENTS	"Charming, warm, and Sue is a superb cook and baker. Just to watch Benny 'hold court' from the upper veranda is worth a visit!" "Hosts were personable; delicious breakfast, airy lacy atmosphere with balconies, close to the Riverwalk."

BULLIS HOUSE INN

621 Pierce Street, San Antonio, TX 78208
Steve & Alma Cross, Resident Owners

210-223-9426
FAX 210-299-1479

LOCATION	From downtown San Antonio, take I-35 northeast 2 miles to the north New Braunfels exit. The inn is directly across from Fort Sam Houston.
OPEN	All year
DESCRIPTION	A 1909 three-story neoclassical inn with Victorian details, listed on the State Historic Register. The mansion has large columns, a carriageway, a wide veranda, 14-foot decorative plaster ceilings, patterned wood floors, and marble fireplaces.
NO. OF ROOMS	One room with a private bathroom, and six rooms share three-and-a-half bathrooms.

RATES	Year-round rate for a single or double with a private bathroom is $79, and a single or double with a shared bathroom is $49-69. A two-night minimum is required on weekends and cancellation requires five days' notice.
CREDIT CARDS	American Express, Discover, MasterCard, Visa
BREAKFAST	Continental plus is served in the dining room or on the veranda and includes assorted cereals, fruits, whipped orange or pineapple juice, pastries, muffins, crepes, cinnamon coffee, tea, or several kinds of hot chocolate. Catering is available for groups or meetings with advance notice.
AMENITIES	Swimming pool, wood-burning fireplaces, video library, heat and air conditioning, telephone, TVs, fax, meeting facilities. Small gift shop on premises, additional dormitory facilities located next door for groups, free off-street parking.
RESTRICTIONS	Smoking is limited, no pets, children are welcome.
REVIEWED	*Fodors Let's Go USA; The National Trust Guide to Historic Bed & Breakfasts, Inns & Small Hotels; Country Inns of Texas*
MEMBER	San Antonio Bed & Breakfast Association
RATED	ABBA 3 Crowns, Mobil 2 Stars

BUTTERCUP BED & BREAKFAST

222 Primrose Place, San Antonio, TX 78209　　　　　*800-814-6116*

CANYON LAKE RANCH

915 South Alamo Street, San Antonio, TX 78205　　　*210-212-5533*
WEBSITE www.texasvacation.com

CHRISTMAS HOUSE BED & BREAKFAST

2307 McCullough Avenue, San Antonio, TX 78212　　　*210-737-2786*
Penny & Grant Estes, Innkeepers　　　　　　　　　*800-268-4187*
EMAIL christmashsb@earthlink.net　　　　　　　*FAX 210-734-5712*
WEBSITE www.texassleepaways.com/christmashouse

LOCATION	From the San Antonio airport, turn left on the access road to Highway 410, exit McCullough, and go south about 5.5 miles.

OPEN	All year
DESCRIPTION	A 1910 two-story host home with wide verandas in front and back, original hardwood floors, and antique furnishings.
NO. OF ROOMS	Five rooms with private bathrooms. Try the Santa Claus Room.
RATES	Year-round rates are $75-125 for a single or double. There is a two-night minimum stay and cancellation requires one week's notice for a refund less 10 percent.
CREDIT CARDS	MasterCard, Visa
BREAKFAST	Full three-course breakfast is served on the weekends and includes fruit, hot breads, and casseroles. Midweek, continental breakfast includes hot breads, fruit, juice, and coffee.
AMENITIES	Handicapped accessible room, home-baked goodies, nonalcoholic drinks, antique furnishings for sale.
RESTRICTIONS	No smoking inside, no pets, well-behaved children are welcome. Dizzy is the resident cat.
MEMBER	Professional Association of Innkeepers International
RATED	AAA 2 Diamonds

CLASSIC CHARMS

302 King William, San Antonio, TX 78204　　　　　　210-271-9016
Edith Stockhardt, Resident Owner

THE COLUMNS ON ALAMO

1037 South Alamo Street, San Antonio, TX 78210　　　210-271-3245
Art & Ellenor Link, Innkeepers　　　　　　　　　　800-233-3364
German spoken　　　　　　　　　　　　　　FAX 210-271-3245
WEBSITE www.bbonline.com/tx/columns

LOCATION	From I-10, take the Durango Street exit and go east on Durango. Go right on South Alamo Street.
OPEN	All year
DESCRIPTION	An 1892 Greek revival inn and an adjacent 1901 guesthouse furnished in an uncluttered way with Victorian antiques and reproductions, situated on 1.3 acres of gardens.
NO. OF ROOMS	Eleven rooms with private bathrooms.

The Columns on Alamo, San Antonio

RATES	Year-round rates are $89-155 for a single or double. There is a two-night minimum stay when a Saturday is involved and cancellation requires seven days' notice.
CREDIT CARDS	American Express, Carte Blanche, Diners Club, Discover, MasterCard, Visa
BREAKFAST	Full breakfast is served in the dining room or guestrooms and includes coffee, tea, milk, fresh orange juice and fruit, granola and yogurt, an egg dish such as omelets or huevos rancheros, and dessert.
AMENITIES	Flowers and champagne for special occasions, soft drinks and coffee, air conditioning, trolley service at the door, large library can be used for meeting facility.
RESTRICTIONS	No smoking, children over 12 are welcome.
REVIEWED	*Frommer's*
MEMBER	San Antonio Bed & Breakfast Association, Texas Hotel & Motel Association
RATED	AAA 4 Diamonds
KUDOS/COMMENTS	"Beautifully restored, elegant accommodations. Excellent hostess."

THE COOK'S COTTAGE

1915 Eagle Meadow, San Antonio, TX 78248   *210-493-5101*
WEBSITE www.aisi.net/patsys-place/cooks.htm   *FAX 210-493-1885*

DR. YRIZARRY'S BED & BREAKFAST

115 West Ashby Place, San Antonio, TX 78212   *210-733-5899*
Ada Yrizarry, Innkeeper   *888-733-0131*
Spanish spoken   *FAX 210-733-5899*

LOCATION	Take Highway 281 south to the Mulberry exit, to Ashby. The B&B is between North Main and San Pedro Streets.
OPEN	All year
DESCRIPTION	A 1906 three-story Victorian antebellum inn decorated with antiques. Listed on the National and State Historic Registers.
NO. OF ROOMS	Three rooms with private bathrooms.
RATES	Year-round rates are $125-150 for a single or double. There is a two-night minimum stay and cancellation requires 48 hours' notice.
CREDIT CARDS	American Express, Discover, MasterCard, Visa
BREAKFAST	Full breakfast is served brunch style in the dining room with formal settings and healthy, fresh selections.
AMENITIES	Flowers, candies, refrigerators with refreshments, air conditioning and heat, antique bathtubs, steam room with vertical showers, VCR, phones with private lines, cozy sitting area with relaxing fountains and birds.
RESTRICTIONS	No smoking, no pets
REVIEWED	*Historic Accommodations of Texas*
MEMBER	San Antonio Bed & Breakfast Association

Inn on the River, San Antonio

INN ON THE RIVER

129 Woodward Place, San Antonio, TX 78204   *210-225-6333*
Dr. A. D. Zucht III, Innkeeper   *800-730-0019*
EMAIL *adz@swbell.net*   *FAX 210-271-3992*
WEBSITE *www.hotx.com/sa/bb*

LOCATION	In downtown San Antonio on the banks of the San Antonio River, about 0.5 mile to the main riverwalk attractions and 0.4 mile to the King William Historic District.
OPEN	All year
DESCRIPTION	A 1916 three-story Victorian inn decorated with period antique furnishings and hardwood floors, situated on the banks of the San Antonio River. There is also a cottage.
NO. OF ROOMS	Twelve rooms with private bathrooms. Try the Penthouse Room.
RATES	February through June and September through December, rates are $99-139 for a single or double. January, July, and August, rates are $80-111 for a single or double. There is a minimum stay during weekends and holidays, and cancellation requires seven days' notice.
CREDIT CARDS	American Express, Discover, MasterCard, Visa

BREAKFAST	Full breakfast is served in the dining room or guestrooms and includes a main course such as Belgian waffles, fruit salad, bagels, muffins, cereals, and bread. Special meals are available for groups at an additional charge.
AMENITIES	All rooms face the beautiful San Antonio River; Jacuzzi tubs in four rooms; fireplaces in two rooms; all rooms with king- or queen-size beds, TV, phone with voice mail, air conditioning, heating.
RESTRICTIONS	No smoking, no pets
REVIEWED	*Recommended Country Inns—The Southwest*
MEMBER	Professional Association of Innkeepers International, San Antonio Bed & Breakfast Association
RATED	AAA 2 Diamonds

JOSKE HOUSE

241 King William, San Antonio, TX 78204　　　　　　210-271-0706
Jessie Simpson, Innkeeper
Spanish spoken

LOCATION	From I-37 south, take the Durango exit to the west, go 1 mile, and turn left onto St. Mary's Street. Take an immediate right onto King William.

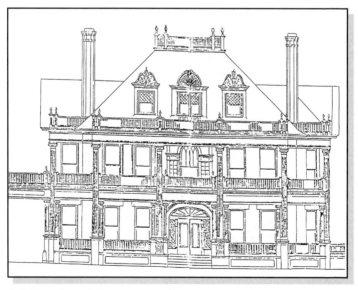

Joske House, San Antonio

OPEN	All year
DESCRIPTION	A 1900 three-story colonial revival guesthouse with original parquet floors, stained-glass, chandeliers, and period antiques.
NO. OF ROOMS	Three rooms with private bathrooms. Try the Antebellum Room.
RATES	Year-round rates are $95-105 for a single or double. There is a two-night minimum stay on weekends and cancellation requires seven days' notice.
CREDIT CARDS	No
BREAKFAST	Continental breakfast is served in the dining room and includes pastries, fruit, cereal, milk, juice, and coffee.
AMENITIES	Advice for personal tours, 2 blocks from the downtown trolley, 8 blocks from the Alamo, half a block from the Riverwalk.
RESTRICTIONS	No smoking. Scratchy is the resident tabby.

LITTLE FLOWER INN

225 Madison Street, San Antonio, TX 78204   *210-354-3116*
Phil & Christine Touw, Innkeepers   *FAX 210-354-3116*
Dutch and German spoken
EMAIL littleflower@satexas.com
WEBSITE members.tripod.com/~little_flower_inn/

LOCATION	In the King William District of San Antonio, close to downtown, 2 blocks from the Riverwalk. From I-10, take the Durango Street exit, travel east (toward downtown) on Durango to South St. Mary's Street, and turn right. Madison is 2 streets down on the right.
OPEN	All year
DESCRIPTION	A 1908 two-story clapboard host home with oversized verandas upstairs and down and decorated with antiques and creature comforts representative of the late 1800s to early 1900s.
NO. OF ROOMS	Two rooms with private bathrooms.
RATES	Year-round rates are $80-95 for a single or double. There is no minimum stay and no cancellation policy.
CREDIT CARDS	No
BREAKFAST	Full breakfast is served in the dining room, garden, or guestrooms and includes coffee, tea, juices, fruit dishes, homemade coffeecake, an entrée such as fancy waffles, decadent French toast, and assorted scrumptious egg dishes. Low-fat breakfasts can be served with advance notice.

AMENITIES	Complimentary afternoon tea by reservation, includes tea, lemonade, finger sandwiches, and sweets; robes, bubble baths, lavish lotions, and fresh flowers in rooms; pool; refrigerator in common area stocked with complimentary juices and soft drinks; TV/VCR and collection of classic movies. Ten percent of room rate is donated to a charitable cause.
RESTRICTIONS	No smoking, no pets, children are welcome. "We love children!" The resident pooches are Annebelle, a 14-year-old dalmatian (the matriarch); Solo, a black Lab mix; Buddy, a yellow Lab mix; and Dempsey, a boxer mix. "Our dogs are our children. Many of our guests come back from touring early just to play ball with the crew! Of course, if you are not a dog person, the pups are kept discreetly away."

LOS ENCINOS TEXAS HILL COUNTRY

24183 Boerne Stage Road, San Antonio, TX 78255   *210-698-1654*

MONARCH HOUSE

128 West Mistletoe, San Antonio, TX 78212   *512-733-3884*
WEBSITE *www.monarchhouse.com*   *800-851-3666*

NOBLE INNS

107 Madison Street, San Antonio TX 78204   *210-225-4045*
Don & Liesl Noble, Innkeepers   *800-221-4045*
Spanish spoken   FAX *210-227-0877*
EMAIL *nobleinns@aol.com*   WEBSITE *www.nobleinns.com*

LOCATION	Downtown, across the street from the Riverwalk.
OPEN	All year
DESCRIPTION	Impeccably restored historic Victorian houses converted to luxury inns, featuring fireplaces, custom bedding, fine period antiques, marble bathrooms, and beautiful gardens; listed on the State Historic Register.
NO. OF ROOMS	Nine rooms with private bathrooms.

RATES	Year-round rates are $115-170 for a single or double and $165-185 for a suite. There is a two-night minimum stay on weekends and cancellation requires 10 days' notice.
CREDIT CARDS	American Express, Discover, MasterCard, Visa
BREAKFAST	Full breakfast is served in the main house. Continental plus is served in the carriage house.
AMENITIES	Private marble baths, some with large Jacuzzi tub; fresh flowers; custom guest robes; fireplaces with antique mantelpiece; pool and heated spa; afternoon refreshments; all rooms have central air conditioning and heating; ceiling fans; turndown service with Godiva chocolates; porch and patios for relaxing; beautiful gardens; classic 1960 Rolls Royce available for transportation.
RESTRICTIONS	No smoking, no pets. Young children are welcome at the carriage house only.
REVIEWED	*America's Favorite Inns, B&B's and Small Hotels; Frommer's San Antonio and Austin*
MEMBER	Professional Association of Innkeepers International, Historic Accommodations of Texas, San Antonio Bed & Breakfast Association
RATED	AAA 3 Diamonds, Mobil 3 Stars

O'CASEY'S BED & BREAKFAST

225 West Craig Place, San Antonio, TX 78212   210-738-1378
John & Linda Fay Casey, Innkeepers   800-738-1378
EMAIL info@ocaseybnb.com   FAX 210-733-9408
WEBSITE www.ocaseybnb.com

LOCATION	Located in the Monte Vista Historic District. From Main Plaza, in the heart of downtown San Antonio, go 1.5 miles north on Main Avenue, then drive one-and-a-half blocks left to the inn.
OPEN	All year
DESCRIPTION	A 1904 two-story Victorian inn with pine floors and cozy, eclectic decor, situated in San Antonio's Monte Vista Historic District.
NO. OF ROOMS	Seven rooms with private bathrooms.
RATES	Year-round rates are $65-105 for a single or double. There is a minimum stay during holiday weekends and cancellation requires seven days' notice.
CREDIT CARDS	American Express, Discover, MasterCard, Visa

BREAKFAST	Full breakfast is served in the dining room and includes cereals, milk, breads, jams, jellies, fruit, juice, coffee, tea, and a hot entrée of the day with a breakfast meat.
AMENITIES	Air-conditioned rooms; off-street parking; facilities for small meetings, receptions, and small garden weddings; handy to downtown attractions.
RESTRICTIONS	No smoking. Connor is the resident golden retriever. Connor stays outside or in the innkeepers' quarters. He is not allowed inside the B&B.
REVIEWED	*Frommer's*
KUDOS/COMMENTS	"A fairly new B&B with lots of charm, charming hosts, the only Irish B&B in town." "Great Irish atmosphere."

THE OGE HOUSE ON THE RIVERWALK

209 Washington Street, San Antonio, TX 78204   210-223-2353
Patrick & Sharrie Magatagan, Resident Owners   800-242-2770
Some Spanish spoken   FAX 210-226-5812
EMAIL *ogeinn@pacbell.com*   WEBSITE *www.ogeinn.com*

LOCATION	Downtown at the corner of Durango and Pancoa Streets.
OPEN	All year
DESCRIPTION	An 1857 three-story Southern antebellum mansion with European and American antiques, located on 1.5 acres on the Riverwalk.
NO. OF ROOMS	Ten rooms with private bathrooms.
RATES	Year-round rates for a single or double are $145, and suites are $175-205. There is a minimum stay on weekends and cancellation requires 14 days' notice.
CREDIT CARDS	American Express, Diners Club, Discover, MasterCard, Visa
BREAKFAST	Full breakfast is served in the dining room and includes gourmet pastries, eggs (some days), cereals, yogurt, seasonal fruit, juices, tea, coffee, Texas biscuits and sausage gravy.
AMENITIES	Scented soaps and bath amenities, fresh fruit bowl and Danish butter cookies in the foyer, decanter of port and chocolates on the mantels.
RESTRICTIONS	No smoking inside, no pets, children over 16 are welcome.
REVIEWED	*Fodor's, America's Wonderful Little Hotels & Inns, Frommer's San Antonio and Austin, Texas Bed & Breakfast*
MEMBER	Independent Innkeepers Association, Texas Hotel & Motel Association, Historic Accommodations of Texas

"Outstanding." "One of the most elegant B&Bs we've ever seen. The Oge House is well-located on the San Antonio Riverwalk and furnished with museum-quality antiques and collectibles." "Elegant European inn; French Victorian decor, on the Riverwalk, beautiful gardens; very good breakfasts." "Lovely antebellum plantation home. Very well done. Owners are very professional and handle everything well."

THE PAINTED LADY

620 Broadway, San Antonio, TX 78215   *830-220-1092*
Cynthia Cesnalis, Resident Owner
WEBSITE www.bestinns.net/usa/tx/paintedlady.html

KUDOS/COMMENTS "Small, romantic hotel. Large, comfortable rooms. Attentive staff and owners."

PANCOAST CARRIAGE HOUSE

102 Turner, San Antonio, TX 78204   *210-225-4045*
WEBSITE www.nobleinns.com

RIVERWALK INN

329 Old Guilbeau Street, San Antonio, TX 78204   *210-212-8300*
Tracy & Jan Hammer, Innkeepers   *800-254-4440*
Spanish   *FAX 210-229-9422*
EMAIL innkeeper@riverwalkinn.com
WEBSITE www.riverwalkinn.com

LOCATION   From the airport, take Highway 281 south to exit 140B
                       (Alamodome-Durango). Go right on Durango and continue
                       through the third traffic light (St. Mary's). Take the first right on
                       Aubrey, which will dead-end at Old Guilbeau Street.

OPEN   All year

DESCRIPTION   The inn comprises five two-story log homes. Originally constructed
                       in Tennessee around 1840, these cabins were relocated and
                       reconstructed along the scenic San Antonio Riverwalk.

NO. OF ROOMS   Eleven rooms with private bathrooms.

RATES	Year-round rates are $110-175 for a single or double. There is a minimum stay on weekends and during holidays and special events. Cancellation requires 10 days' notice with a $15 charge.
CREDIT CARDS	American Express, Discover, MasterCard, Visa
BREAKFAST	Continental plus breakfast is served in the dining room. Evening desserts are also available.
AMENITIES	Gas-burning fireplaces, small refrigerators, coffee-makers, cable TV, voice mail, dual jacks for laptops, porches and balconies with rocking chairs overlooking the Riverwalk.
RESTRICTIONS	No smoking, no children. A gray tiger cat named Annie shares the inn.
REVIEWED	*Frommer's, Fodor's*
MEMBER	San Antonio Bed & Breakfast Association, Professional Association of Innkeepers International
RATED	AAA 3 Diamonds, Mobil 3 Stars
KUDOS/COMMENTS	"Charming real log house on Riverwalk with excellent attention to detail, service and amenities."

THE ROYAL SWAN GUEST HOUSE

236 Madison, San Antonio, TX 78204　　　　　210-223-3776
Curt & Helen Skredergard, Innkeepers　　　　800-368-3073
EMAIL *theswan@onr.com*　　　　　　　　FAX 210-271-0373
WEBSITE *www.royalswan.com*

LOCATION	Located downtown, 1 block from the Riverwalk and the trolley.
OPEN	All year
DESCRIPTION	An 1892 two-story Victorian inn with Victorian decor, original stained-glass windows, and ornate woodwork.
NO. OF ROOMS	Five rooms with private bathrooms. Try the Emerald Room.
RATES	Year-round rates for a single or double are $95-140. There is a minimum stay during holidays and special events, and cancellation requires 10 days' notice.
CREDIT CARDS	Discover, MasterCard, Visa
BREAKFAST	Full breakfast is served family style in the dining room and includes coffee, teas, juice, fresh fruit, an entrée with meat, and a desert pastry.
AMENITIES	Complimentary sodas, snacks in the evening, free trolley passes, flowers, champagne for special occasions, great breakfast conversation.

RESTRICTIONS	No smoking, no pets, children over 12 are welcome.
REVIEWED	*Frommer's, Texas Highways, Southern Living*
MEMBER	Professional Association of Innkeepers International, San Antonio Bed & Breakfast Association, Historic Accommodations of Texas
RATED	AAA 3 Diamonds, ABBA 3 Crowns, Mobil 3 Stars
KUDOS/COMMENTS	"Magnificent common areas."

TARA INN BED & BREAKFAST

307 Beauregard, San Antonio, TX 78204	*210-223-5875*
Douglas & Donna West, Innkeepers	*800-356-1605*
WEBSITE *www.xyber.com/tarainn*	*FAX 210-479-1172*

LOCATION	From I-10 west, take the South Alamo Street exit, take a right, drive to Beauregard, and turn left.
OPEN	All year
DESCRIPTION	A 1905 two-story grand antebellum home with Victorian decor and rooms with decorations inspired by *Gone with the Wind*. A private garden cottage features country Victorian decor.
NO. OF ROOMS	Six rooms with private bathrooms.
RATES	Year-round rates are $79-135 for a double. There is a two-night minimum stay on weekends and cancellation requires seven days' notice.
CREDIT CARDS	American Express, Diners Club, Discover, MasterCard, Visa
BREAKFAST	Full breakfast is served in the dining room and includes fruit, muffins, egg dishes such as quiche or baked French toast, juice, coffee. Early morning continental is served prior to the full breakfast.
AMENITIES	Air conditioning; chocolates; hot tub on back courtyard; fireplaces; grand verandas; sodas, tea, coffee, ice in kitchen; some rooms with feather beds, TV/VCR, clawfoot tubs, Jacuzzi tubs, porches, kitchenettes.
RESTRICTIONS	No smoking, no pets, children over 10 are welcome.
MEMBER	Historic Accommodations of Texas, San Antonio Bed & Breakfast Association, Greater San Antonio Area Hotel & Motel Association

TERRELL CASTLE BED & BREAKFAST

950 East Grayson Street, San Antonio, TX 78208   210-271-9145
800-356-1605
FAX 210-824-8036

THE VICTORIAN LADY INN

421 Howard Street, San Antonio, TX 78212   210-224-2524
Joe & Kate Bowski, Resident Owners   800-879-7116
WEBSITE www.viclady.com   FAX 210-224-5123

LOCATION	Six blocks north of the entrance to the Riverwalk.
OPEN	All year
DESCRIPTION	An 1898 three-story Greek revival home furnished with Victorian antiques and listed on the State Historic Register.
NO. OF ROOMS	Eight rooms with private bathrooms.
RATES	Please inquire about current rates. There is a two-night minimum stay on weekends and holidays, and cancellation requires 14 days' notice.
CREDIT CARDS	American Express, Discover, MasterCard, Visa
BREAKFAST	Full breakfast is served in the dining room and includes a hot entrée, a side dish, homemade muffins and breads, hot and cold cereals, fresh fruit, toast basket, coffee, tea, orange juice, and milk.
AMENITIES	Hot tub, swimming pool, cable TV, telephones, fireplaces, verandas, complimentary beverages, air conditioning, ceiling fans, bicycles, books, small meeting facilities, discount coupons for area attractions.
RESTRICTIONS	No smoking, no pets, children over 12 are welcome.
REVIEWED	The Non-smokers Guide to Bed & Breakfasts
MEMBER	San Antonio Bed & Breakfast Association, Texas Hotel & Motel Association, Historic Accommodations of Texas
RATED	AAA 3 Diamonds

WHIPPOORWILL COTTAGES BED & BREAKFAST

930 East Grayson Street, San Antonio, TX 78208   *210-271-3566*

A YELLOW ROSE

229 Madison, San Antonio, TX 78204   *210-229-9903*
Deb & Kit Walker, Innkeepers   *800-950-9903*
EMAIL *yellowrs@express-news.net*   *FAX 210-229-1691*
WEBSITE *www.bbonline.com/tx/yellowrose/*

LOCATION	From the center of town (Houston and South St. Mary), go south on St. Mary to Madison, turn right, and go to the middle of the second block.
OPEN	All year
DESCRIPTION	An 1865 brick Victorian inn with English period decor, situated in the Historic King William District two blocks from the Riverwalk.
NO. OF ROOMS	Five rooms with private bathrooms. Try the Magnolia Room.
RATES	Year-round rates are $100-165 for a single or double. There is a minimum stay during weekends and holidays, and cancellation requires 14 days' notice.
CREDIT CARDS	American Express, MasterCard, Visa
BREAKFAST	Full breakfast is served in the dining room and includes fresh-ground coffee, tea, juice, fruit, and muffins fresh from the oven, plus an entrée with a meat side.
AMENITIES	All rooms have ceiling fans and central heat and air conditioning; cold drinks in the refrigerator; sherry in a decanter in the parlor; each day begins with the local paper and *The New York Times*; Godiva chocolates on bedside tables.
RESTRICTIONS	No smoking inside, children over 12 are welcome.
MEMBER	Texas Hotel & Motel Association, Professional Association of Innkeepers International, Historic Accommodations of Texas, San Antonio Bed & Breakfast Association
RATED	AAA 3 Diamonds, Mobil 3 Stars
AWARDS	1998, First Place: Xeriscape Contest and Garden Tour, San Antonio Botanical Gardens and Bexar County Master Gardeners
KUDOS/COMMENTS	"Victorian charm in historic district, wonderful host and hostess." "Beautifully decorated Queen Anne with wonderful antiques."

San Augustine

Main Street Bed & Breakfast

409 East Main Street, San Augustine, TX 75972   409-275-5013

The Wade House

202 East Livingston Street, San Augustine, TX 75975   409-275-5489
Julia & Nelsyn Wade, Resident Owners

KUDOS/COMMENTS   "Large, very nice, historical old home."

San Benito

Close to South Padre Island and 20 miles north of Matamoros, Mexico, on Highway 77/83, San Benito features an annual birding festival, and a good zoo and wildlife refuge. Local fiestas include Rio Fest and Charro Days.

Vieh's Bed & Breakfast

Route 4, Box 75A, San Benito, TX 78586   956-425-4651
Charles & Lana Vieh, Innkeepers   FAX 956-425-9223
Spanish spoken
EMAIL clvieh@aol.com
WEBSITE www.vieh.com

LOCATION	Take exit 509 to the south off Highway 77/83. Drive approximately 6 miles to the second blinking light and turn right onto Highway 675. Drive 0.6 mile to the big white mailbox on the right.
OPEN	All year
DESCRIPTION	A 1982 ranch-style host home with western decor and Mexican flavor, located on a 15-acre palm-tree farm with a large lake in the heart of the Rio Grande Valley.
NO. OF ROOMS	Three rooms with private bathrooms and two rooms share one bathroom. Try Hailey's Room.

RATES	Year-round rates for a single or double with a private or shared bathroom are $55-65. There is no minimum stay and cancellation requires 30 days' notice for a full refund.
CREDIT CARDS	No
BREAKFAST	Full hearty breakfast is served in the dining room and includes eggs, bacon, grits, biscuits, gravy, or whatever the guests request. Lunch, dinner, and special meals are available upon request.
AMENITIES	A 10-acre lake with birding trails (104 bird species have been sighted on the property), a large palm tree nursery, ice cream in the evenings, telephone, computer, fax, guided tours of local birding habitat.
RESTRICTIONS	No smoking inside. Four horses, a dog, a burro, and an emu are the resident pets.

SAN MARCOS

About 30 miles south of Austin on I-35, San Marcos is named after the crystalline, spring-fed river that flows past town. Stroll along the lovely river walkway and check out Aquarena Springs, a water-oriented theme park on the headwaters of the San Marcos. In September, stop in for the world's largest CASI-sanctioned chili cook-off.

AQUARENA SPRINGS INN

One Aquarena Springs Drive, San Marcos, TX 78666   512-245-7500

CRYSTAL RIVER INN

326 West Hopkins, San Marcos, TX 78666   512-396-3739
Mike & Cathy Dillon, Resident Owners   888-396-3739
Spanish spoken   FAX 512-353-3248
EMAIL *cri@haysco.net*   WEBSITE *www.crystalriverinn.com*

LOCATION	From I-35, take exit 205 and drive west. The inn is 3 blocks west of the courthouse, on the right.
OPEN	All year
DESCRIPTION	A 1883 two-story Victorian/Georgian with "pure designer" interior, "no heavy hand with antiques."

NO. OF ROOMS	Ten rooms with private bathrooms and two rooms share one bathroom. There is also a two-bedroom corporate apartment for extended stays.
RATES	Year-round rates for a single or a double with a private bathroom are $80-135, a single or a double with a shared bathroom is $80-85, and the apartment rents for $50-75 per day. Midweek rates are lower. There is a minimum stay on weekends and cancellation requires seven days' notice.
CREDIT CARDS	American Express, Diners Club, Discover, MasterCard, Visa
BREAKFAST	Full breakfast is served in the dining room and includes fruit, bread, and a main course such as raspberry French toast, Texas lasagna, or eggs Benedict. Lunch and dinner are served on a catered basis.
AMENITIES	Fresh flowers, fruit in all rooms, brandy and chocolates at bedtime, rose garden, fountains, library, and vintage magazines.
RESTRICTIONS	No smoking, no pets
REVIEWED	*Country Inns* magazine
MEMBER	Historic Accommodations of Texas, Professional Association of Innkeepers International
RATED	Mobil 3 Stars
AWARDS	1998, Texas' Featured Inn, America Online's B&B Guide
KUDOS/COMMENTS	"Fabulous B&B. Hosts do all the right things." "Outstanding."

THE HOMESTEAD BED & BREAKFAST

RR 12 at County Road 316, San Marcos, TX 78676   800-918-8788

TRAILS END BED & BREAKFAST

8909 Ranch Road 12, San Marcos, TX 78666   512-392-0430

SEABROOK

Southeast of Houston on Galveston Bay, Seabrook is less than a dozen miles northeast of LBJ Space Center. Explore the lovely Old Seabrook District and the Armand Bayou Nature Center. Local fetes include the Seabrook Celebration, the Fourth of July fireworks over Clear Lake, and the Christmas Boat Parade.

BEACON HILL GUEST HOUSE BED & BREAKFAST

3705 NASA Road One, Seabrook, TX 77586   281-326-7643
FAX 281-326-2883
WEBSITE *www.texasguides.com/beaconhillguesthouses.html*

THE PELICAN HOUSE BED & BREAKFAST INN

1302 1st Street, Seabrook, TX 77044   281-474-5295
Suzanne Silver, Resident Owner   FAX 713-474-7840
WEBSITE *www.pelicanhouse.com*

LOCATION	From Houston or Galveston, take the Nasa Road 1 exit from I-45 (Gulf Freeway) south. Go east on Nasa Road 1 for 7.8 miles. Cross Highway 146 to 2nd Street and go 4 blocks to Hall Street. Turn left, then take another left onto 1st Street. The B&B is the first house on the right.
OPEN	All year
DESCRIPTION	A 1910 country inn decorated in a whimsical nautical style, located in the old Seabrook art and antique colony.
NO. OF ROOMS	Four rooms with private bathrooms. Suzanne suggests the Pelican Room.
RATES	Year-round rates for a single or double room are $75-85. Cancellation requires three days' notice.
CREDIT CARDS	American Express, Discover, MasterCard, Visa.
BREAKFAST	Full breakfast is served wherever the guests request (dining area, porches, or rooms) and includes an entrée, meat, fresh fruit, and homemade pastry. Specialties are French toast and crepes.
AMENITIES	Wine, tea, or champagne at check-in; water views, bird watching, air conditioning, eight-person hot tub, paddleboat, use of kitchen facilities.

RESTRICTIONS	No smoking inside, no pets, children over 10 are welcome.
REVIEWED	*Texas Highways, Houston Life* magazine, *Bay Runner*
MEMBER	Texas Hotel & Motel Association, Historic Accommodations of Texas

SEADRIFT

North of Corpus Christi, Seadrift is a small community overlooking San Antonio Bay. Pristine Matagorda Island lies just across Espiritu Santo Bay.

HOTEL LAFITTE B&B

302 Bay Avenue, Seadrift, TX 77983　　　　　　　　512-785-2319

LOCATION	Take Highway 185 and go right at Barkett's Restaurant. At the bay front, go left and the inn is 1 block down on the left.
OPEN	All year
DESCRIPTION	A restored 1909 three-story Victorian hotel furnished with antiques and situated on San Antonio Bay.
NO. OF ROOMS	Four rooms with private bathrooms, and six rooms share two-and-a-half bathrooms.
RATES	Please inquire about current rates and cancellation information.
CREDIT CARDS	American Express, MasterCard, Visa
BREAKFAST	Full breakfast is served in the dining room.
AMENITIES	Air conditioning, Jacuzzi.
RESTRICTIONS	No pets, children over 12 are welcome.
REVIEWED	*The Birder's Guide to Bed & Breakfasts, Recommended Country Inns—The Southwest*

SEGUIN

WEINERT HOUSE BED & BREAKFAST

1207 North Austin, Seguin, TX 78155　　　　　　　　830-372-0422
Tom & Lynna Thomas, Resident Owners
WEBSITE *www.texasbedandbreakfast.com/weinerthouse.html*

SHAMROCK

YE OLDE HOME PLACE

311 East 2nd Street, Shamrock, TX 79079   *806-256-2295*

SHERMAN

Just south of Lake Texoma on Highway 75, Sherman is home to 150-year-old Austin College. President Eisenhower's birthplace and historical site is about 10 miles north, in Denison.

HART'S COUNTRY INN

601 North Grand Avenue, Sherman, TX 75090   *903-892-2271*
Rhay & Jim Blevins, Resident Owners

LOCATION   Follow signs to Austin College. The inn is across the street from the college.

OPEN   All year

Hart's Country Inn, Sherman

DESCRIPTION	An 1898 two-story Victorian country inn decorated with Victorian antiques and reproductions. The inn was originally built as Sherman's first hospital.
NO. OF ROOMS	Six rooms with private bathrooms. Try the Bride's Room.
RATES	Year-round rates are $50-60 for a single or double. There is no minimum stay requirement. Ask about a cancellation policy.
CREDIT CARDS	No
BREAKFAST	Full breakfast is served in the dining room and includes ham, bacon, or sausage with eggs, homemade breads, juice, and coffee.
AMENITIES	Air conditioning, heat, ceiling fans, goose-down comforters.
RESTRICTIONS	No smoking, no pets
REVIEWED	*Texas—Off the Beaten Path*
AWARDS	1996, Adaptive Re-Use winner, Sherman Preservation League

SHINER

A regional cotton and cattle trade center for farmers of historically Czech and German heritage, Shiner attracts out-of-towners to its Shiner Brewery, the home of scrumptious Shiner Bock beer. Less heady draws include Kaspar Wire Works and the Gonzales Historic Jail. Shiner is 82 miles east of San Antonio on I-10 and Alternate Highway 90.

THE OLD KASPER HOUSE

219 North Avenue C, Shiner, TX 77984   *512-594-4336*
Mary & Hank Novak, Resident Owners
Czech spoken
WEBSITE www.texaslodging.com/ads/3059.phtml

LOCATION	Two blocks left of Highway 95 in downtown Shiner.
OPEN	All year
DESCRIPTION	A 1905 two-story Victorian inn.
NO. OF ROOMS	Nine rooms with private bathrooms.
RATES	Year-round rates for a single or double are $50-100. There is no minimum stay and cancellation requires 72 hours' notice.
CREDIT CARDS	American Express, Diners Club, Discover, MasterCard, Visa
BREAKFAST	Full breakfast is served in the dining room.

AMENITIES	Air conditioning, cable TV, microwaves and refrigerators in some rooms, deck, one room with a Jacuzzi and fireplace.
RESTRICTIONS	No smoking, no pets, ask about children.
MEMBER	Texas Hotel & Motel Association

SMITHVILLE

Smithville is 43 miles southeast of Austin on Highway 71. Check out the annual Jamboree Festival during the first weekend after Easter. In December, enjoy the nighttime Christmas parade and Festival of Lights.

KATY HOUSE BED & BREAKFAST

201 Romana Street, Smithville, TX 78957
Sallie & Bruce Blalock, Innkeepers
EMAIL thekatyh@onr.com
WEBSITE www.katyhouse.com

512-237-4262
800-843-5289
FAX 512-237-2239

LOCATION	One block west of historic Main Street, on the corner of 2nd and Romana.
OPEN	All year
DESCRIPTION	A 1909 classical revival and Romanesque lodge decorated with railroad memorabilia and American antiques; listed on the State and National Historic Registers. The home is named after the Missouri–Kansas–Texas Railroad (the "Katy").
NO. OF ROOMS	Four rooms with private bathrooms.
RATES	Year-round rates are $56-110 for a single or double. There is no minimum stay and cancellation requires seven days' notice.
CREDIT CARDS	American Express, MasterCard, Visa
BREAKFAST	Full country breakfast is served in the dining room and always includes eggs, meat, homemade breads, jellies, fruit plates, two juices, coffee, and tea. Jalapeno cheese grits, cinnamon rolls, and other specialties are also served. Special dietary needs can be accommodated.
AMENITIES	Large collection of railroad photographs and memorabilia, all rooms have ceiling fans and air conditioning, cable TV/VCR; each bath has a clawfoot tub with overhead shower; two rooms have private balconies with rocking chairs.
RESTRICTIONS	No smoking. Children are welcome in certain rooms. Jake is the resident Welsh corgi.

REVIEWED	*Houston Chronicle, Dallas Morning News, The Texas Monthly: Texas Bed & Breakfast, Bed & Breakfasts and Country Inns*
MEMBER	Professional Association of Innkeepers International, Historic Accommodations of Texas, Texas Hotel & Motel Association

SNYDER

About 75 miles northwest of Abilene on Highway 84, Snyder is in the heart of West Texas cattle country. If it1s wide-open country and long horizons you crave, this is the place for you.

THE BUNKHOUSE BED & BREAKFAST

Highway 380, Snyder, TX 79549   806-237-2700
Mary Ellen Kyle, Innkeeper

LOCATION	On Highway 380 between Jayton and Post.
OPEN	All year
DESCRIPTION	A 1940 redbrick ranch house situated on a working west Texas ranch.
NO. OF ROOMS	Two rooms with a shared bathroom.
RATES	Year-round rates are $50-60 for a single or double. There is no minimum stay. Ask about a cancellation policy.
CREDIT CARDS	No
BREAKFAST	Full breakfast is served in the dining room and includes eggs, meat, biscuits, fruit, and juice. Lunch and dinner are also available.
AMENITIES	Air conditioning, guided hunting tours, tank for fishing, horse boarding.
RESTRICTIONS	None. There are hunting and cattle dogs, cats, horses, and cattle on the property.

WAGON WHEEL RANCH

5996 County Road 2128, Snyder, TX 79549   915-573-2348
WEBSITE www.wagonwheel.com

SPRING

McLachlan Farm B&B

PO Box 538, Spring, TX 77383   *281-350-2400*
Joycelyn Clairmon, Resident Owner
WEBSITE www.macfarm.com

KUDOS/COMMENTS   "Hosts are very friendly. The inn is set off the road and is very quiet." "Comfortable and relaxing."

SWEETWATER

Site of the World's Largest Rattlesnake Roundup in March and the former training ground for WWII women pilots, Sweetwater is 42 miles west of Abilene on I-20.

Mulberry Mansion

1400 Sam Houston Street, Sweetwater, TX 79556   *915-235-3811*
Raymond & Beverly Stone, Resident Owners   *800-235-3811*
EMAIL brstone@swbell.net   *FAX 915-235-4701*
WEBSITE www.texassleepaways.com/mulberrymansion/

LOCATION	Four blocks north of I-20 (exit 244). Sam Houston Street is the first street west of the Holiday Inn off the access road.
OPEN	All year
DESCRIPTION	A 1911 two-story California-style Spanish inn and cottage furnished with elegant French antiques and featuring marble bathtubs. Listed on both the National and State Historic Registers.
NO. OF ROOMS	Eight rooms with private bathrooms. The cottage has two rooms with private bathrooms.
RATES	Year-round rates for a single or double with a private bathroom are $65-225. Senior citizens receive a discount and there are corporate rates. There is no minimum stay and cancellation requires 48 hours' notice.
CREDIT CARDS	American Express, Diners Club, Discover, MasterCard, Visa

BREAKFAST	Full four-course, custom-made breakfast is served at guests' convenience in the dining room or guestrooms and includes quiche, omelets, French toast, biscuits and gravy, eggs, fresh fruit, coffee and tea, juice and strawberry croissants. Lunch, candlelight dinners, and special meals are available in the glass-roofed atrium.
AMENITIES	Complimentary snack trays, bottle of wine, beverages, TV, telephones and stereos in all rooms, fireplace in one suite, handicapped accessible, meeting facilities, air conditioning, robes, bar with large-screen TV, two suites with 90-gallon Roman marble tubs, romantic candlelit dinners available upon request. The cottage has a kitchen and living room.
RESTRICTIONS	None
REVIEWED	*Texas Highways, Southern Living*
MEMBER	Texas Hotel & Motel Association, Historic Hotel Association
RATED	AAA 3 Diamonds
AWARDS	1995, Best Bed & Breakfast in Texas, *San Angelo Standard Times*

TERRELL

About 20 miles east of Dallas on Highway 80, Terrell offers a tour of historical homes, the annual Heritage Jubilee, Tanger Outlet Mall, and beautiful city parks and area lakes.

THE BLUEBONNET INN

310 West College Street, Terrell, TX 75160   972-524-2534
Bryan & Jan Jobe, Resident Owners   888-258-4124
EMAIL *bjobe@flash.net*   FAX 972-524-3017
WEBSITE *www.virtualcities.com/ons/tx/d/txdc702.htm*

LOCATION	Take Highway 80 into Terrell and turn north on Rockwall Avenue. Go 3 blocks to West College Street.
OPEN	All year
DESCRIPTION	An 1880 two-story Victorian inn decorated with eclectic antiques.
NO. OF ROOMS	Four rooms with private bathrooms. Try the Judge's Suite.
RATES	Year-round rates are $75-85 for a single or double and $95-105 for a suite. There is no minimum stay. Ask about a cancellation policy.
CREDIT CARDS	American Express, Discover, MasterCard, Visa

BREAKFAST	Guests can choose between a full gourmet or continental breakfast served in the dining room. Candlelight dinners are also available with 24 hours' notice and an additional charge.
AMENITIES	Service area with fountain sodas, coffees, tea, and snacks; two parlors; sunroom; fireplace.
RESTRICTIONS	No smoking, no pets, children over 12 are welcome.

TEXARKANA

In the far northeast corner of Texas on I-30, Texarkana is split in half, literally, by the state line that separates Texas and Arkansas. Two towns in one, Texarkana, whose motto is "twice as nice," exists in two states and has two mayors, yet only one post office, one court building, and one rail station. President Clinton's birthplace and boyhood home, Hope, is 30 miles across the Arkansas border.

MAIN HOUSE

3419 Main Street, Texarkana, TX 75503   903-793-5027
Zona & Jim Farris, Resident Owners

MANSION ON MAIN BED & BREAKFAST INN

802 Main Street, Texarkana, TX 75501   903-792-1835
Inez & Lee Hayden, Innkeepers   FAX 903-793-0878
Cajun and "Deep South" spoken
EMAIL *mansionbnb@aol.com*
WEBSITE *www.bbonline.com/tx/mansion/*

LOCATION	Exit I-30 at State Line Avenue in Texarkana and head south toward downtown (the boundary between Texas and Arkansas runs down the center of the street). Drive about 1.5 miles. At 8th Street (M. L. King), turn right and go 3 blocks, to the corner of 8th and Main.
OPEN	All year
DESCRIPTION	A restored 1895 two-story neoclassical Victorian inn with Doric columns, documented wallpapers, fine woodwork, and furnished with antiques. When the 1905 World's Fair closed in St. Louis, the 22-foot-tall Doric columns from the Mississippi exhibit were salvaged and used to construct a marvelous veranda on three sides of the mansion. Listed on the State Historic Register.

Mansion on Main Bed & Breakfast Inn, Texarkana

NO. OF ROOMS	Six rooms with private bathrooms. Try the Penthouse Suite.
RATES	Year-round rates are $60-109 for a single or double and $99-109 for a suite. There is no minimum stay and cancellation requires three days' notice.
CREDIT CARDS	American Express, MasterCard, Visa
BREAKFAST	Full "gentleman's breakfast" is served in the dining room and features Creole and Cajun touches. The innkeeper/chef was trained and taught a cooking school in New Orleans. First treat each morning is the rich, aromatic Cajun coffee, brewed for early risers. Breakfast may include blueberry-stuffed French toast with homemade huckleberry topping or genuine maple syrup, orange-pecan French toast, shirred eggs with honey-cured ham, grits and French/Cajun sausage.
AMENITIES	Victorian hats furnished for guests to wear to breakfast, romantic nightgowns and old-time nightshirts, cable TV and telephones in each room with data ports and desks, 24-hour refreshments, fax, veranda, flower gardens, Inez's culinary treats.
RESTRICTIONS	No smoking, no pets
REVIEWED	*Texas Highways, Frommer's*
MEMBER	Arkansas Bed & Breakfast Association, Texas Hotel & Motel Association
RATED	AAA 3 Diamonds, Mobil 2 Stars
KUDOS/COMMENTS	"Very comfortable, nice rooms, great host who makes you feel welcome."

TEXAS CITY

MOORE MANOR

8 9th Avenue North, Texas City, TX 77590   409-945-8042

TRINITY

SANDERSON ESTATE BED & BREAKFAST

Highway 19 North, Trinity, TX 75862   409-594-2007

TROUP

Eighteen miles south of Tyler on Highway 110, Troup is very handy to Lake Tyler and not far from Lakes Palestine and Striker.

THOMAS HOUSE AND ROSE ARBOR B&B

202 Alabama Street, Troup, TX 75789   903-842-2466
Mary Thomas, Resident Owner

LOCATION	Five blocks east of the four-way stop in the center of town.
OPEN	All year
DESCRIPTION	An 1889 farmhouse-style host home, with rocker on the front porch, country English gardens with a gazebo, and a porch and patio in back connected to the yard by a 20-foot bridge.
NO. OF ROOMS	One room with a private bathroom and one room shares a bathroom.
RATES	Year-round rates for a single or double with a private bathroom is $55 and a single or double with a shared bathroom is $50. Weekly rates are available. There is no minimum stay and cancellation requires one week's notice.
CREDIT CARDS	No

BREAKFAST	Full breakfast is served in the dining room, guestrooms, on the deck, or in the gazebo and includes homemade bread, jellies, fresh fruit, orange juice, coffee, country omelet with potatoes and onions or quiche, pancakes with local cured ham or sausage. Special meals are also available upon request.
AMENITIES	Fresh flowers, robes, air conditioning, deck, patios, gardens, gazebos. Hosts will take guests antiquing.
RESTRICTIONS	No smoking, no pets. Children over 12 are welcome. The resident cat is Shera.

TULIA

BILL'S BED & BREAKFAST

113 North Armstrong Avenue, Tulia, TX 79088   806-995-2264

TURKEY

One hundred miles southeast of Amarillo and 100 miles northeast of Lubbock, Turkey is 15 miles from beautiful Caprock Canyons State Park. During the last Saturday in April, check out Bob Wills Day for a little western swing music.

HOTEL TURKEY

3rd and Alexander, Turkey, TX 79261   806-423-1151
Gary L. Johnson, Innkeeper   800-657-7110
EMAIL *suziej@caprock-spur.com*
WEBSITE *www.llano.net/turkey/hotel*

LOCATION	One block north of Main Street, in the center of town.
OPEN	All year
DESCRIPTION	A 1927 two-story west Texas brick hotel with Victorian decor and "full of antiques"; listed on the State and National Historic Registers.
NO. OF ROOMS	Nine rooms with private bathrooms and six rooms share three bathrooms.
RATES	Year-round rates are $69 for a single or double with a private or shared bathroom and $89 for a suite. There is no minimum stay.

CREDIT CARDS	American Express, MasterCard, Visa
BREAKFAST	Full country breakfast is served in the dining room and includes sweet potato pancakes (the hotel's specialty), eggs, sausage, coffee, and juice. Breakfast will vary during extended stays. Special meals for groups of 15 or more are available by reservation.
AMENITIES	Air conditioning; horse boarding; three blocks from hiking, biking, horseback riding; conference/meeting room; occasional live western swing music performed on the patio; one room handicapped accessible; homemade muffins and cookies; magnificent sunsets.
RESTRICTIONS	No smoking, no pets, children over five are welcome.
REVIEWED	*The Official Guide to American Historic Inns, Texas—Off The Beaten Path, The Texas Monthly*

TYLER

A town for rose lovers, Tyler is home to the world's largest municipal rose garden and museum. Celebrate the Rose Festival during the third weekend in October. Tour the beautiful homes and historic mansions constructed during the East Texas oil boom of the 1930s. Other area hot spots are the Goodman and the East Texas Oil Museums, Azalea Trails, Brookshire's World of Wildlife, the East Texas State Fair, Hudnall Planetarium, and the Caldwell Zoo. Tyler is 75 miles west of Dallas, 10 miles south of I-20.

CHARNWOOD HILL

223 East Charnwood Road, Tyler, TX 75701   *903-597-3980*
WEBSITE *www.tyler.com/charnwood*

CHILTON GRAND AND THE IVY COTTAGE

433 South Chilton, Tyler, TX 75702   *903-595-3270*
Jerry & Carole Glazebrook, Innkeepers   *FAX 903-595-3270*

LOCATION	From downtown Tyler, travel 2 blocks south on Broadway to Front Street (Highway 31), then turn right and drive 3 blocks to Chilton. Turn left and drive 1 block.
OPEN	All year

Chilton Grand and the Ivy Cottage, Tyler

DESCRIPTION	A 1910 two-story redbrick Greek revival inn with Corinthian columns, an upstairs balcony, and an interior that features antiques, hardwood floors, and decorative painting. The Ivy Cottage is a separate, 10-room luxurious guesthouse for one or two couples.
NO. OF ROOMS	Four rooms with private bathrooms. Carole recommends the Ivy Cottage guesthouse.
RATES	Year-round rates are $75-150 for a double. There is no minimum stay. Ask about a cancellation policy.
CREDIT CARDS	American Express, MasterCard, Visa
BREAKFAST	Full hearty breakfast is served in the dining room and includes Mennonite Pie with vegetables, cheese, eggs, and meat; plus sweet breakfast breads, strawberry-banana delight or blackberry parfait, juice, coffees, and tea.
AMENITIES	Each room has guest-controlled central heat and air conditioning, feather beds, coffee-makers; two-person indoor Jacuzzi on gazebo, sunroom.
RESTRICTIONS	No smoking, no pets, children over 12 are welcome. The Maine coon cat, Spike, "likes to greet guests, especially ladies, is talkative, and likes to be admired."
REVIEWED	*The Official Guide to American Historic Inns, Texas Bed & Breakfast Cookbook*
MEMBER	East Texas Bed & Breakfast Association

HISTORIC 1859 WOLDERT–SPENCE MANOR

611 West Woldert Street, Tyler, TX 75702   903-533-9057
Richard & Patricia Heaton, Innkeepers   800-965-3378
Spanish spoken   FAX 903-531-0293
EMAIL *woldert-spence@tyler.net*
WEBSITE *www.woldert-spence.com*

LOCATION	Eighty-five miles east of Dallas and 7 miles east of I-20, in Tyler.
OPEN	All year
DESCRIPTION	An 1859 two-story Queen Anne Victorian inn with Victorian decor. Listed on the State Historic Register.
NO. OF ROOMS	Seven rooms with private bathrooms. Try Alma Mary & Robert Spence's Room.
RATES	Ask about current rates. There is no minimum stay and cancellation requires 10 days' notice.
CREDIT CARDS	American Express, Diners Club, Discover, MasterCard, Visa
BREAKFAST	Full all-you-can-eat breakfast is served in the dining room.
AMENITIES	Private off-street parking, several decks and porches, spa in courtyard, gazebo, fish garden, close to downtown Tyler.
RESTRICTIONS	Children over 10 are welcome.
REVIEWED	*Southern Living* magazine
MEMBER	Historic Accommodations of Texas, Tyler Hotel & Motel Association, Texas Hotel & Motel Association, Smith County Historic Society, Heart of Tyler Main Street, Historic Tyler, Inc., Bed & Breakfasts of East Texas
RATED	ABBA 3 Crowns

MARY'S ATTIC BED & BREAKFAST

417 South College Avenue, Tyler, TX 75702   903-592-5181
WEBSITE *www.marysatticbb.com*

Rosevine Inn Bed & Breakfast, Tyler

ROSEVINE INN BED & BREAKFAST

415 South Vine, Tyler, TX 75702
Bert & Rebecca Powell, Innkeepers
EMAIL *rosevine@iamerica.net*

903-592-2221
FAX 903-593-9500
WEBSITE *www.rosevine.com*

LOCATION	From Dallas, take I-20 east, and from Shreveport, take I-20 west. Take the Highway 69 exit and go south to Loop 323. Go right on the Loop to Highway 31 (Front Street), turn left, and go 2 miles on Front Street to Vine Avenue. Turn right, and the B&B is the first house on the right.
OPEN	All year
DESCRIPTION	A 1986 two-story Georgian inn with 1920s and 1930s-era decor including antiques and wallpaper, situated high on a terraced lawn.
NO. OF ROOMS	Six rooms with private bathrooms. Try the suite.

RATES	Year-round rates are $75-150 for a single or double and the suite is $150. There is no minimum stay and cancellation requires five days' notice.
CREDIT CARDS	American Express, Diners Club, Discover, MasterCard, Visa
BREAKFAST	Full breakfast is served in the dining room and includes coffee, tea, orange juice, fresh fruits, homemade muffins, coffeecake, pastries, and egg dishes such as frittatas, herb eggs, and casseroles. Picnic lunches are available upon request.
AMENITIES	Hot tub outdoors, robes, extra towels, fresh flowers in rooms, hot water for tea, game room, courtyard with fountain, fireplace, ceiling fans.
RESTRICTIONS	No smoking, no pets, children over two are welcome. There are four outdoor cats: Boots, Cal, Fluffy, and Mr. Cross.
REVIEWED	*Best Places to Stay in the Southwest, Recommended Country Inns—The Southwest, Texas Bed & Breakfast, The Great Stays of Texas, Bed & Breakfast USA, The Complete Guide to Bed & Breakfasts, Inns & Guesthouses in the United States, Canada & Worldwide*
MEMBER	Professional Association of Innkeepers International, Texas Hotel & Motel Association, Historic & Hospitality Accommodations of Texas
KUDOS/COMMENTS	"A comfortable, clean, attractive place that is made outstanding by very charming and hospitable owners."

SEASONS BED & BREAKFAST INN

313 East Charnwood Street, Tyler, TX 75701   903-533-0803
Jim & Myra Brown   FAX 905-533-8870
EMAIL *theseasons@worldnet.att.net*   WEBSITE *www.theseasonsinn.com*

LOCATION	Ninety miles east of Dallas, south of the downtown square on Highway 69, 0.5 mile from downtown Tyler.
OPEN	All year
DESCRIPTION	A 1910 two-story Greek revival host home with handmade furniture, some antiques, and rooms decorated with seasonal themes. Listed on the National Historic Register.
NO. OF ROOMS	Four rooms with private bathrooms.
RATES	Year-round rates are $85-125 for a single or double and $150 for a suite. For single business travelers, the corporate rate is $70. There is no minimum stay and cancellation requires 10 days' notice.
CREDIT CARDS	American Express, Discover, MasterCard, Visa

Seasons Bed & Breakfast Inn, Tyler

BREAKFAST	Full breakfast is served in the formal dining room.
AMENITIES	Fresh flowers in rooms, water and candy, snack tray on request, picnic baskets in season, brunches or teas for small groups.
RESTRICTIONS	No smoking, no pets, children over 14 are welcome.
REVIEWED	*The Great Stays of Texas, Texas Bed & Breakfast*
MEMBER	Historic Accommodations of Texas, Professional Association of Innkeepers International

UNCERTAIN

One of the most interesting town names in all of Texas, Uncertain is reputed to have gotten its moniker from steamboat skippers who couldn't quite find the right place to land. This nice little place is northeast of Longview, just south of Caddo Lake.

BLUE BAYOU INN ON CADDO LAKE

Uncertain, TX 75661 903-789-3371
Sherry Hanson, Innkeeper
WEBSITE *www.jefferson-texas.com/5-bbic.htm*

CADDO COTTAGE GUEST HOUSE

Mossy Brake Drive, Uncertain, TX 75661   *903-789-3988*
Bubba & Ginger Nixon, Resident Owners   *FAX 903-789-3916*
WEBSITE *www.mistycal.com/caddocottage*

LOCATION	From downtown Uncertain, from the end of Farm Market Road, turn left on Cypress Drive and go 0.75 mile. Turn right at the first corner (Bois d'Arc) and go over the bridge onto Taylor Island. At the stop sign, turn right. The inn is the second drive on the left.
OPEN	All year
DESCRIPTION	A 1981 two-story lakeside cottage with modern traditional interior. The house has an open deck upstairs that overlooks moss-draped cypress trees.
NO. OF ROOMS	Two rooms with private bathrooms.
RATES	Year-round rate is $100 for a double with a $15 charge for each additional person. Children 12 and under are free. There is a two-night minimum stay on weekends.
CREDIT CARDS	No
BREAKFAST	Full breakfast is left in the kitchen.
AMENITIES	Flowers, patio, ceiling fans on upstairs lakeside deck, boathouse, dock, pier, gas grill, bird-watching, fax available.
RESTRICTIONS	No smoking
KUDOS/COMMENTS	"Casual lake house on a beautiful part of Lake Caddo with Spanish moss in the Cypress trees."

CYPRESS MOON COTTAGE

500 Big Oak Road/Private Road 2422, Uncertain, TX 75661 903-679-3154
Lady Margaret & True Redd, Innkeepers

Mossy Brake Lodge

Route 2, Box 63AB, Uncertain, TX 75661   903-789-3440
Norman & Pat Presson, Resident Owners   800-607-6002
EMAIL nipjr@prysm.net
WEBSITE www.jefferson-texas.com/5-mblo.htm

River's Bend Bed & Breakfast

Route 2, Box 91, Uncertain, TX 75661   903-789-3293
Beverly Warren, Innkeeper

Utopia

Northwest of San Antonio, between Lost Maple and Garner State Parks, Utopia is
a lovely small Texas town at the junction of scenic Route 1050 and Route 187. Just
to the southwest, Garner State Park lays claim to the largest live oak in the nation.
Enjoy the Arts and Crafts Fall Fair during the first two Saturdays of November.
Other local and nearby events include the Christmas Tour of Homes, the July
Jubilee in Leakey, and the August Apple Fest in Medina.

Blue Bird Hill Bed & Breakfast

PO Box 697, Utopia, TX 78884   830-966-3525
Lora & Roger Garrison, Innkeepers
Texan spoken

LOCATION	Ten miles west of Utopia on FM 1050 and 5 miles east of Highway 83.
OPEN	All year
DESCRIPTION	A 1973 two-story early Texas ranch house with saltillo tile floors, tin roof, patios, and a deck over the creek. There is also a hideaway cabin on the ranch that has been in the family for 92 years.
NO. OF ROOMS	Three rooms with private bathrooms. Try the Texas Star Suite.
RATES	Year-round rates are $65-75 for a single or double, $85 for a suite, and $95 for the cabin. There is a two-night minimum stay in the suite or cabin, three days during holidays. Cancellation requires seven days' notice.

CREDIT CARDS	No
BREAKFAST	Full breakfast is served in the dining room and is delivered to the cabin and includes juice, casseroles, eggs Benedict, biscuits and gravy, home-baked breads, special hot-cereal mixes, fruit compote, homemade jellies, bread pudding, French roast coffee, tea.
AMENITIES	Robes, garden room in main house with hot tub, fireplace, extensive library, bird-watching, butterfly migrations, hiking, mountain climbing, swimming in the cold spring at the cabin, hot tub under the stars, cool breezes at the cabin, air conditioning at the main house, wine for honeymoons and anniversaries, desserts in evenings, handicapped accessible.
RESTRICTIONS	No smoking inside, no pets, children over seven are welcome at the main house, children of all ages are welcome at the cabin. Digger is the resident dog, Bug is the cat, and there are black Angus cattle on the ranch.
REVIEWED	*Texas Highways, Texas Bed & Breakfast, A Lady's Day Out in the Texas Hill Country*
MEMBER	Bed & Breakfast Texas Style
KUDOS/COMMENTS	"Wonderfully designed; warm and friendly hosts. Excellent conversation." "Variety of accommodations, landscaped grounds. My favorite is the Hideaway Cabin."

THE DAISY INN

HC02, Box 1240, Utopia, TX 78884   830-966-3511
David & Wanetta Hillis, Resident Owners

LOCATION	On the corner of Highways 1050 and 187 in Utopia.
OPEN	All year
DESCRIPTION	A 1906 one-and-a-half-story country home on the Sabinal River.
NO. OF ROOMS	Three rooms share two bathrooms.
RATES	The two-night rate for a couple is $240. There is a two-night minimum and reservations are required.
CREDIT CARDS	No
BREAKFAST	Continental breakfast of coffee and rolls or juice and fruit is provided.
AMENITIES	Central air conditioning, two dozen species of trees on the property, barbecue pits, patio furniture, TV, no telephones.
RESTRICTIONS	No smoking, no pets, no alcohol

GINGERBREAD HAUS

HC02, Box 1240, Utopia, TX 78884   830-966-3511
David & Wanetta Hillis, Innkeepers

OPEN	All year
DESCRIPTION	A restored 1882 gingerbread house decorated with antiques. It is the oldest home in Utopia.
RATES	Year-round rates are $240 for a double for a two-night stay. There is a two-night minimum stay.
CREDIT CARDS	No
BREAKFAST	Continental breakfast of coffee and rolls or juice and fruit is provided.
AMENITIES	Fireplace, air conditioning and heat, barbecue pit.
RESTRICTIONS	No smoking, no pets, no alcohol

RIO FRIO BED & BREAKFAST AND LODGING

Ranch Road 1050, Rio Frio, TX 78879   830-966-2320
LeAnn & Anthony Sharp, Innkeepers
WEBSITE *www.friolodging.com*

LOCATION	On the north side of Ranch Road 1050, 10 miles west of Utopia, 4 miles east of Garner State Park, and 24 miles southwest of Lost Maples State Natural Area.
OPEN	All year
DESCRIPTION	A secluded Spanish-style home, plus a cedar cabin and several vacation homes and cottages; situated in Texas Hill Country on the Frio and Sabinal Rivers.
NO. OF ROOMS	Twenty rooms with private bathrooms.
RATES	Year-round rates are $75-150 for a single or double. There is a two- or three-night minimum stay and cancellation requires seven days' notice.
CREDIT CARDS	No
BREAKFAST	Full breakfast is served in the dining room and includes casseroles, quiche, fruit salads, muffins, juice, teas, coffee, and more.
AMENITIES	Mountain biking and hiking trails, bird-watching, fishing, swimming, scenic drives.
RESTRICTIONS	No smoking, no pets

SETTLER'S CROSSING

HCO2, Box 1240, Utopia, TX 78884   830-966-3511
David & Wanetta Hillis, Innkeepers

LOCATION	Off Highway 187, 1 mile south of Utopia.
OPEN	All year
DESCRIPTION	A restored 1882 ranch-style home decorated with antiques and country furnishings, situated 3 blocks from the Sabinal River on 5 acres.
NO. OF ROOMS	Two rooms share one-and-a-half bathrooms.
RATES	Year-round rate is $100 for a double.
CREDIT CARDS	No
BREAKFAST	Continental breakfast is stocked and includes coffee, rolls, juice, and fruit.
AMENITIES	Air conditioning, lawn furniture, long porch, TV, gas stove, microwave, no telephone.
RESTRICTIONS	No smoking, no pets, no alcohol

UTOPIA ON THE RIVER

PO Box 14, Utopia, TX 78884   830-966-2444
Brian & Karyn Jones, Innkeepers   888-239-0179
EMAIL riverlod@swtexas.net   WEBSITE *riverlodge.com*

LOCATION	Go 2 miles south of Utopia on Highway 187, then turn west onto County Road 360 and drive 0.25 mile.
OPEN	All year
DESCRIPTION	A 1986 two-story German-style Texas lodge built of native limestone and cedar with hardwood floors and country decor.
NO. OF ROOMS	Twelve rooms with private bathrooms.
RATES	Year-round rates for a double are $85 and $15 for each additional person. Children under six are free.
CREDIT CARDS	American Express, Diners Club, Discover, MasterCard, Visa
BREAKFAST	Full country breakfast is served in the dining room and may include eggs, sausage, fried potatoes, fresh fruit, cinnamon French toast, and hot peaches and biscuits (the signature dish).

| AMENITIES | Ten acres on the Sabinal River, pool, Jacuzzi, some rooms with small refrigerators and microwaves, smoker and barbecue pit with picnic tables. |
| RESTRICTIONS | No smoking inside, no pets. Wildlife roams the property. |

THE WEDGWOOD HOUSE

PO Box 547, Utopia, TX 78884

830-966-2325
FAX 830-966-2239

UVALDE

At the junction of Highways 83 and 90, 80 miles west of San Antonio, this west Texas town is about 20 miles south of Garner State Park. Annual fetes include the Cactus Jack Festival and Southwest Badland Festival. Explore Fort Inge, the Garner Museum, the Briscoe Art and Antique Collection, and the Grand Opera House.

CASA DE LEONA BED & BREAKFAST

1149 Pearsall, Uvalde, TX 78802
Ben & Carolyn Durr, Resident Owners
Spanish spoken

830-278-8550

LOCATION	From the intersection of Highways 90 and 83, go south on 83 toward Batesville for 1.5 miles. At Highway 140, go left (east) for 0.9 mile. Casa de Leona is on the right side of the highway.
OPEN	All year
DESCRIPTION	A 1975 Spanish hacienda. Situated on 17 acres, the home faces the river.
NO. OF ROOMS	Four rooms with private bathrooms and two rooms share one bathroom.
RATES	Please inquire about current rates and cancellation information.
CREDIT CARDS	American Express, MasterCard, Visa
BREAKFAST	Continental plus is served in the guestrooms or the dining room.
AMENITIES	Fishing pier, gazebo on the river, fountain and courtyard, meeting room, air conditioning.
RESTRICTIONS	No smoking, no pets

MEMBER	Texas Hotel & Motel Association, Bed & Breakfast of America, Bed & Breakfast U.S. and Canada, Bed & Breakfast International, Bed & Breakfast of Texas
RATED	AAA 3 Diamonds
KUDOS/COMMENTS	"Ben and Carolyn are friendly and helpful. Breakfast is very gourmet."

VAN

GOLDEN POND COUNTRY INN

Highway 110 North, Van, TX 75790 903-963-5128
Charlotte Bicking, Manager 800-687-1580

IVY COVERED COTTAGE

615 East Main Street, Van, TX 75790 903-963-7272

VAN ALSTYNE

THE DURNING HOUSE BED & BREAKFAST

205 West Stephens, Van Alstyne, TX 75495 903-482-5188
Brenda Hix & Sherry Heath, Resident Owners

VANDERPOOL

A ranching community 100 miles northwest of San Antonio on the Sabinal River, Vanderpool is the gateway to the Lost Maples State Natural Area and boasts of being the "Apple Capital of Texas." Vanderpool offers scenic drives, wildflowers, bird-watching, stargazing, and three rivers for swimming and inner-tubing. Nearby Leakey celebrates July Jubilee.

THE LODGES AT LOST MAPLES

RR 337 West, Vanderpool, TX 78885
Fred & Jeralyn Hathorn, Innkeepers
EMAIL lodges@peppersnet.com

830-966-5178
877-216-5627
FAX 830-966-5179

LOCATION	Approximately 90 miles from San Antonio. Take Highway 16 northwest to Medina. From Medina, take Ranch Road 337 west to Highway 187 (Vanderpool). Turn right, drive 1 mile, turn left, and resume driving west on RR 337 toward Leakey. The Lodges are 4 miles from this intersection, on the left.
OPEN	All year
DESCRIPTION	A 1999 masonry guesthouse with a metal roof, decorated with antiques, the artwork of local artisans, and Hill Country rustic elegance.
NO. OF ROOMS	All rooms with private bathrooms.
RATES	Year-round rate is $105. There is a minimum stay during holidays and cancellation requires 14 days' notice.
CREDIT CARDS	No
BREAKFAST	Continental breakfast is delivered to the guestrooms and includes fresh-baked treats such as pumpkin bread, country ham and cheese biscuits, scones, and fresh peach muffins with crumb topping.
AMENITIES	Central air conditioning and heat, TV/VCR, firewood, fireplaces, hammocks, campfire rings, private front porch and rear screened-in sleeping porch, fully equipped kitchens, linens and towels, stargazing, turndown service, coffee pot in lodge, ceiling fans, wildlife viewing. Special occasion cakes (Texas praline ice-box cake, chocolate strawberry shortcake) are available with advance notice. Babysitting, nighttime sky tours guided by a knowledgeable astronomer, hay rides, and grocery shopping services are available for a small fee.
RESTRICTIONS	No smoking, no pets, no fireworks or firearms. Punkin is the resident tabby cat; JoJo and Chico are the horses. There are also plenty of wildlife on the property, such as turkey, whitetail and axis deer, raccoons, jack rabbits, ringtails, armadillos, and over 200 species of birds including such rare species as the Golden-Cheeked Warbler, Green King Fisher, and Black-Capped Vireo.

ORCHARD INN

PO Box 277, Vanderpool, TX 78885   830-966-3591
WEBSITE *www.foxfirecabins.com*

TEXAS STAGECOACH INN

HC02, Box 166, Vanderpool, TX 78885   830-966-6272
Karen & David Camp, Innkeepers   888-965-6272
EMAIL *stageinn@swtexas.net*   FAX 830-966-6273
WEBSITE *bbhost.com/txstagecoachinn*

LOCATION	Located in western Bandera County on Highway 187, halfway between Utopia and Vanderpool. On the west side of the road, 4 miles south of the T intersection of Highways 187 and 337. The inn is 9 miles south of Lost Maples State Natural Area on Highway 187.
OPEN	All year
DESCRIPTION	An 1885 two-story ranch-style inn, remodeled to resemble an early Texas stagecoach inn, decorated with Hill Country elegance, and situated on 3 picturesque acres along the Sabinal River in the Texas Hill Country near Lost Maples State Natural Area.
NO. OF ROOMS	Four rooms with private bathrooms. Try the Cottonwood Canyon Suite.
RATES	Mid-March to mid-August and mid-September through December, rates are $85-95 for a single or double and $95-115 for a suite. The remainder of the year, rates are $75-85 for a single or double and $85-105 for a suite. There is a minimum stay during major holidays and weekends, and cancellation requires 14 days' notice during high season, 7 days during low.
CREDIT CARDS	No
BREAKFAST	Full breakfast is served in the dining room and includes fresh-ground coffee, juice, a cut-fruit plate, a meat platter, breads, muffins, or biscuits; accompanied by house specialties such as breakfast bread pudding or pumpkin pancakes with praline sauce.
AMENITIES	Located in the heart of the pristine Texas Hill Country.
RESTRICTIONS	No smoking, no pets. Ask about children. Abby is the resident schnauzer, Gus is the dachshund, and Maggie is the cat. "The pets are not allowed in guest areas, though many guests ask to meet the rest of the family."

REVIEWED	*The Texas Monthly: Texas Bed & Breakfast; The Great Stays of Texas; Frommer's San Antonio and Austin; Great Destinations: The Texas Hill Country; Recommended Country Inns—The Southwest; America's Wonderful Little Hotels & Inns; Texas Bed & Breakfast Cookbook; Southern Living* magazine; *Texas Highways; Outside* magazine
MEMBER	Professional Association of Innkeepers International, Historic & Hospitality Accommodations of Texas
KUDOS/COMMENTS	"Charming, beautiful rural setting, warm welcome and gourmet breakfast."

VICTORIA

About 100 miles southwest of Houston on Highway 59, Victoria is an old Texas town with a large historic district of carefully preserved homes. Come for ballet, symphony, and theater events and year-round ethnic and specialty festivals and fairs. The Gulf of Mexico is about 30 miles south.

FRIENDLY OAKS BED & BREAKFAST

210 East Juan Linn Street, Victoria, TX 77901   361-575-0000
CeeBee McLeod, Innkeeper
EMAIL *innkprbill@aol.com*
WEBSITE *www.bbhost.com/friendlyoaks*

LOCATION	From the junction of Highways 87, 77, and 59 go south on Main Street for 1 mile. Turn left (east) on East Juan Linn Street and go one-and-a-half blocks. The B&B is on the left at the corner of Juan Linn and William Streets.
OPEN	All year
DESCRIPTION	A 1915 tree-shaded Craftsman host home with eclectic decor. Listed on the National Historic Register.
NO. OF ROOMS	Four rooms with private bathrooms.
RATES	Year-round rates are $55-80 for a single or double. There is no minimum stay and cancellation requires 72 hours' notice.
CREDIT CARDS	American Express, Discover, MasterCard, Visa
BREAKFAST	Full breakfast is served in the dining room or on the patio and includes seasonal fresh fruit, a choice of several entrées including orange or pecan French toast, royal Scottish pancakes, frittata, and assorted muffins and scones, coffee, tea, or juice. Catering is also available.

AMENITIES	Fully air conditioned, fresh flowers in each room, homemade sorbets on arrival, ticket and dinner reservations made on request, guided walking tours of historic district, business center for guests to spread out and work, one room handicapped accessible, TVs in most rooms and lounge, historic tiled fireplace.
RESTRICTIONS	No smoking, no pets, children over 10 are welcome.
MEMBER	Professional Association of Innkeepers International, Gulf Coast Region Bed & Breakfasts

GINGERBREAD COTTAGE BED & BREAKFAST

101 South Depot Street, Victoria, TX 77901   512-788-4570

WACO

About 90 miles south of Dallas on I-35, Waco is home to Baylor University, the Robert and Elizabeth Barrett Browning Library, the Texas Rangers Museum, and the Cameron Park Zoo. The Old Fort Parker State Historic Site is 45 miles east.

BRAZOS HOUSE

1316 Washington Avenue, Waco, TX 76701   254-754-3565

COLCORD HOUSE

2211 Colcord, Waco, TX 76707   254-753-6856
WEBSITE *www.bbchannel.com/*   FAX 254-753-6825

JUDGE BAYLOR HOUSE

908 Speight Avenue, Waco, TX 76706   254-756-0273
Bruce & Dorothy Dyer, Innkeepers   888-522-9567
EMAIL *jbaylor@iamerica.net*   FAX 254-756-0711
WEBSITE *www.judgebaylorhouse.com*

Judge Baylor House, Waco

LOCATION	From I-35 north, take exit 334 B, turn right onto 8th, then left onto Speight Avenue. From I-35 south, take exit 335 A, turn left under the interstate on 5th, stay in the far right lane, turn right onto Sutton, left onto 8th, then right onto Speight Avenue.
OPEN	All year
DESCRIPTION	A 1940 two-story redbrick English country inn with English country decor.
NO. OF ROOMS	Five rooms with private bathrooms. Try the Judge Baylor Suite.
RATES	Year-round rates are $72-90 for a single or double and $89-105 for a suite. There is a minimum stay during football weekends and cancellation requires 48 hours' notice.
CREDIT CARDS	American Express, MasterCard, Visa
BREAKFAST	Full breakfast is served in the dining room and includes juice, yogurt, homemade granola, and a main course such as bacon and eggs, French toast, and pancakes. A special "Weekend with the Brownings" dinner is also available.
AMENITIES	Air conditioning, off-street parking, flower gardens, TV and grand piano in living room.
RESTRICTIONS	No smoking

WARRENTON

WARRENTON INN BED & BREAKFAST

4339 South Highway 237, Warrenton, TX 78961   409-249-3074
Carolyn & Ray Fox, Resident Owners

WAXAHACHIE

Thirty miles south of Dallas on I-35, Waxahachie's name derives from an Indian word meaning "cow or buffalo creek." Today this "Gingerbread City" is known for its abundance of Victorian buildings. Enjoy the Scarborough Faire Renaissance Festival from mid-April to mid-June and the Gingerbread Trail Home Tour during the first weekend in June. The Elvis Celebration rocks Waxahachie's world in August.

THE BONNYNOOK INN

414 West Main, Waxahachie, TX 75165   972-938-7207
Vaughn & Bonnie Franks, Innkeepers   800-486-5936
                                         FAX 972-937-7700

LOCATION	From I-35, take exit 401-B and drive east past the library and art museum on the right. The inn is on the left. If you reach the fire station, you've gone two houses too far.
OPEN	All year
DESCRIPTION	An 1887 two-story Queen Anne Victorian Painted Lady furnished with Victorian antiques: "elegant decor but not frilly; refined, yet comfy."
NO. OF ROOMS	Five rooms with private bathrooms. Try the Sterling Room.
RATES	Year-round rates are $65-115 for a single or double. There is no minimum stay and cancellation requires 24 hours' notice, seven days during special events.
CREDIT CARDS	American Express, Diners Club, Discover, MasterCard, Visa
BREAKFAST	Full breakfast is served in the dining room and includes coffeecake, hot fruit dish, and an entrée, plus juice and coffee. Seven-course dinners for two are available by reservation.

The Bonnynook Inn, Waxahachie

AMENITIES	Whirlpool tub in rooms, king-size beds, fresh flowers, cookies, robes, feather mattresses, candies, candles, coffee nook with refrigerator, hair dryers, assorted bath amenities.
RESTRICTIONS	No smoking. Bean is the resident yellow Lab and Patches is the cat.
REVIEWED	*American Bed & Breakfast Association's Inspected, Rated & Approved Bed & Breakfasts & Country Inns; The Great Stays of Texas: The Official Guide to Texas' Finest B&Bs; Quick Escapes from Dallas/Fort Worth; Recommended Country Inns—The Southwest; America's Wonderful Little Hotel & Inns; The Complete Guide to Bed & Breakfasts, Inns & Guesthouses in the United States, Canada and Worldwide; The Official Guide to American Historic Inns*
MEMBER	Professional Association of Innkeepers International, Texas Hotel & Motel Association
RATED	ABBA 3 Crowns, Mobil 3 Stars

CHASKA HOUSE BED & BREAKFAST

716 West Main Street, Waxahachie, TX 75165   972-937-3390
Louis & Linda Brown, Resident Owners   800-931-3390

KUDOS/COMMENTS   "Beautifully furnished, charming and gracious hosts, exceptional. We highly recommend it."

Harrison Bed & Breakfast

717 West Main Street, Waxahachie, TX 75165   972-938-1922
WEBSITE www.harrisonbb.com

The Rose of Sharon Bed & Breakfast

205 Bryson, Waxahachie, TX 75165   972-938-8833
Sharon Shawn, Resident Owner

Rosemary Mansion on Main Street

903 West Main Street, Waxahachie, TX 75165   972-923-1181
WEBSITE www.texasguides.com/rosemarymansion.html

Weatherford

Weatherford is an old cattle drive town and was portrayed in the book and TV mini-series *Lonesome Dove*. Established in 1856, its courthouse and historic city center date from 1886, and its neighborhoods are graced with over 100 Victorian period homes. Stop by for the Peach Festival in July and take the Christmas tour of homes in December. Weatherford is 35 miles west of Fort Worth on I-20.

Angel's Nest & Breakfast

1105 Palo Pinto Street, Weatherford, TX 76086   817-599-9600
EMAIL angelsnest@airmail.net   800-687-1660
          FAX 817-613-1330

LOCATION	One mile west of the Weatherford Courthouse on Highway 180.
OPEN	All year
DESCRIPTION	An 1896 three-story Queen Anne Victorian inn situated on 3.5 landscaped acres.
NO. OF ROOMS	Ten rooms with private bathrooms.

RATES	Year-round rates for a single or double are $99-175. There is no minimum stay.
CREDIT CARDS	MasterCard, Visa
BREAKFAST	Full country-style breakfast is served on china with 200-year-old sterling silver and crystal. Romantic, private candlelight dinners are also available. Picnic lunches are prepared as well.
AMENITIES	Drinks available at all times; cable TV and telephones in all rooms; antique armoires; monogrammed robes; antique sitting areas; coffee in rooms; private balconies in some rooms; large marble, two-person Jacuzzi tubs; fireplaces; sweetheart packages include rose, champagne, and chocolate-covered strawberries; weddings, receptions, corporate retreats are accommodated; dinners for large groups available.
RESTRICTIONS	No smoking, no pets, children over 12 are welcome.
REVIEWED	*The Complete Guide to Bed & Breakfasts, Inns & Guesthouses in the United States, Canada & Worldwide; Bed & Breakfast Texas Style*

St. Botolph Inn Bed & Breakfast

808 South Lamar Street, Weatherford, TX 76086   817-594-1455
Dan & Shay Buttolph, Resident Owners   800-868-6520
FAX 817-594-1455

LOCATION	From I-20 west, take exit 408 into town. At the fourth stoplight, turn left onto West Russell Street. Go to the second stop sign and turn right on South Lamar. Park in the rear of the house.
OPEN	All year
DESCRIPTION	An 1897 two-story Queen Anne Victorian Painted Lady with a wraparound gingerbread front porch, a two-story tower, Victorian ballroom, Tudor-style wainscoting, and original interior woodwork.
NO. OF ROOMS	Six rooms with private bathrooms. Try the King David Suite.
RATES	Year-round rates for a single or double with a private bathroom are $80-165, $135 for a suite, and $165 for the carriage house. There is no minimum stay and cancellation requires seven days' notice.
CREDIT CARDS	American Express, Discover, MasterCard, Visa
BREAKFAST	Full gourmet breakfast is served either in guestrooms, in the dining room, on the veranda, or poolside. Guests order breakfast from a 12-item menu that includes homemade breads and muffins, special egg dishes, and a house special each morning.

St. Botolph Inn Bed & Breakfast, Weatherford

AMENITIES	Victorian tea served on the veranda, clawfoot tubs or whirlpools, hot tub, cable TV/VCR, turndown service with chocolate, ballroom for wedding parties and conferences, central air and heat, handicapped accessible.
RESTRICTIONS	No smoking inside, no pets, well-behaved children under parental control are welcome. Ahn is the resident Llasa apso.
REVIEWED	*Recommended Country Inns—The Southwest*
KUDOS/COMMENTS	"Lovely home, gracious hosts."

TWO PEARLS BED & BREAKFAST

804 South Alamo Street, Weatherford, TX 76086   *817-596-9316*
Janet Davee & Beth Llewellyn, Innkeepers   *FAX 817-596-9342*
French spoken

LOCATION	Take I-20 west of Fort Worth for 25 miles to the fourth Weatherford exit, at Tin Top Road. Turn right onto South Main Street (Highway 51), drive 1.5 miles to Akard Street, and turn left. Go 2 blocks to South Alamo Street. The house is on the corner.
OPEN	All year
DESCRIPTION	An 1898 two-story, prairie-style Greek revival host home decorated with antiques, reproductions, and original art, situated on a beautifully landscaped terraced acre.
NO. OF ROOMS	Three rooms with private bathrooms and two rooms share one bathroom. Try the Island Cottage.
RATES	Year-round rates are $95-125 for a single or double with a private bathroom, $70-80 for a single or double with a shared bathroom, and $125 for the guesthouse. There is no minimum stay. Ask about a cancellation policy.
CREDIT CARDS	MasterCard, Visa
BREAKFAST	Full breakfast is served in the guestrooms and includes homemade quiche, southwestern soufflé, Texas-shaped waffles, home-baked muffins and pastries, seasonal fruit, juice, and gourmet coffee.
AMENITIES	Large pool with outdoor shower and restroom; robes; beach towels; home-baked cookies; complimentary wine, beer, or soft drinks upon arrival; Jacuzzi tub in cottage; antique clawfoot tubs; library with books and games; custom toiletries; candles and matches.
RESTRICTIONS	No smoking, no pets, and children are welcome when the entire facility is rented by the same party. Louis XIV and Kate the Great are the resident tabbies. The cats are not allowed to roam the guest quarters.

WELLBORN

7F LAND & CATTLE COMPANY LODGE

PO Box 402, Wellborn, TX 77881   *409-690-0073*

WEST

THE ZACHARY DAVIS HOUSE

400 North Roberts Street, West, TX 76691   254-826-3953
Marjorie E. Devlin, Resident Manager

WHITEWRIGHT

HOLIDAY HOUSE

402 East Grand Street, Whitewright, TX 75491   903-364-2592

WICHITA FALLS

Wichita Falls sprang up from virtually nothing during the oil boom of the 1920s. Today it's home to Sheppard Air Force Base. Wichita Falls celebrates many agricultural festivals in spring and the Hotter N' Hell Bicycle ride in summer. Wichita Falls is 137 miles northwest of Dalls on I-44, about a dozen miles south of the Red River and the Oklahoma border.

HARRISON HOUSE BED & BREAKFAST AND WEDDINGS

2014 11th Street, Wichita Falls, TX 76301   940-322-2299
Suzanne Staha, Innkeeper
EMAIL suzanne@hhbb.com
WEBSITE www.hhbb.com

LOCATION	Two miles west of Highway 287 on the corner of 11th Street and Harrison Avenue.
OPEN	All year
DESCRIPTION	A 1919 three-story prairie-style inn home decorated with antiques and specializing in wedding-related events and upscale catering.

NO. OF ROOMS	One room with a private bathroom and four rooms share two bathrooms.
RATES	Year-round rates are $85-150 for a single or double with a private bathroom, $65-75 for a single or double with a shared bathroom, and $150 for a suite. There is no minimum stay and cancellation requires 48 hours' notice.
CREDIT CARDS	American Express, Discover, MasterCard, Visa
BREAKFAST	Full breakfast is served in the dining room and includes homemade muffins or coffeecake, eggs, bacon or sausage, fresh fruit, coffee, and juice. Special meals are available with advance notice.
AMENITIES	Central air conditioning, fresh flowers, robes, soft drinks and bottled water, fresh fruit, balcony with table and chairs, a backyard pond with shaded seating.
RESTRICTIONS	No smoking. Buddy, Bea, and Lucy are the resident outside cats.
RATED	1997, 1998, and 1999, voted Texoma's Best B&B, Historic Renovation—Adaptive Use, published by the local historic commission

WIMBERLEY

An unincorporated village along the Blanco River in beautiful Texas Hill Country, Wimberley celebrates Market Days during the first Saturday of the month from April through December. It is home to the National Wildflower Research Center. Wimberly lies between Austin and San Antonio on Highway 12.

BANDIT'S HIDEAWAY

2324 Flite Acres Road, Wimberley, TX 78676   512-847-9088
                                                    FAX 512-847-2004

BELLA VISTA BED & BREAKFAST

2121 Hilltop, Wimberley, TX 78676   512-847-6425
Max LeBlanc, Innkeeper
WEBSITE *www.texhillcntry.com/bellavista/*

LOCATION	Approximately 2 miles from the town square. Take Valley Drive (County Road 315) off of Rural Route 12 to Blanco and turn right. Cross the low-water bridge, turn right onto Brinkley, and drive to the top of the hill.

OPEN	All year
DESCRIPTION	A 1997 two-story Texas Hill Country host home with traditional decor and some antiques.
NO. OF ROOMS	Two rooms with private bathrooms. Both rooms are poolside.
RATES	Year-round rates are $95-125 for a single or double. There is a two-night minimum stay during weekends and cancellation requires two weeks' notice.
CREDIT CARDS	No
BREAKFAST	Continental breakfast is served in the guestrooms and includes coffee, juice, muffins or sweet rolls, and fruit. Snacks are also available.
AMENITIES	Pool on the hillside overlooking the Wimberley Valley, TV/VCR, microwave, refrigerator, patio, air conditioning, ceiling fans, deer graze outside rooms. Both rooms are poolside.
RESTRICTIONS	No smoking, no pets, no children. Sabina is the resident Maltese. "The sweetest little dog you ever met," says Max.

BLAIR HOUSE

100 Spoke Hill Road, Wimberley, TX 78676   *512-847-1111*
WEBSITE www.blairhouseinn.com   *FAX 512-847-8820*

KUDOS/COMMENTS   "Fabulous! The gracious essence of the Hill Country." "Class act."

COLEMAN CANYON RANCH

Route 3, Box 988, Wimberley, TX 78676   *512-847-2129*
FAX 512-327-0625

COUNTRY INNKEEPERS

105 Scudder Lane, Wimberley, TX 78676   *512-847-1119*
WEBSITE www.texashillco.com

Dancing Water Inn

1405 Mount Sharp Road, Wimberley, TX 78676   512-847-9391
Kimberley & David Bear, Resident Owners

LOCATION	From the center of town, take Highway 12 south for 3.5 miles. Turn left on County Road 182 and follow it for 1.5 miles to County Road 220. Turn right and go 100 yards, to the first driveway on the left.
OPEN	All year
DESCRIPTION	A 1940 one-story Texas native stone inn with folk art and original artwork in the interior.
NO. OF ROOMS	Four rooms with private bathrooms.
RATES	Please inquire about current rates and cancellation information.
CREDIT CARDS	No
BREAKFAST	Continental plus is served in the guestrooms.
AMENITIES	Jacobs Well (a natural spring), fireplaces, hot tub in the meadow, air conditioning, ceiling fans, screened porches, reading library, music collection, swimming, snorkeling, yoga, massage therapy, art gallery.
RESTRICTIONS	Smoking in designated areas only, no pets

Heart House Bed & Breakfast

12711 Ranch Road 12, Wimberley, TX 78676   512-847-1414
WEBSITE www.virtualcities.com/ons/tx/a/txa5601.htm   800-733-7968

Highpoint Manor

900 FM 32 Wimberley, Wimberley, TX 78676   512-847-5225
WEBSITE www.highpointmanor.com

THE HOMESTEAD COTTAGES BED & BREAKFAST

105 Seudder Lane, Wimberley TX 78676
Clark Aylsworth, Innkeeper
EMAIL clarka@homestead-tx.com
WEBSITE www.homestead-tx.com

512-847-8788
800-918-8788
FAX 512-847-1110

LOCATION	From San Marcos, take I-35 to Rural Route 12 west. Turn left onto County Road 316 (half a mile past the Dairy Queen).
OPEN	All year
DESCRIPTION	A collection of 12 cottages, built between 1947 and 1997, with eclectic decor, situated on 7.5 wooded acres along Cypress Creek.
NO. OF ROOMS	Twelve cottages with private bathrooms. Clark recommends the Overlook Cottage.
RATES	Year-round rates are $85-95 for a single or double. There is a two-night minimum stay on weekends, three nights during holidays. Ask about a cancellation policy.
CREDIT CARDS	Discover, MasterCard, Visa
BREAKFAST	Continental plus breakfast is provided in the guestrooms and includes coffee, orange juice, sausage, and muffins. Lunch, dinner, and catered meals are also available.
AMENITIES	Two six-person hot spring spas, air conditioning, fully equipped kitchens, decks, barbecue, fireplaces and firewood, meeting room.
RESTRICTIONS	None. The Siamese cat is Sheba and the Shih Tzu is Phoebe.
MEMBER	Texas Hotel & Motel Association

THE INN ABOVE ONION CREEK

4444 Highway 150 West, Kyle, TX 78640
Janie & John Orr, Resident Owners
Spanish spoken
WEBSITE www.innaboveonioncreek.com

512-268-1617
FAX 512-268-1090

LOCATION	From I-35, take exit 213 to Highway 150 West through Kyle. The inn is located 5.3 miles west of Kyle on Highway 150 West.
OPEN	All year
DESCRIPTION	A country inn, comprising two Texas settler–style buildings, set on 500-acres with panoramic views of Texas Hill Country. The interior decor is both rustic and elegant, with period furnishings and contemporary amenities.

NO. OF ROOMS	Nine rooms with private bathrooms.
RATES	Year-round weekend rates for a single or double are $150-250. Midweek rates are $120-200. A minimum stay is required on weekends and cancellation requires seven days' notice.
CREDIT CARDS	American Express, MasterCard, Visa
BREAKFAST	Full breakfast with a Hill Country/southwestern flair is prepared by the resident chef and is served in the dining room, and includes fresh fruit, homemade granola and breads, yogurt, egg dishes, green-chile strata, bacon, sausage, and potatoes. A three-course dinner is also available and is included in the price of a room.
AMENITIES	All rooms have fireplaces, feather beds, down comforters, entertainment centers concealed in armoires, balconies, and individual climate controls. Four rooms have oversize whirlpool tubs. Library, rocking chairs, trails, facilities and packages for weddings and retreats. One room is handicapped accessible.
RESTRICTIONS	No smoking, no pets, children over 12 are welcome. There are many deer, turkeys, armadillos, hummingbirds, swallows, and butterflies on the property.
MEMBER	Professional Association of Innkeepers International, Texas Hotel & Motel Association
RATED	ABBA 3 Crowns
AWARDS	Inn of the Month, *Country Inns* magazine

LITTLE JUTLAND

Wimberley, TX   800-460-3909

THE LODGE AT CREEKSIDE

310 Mill Race Lane, Wimberley, TX 78676   512-847-8922
Sally, Ashley, & Merry Gibson, Innkeepers   800-267-3925
Spanish spoken   FAX 512-847-9672
EMAIL *lodgeatcreekside@juno.com*
WEBSITE *www.lodgeatcreekside.com*

LOCATION	From I-35 in San Marcos, travel on Ranch Road 12 to Wimberley. Go through the town square, cross Cypress Creek, and take an immediate right onto Mill Race Lane. Travel approximately 0.25 mile on Mill Race—you will see the lodge toward the end of the lane, on the right.

OPEN	All year
DESCRIPTION	Six log-and-stone luxury cabins and two suites, built in 1994, located along the banks of Cypress Creek.
NO. OF ROOMS	Eight rooms with private bathrooms.
RATES	Year-round rates are $95-145 for a single or double. There is a minimum stay on weekends and holidays, and cancellation requires seven days' notice.
CREDIT CARDS	American Express, Discover, MasterCard, Visa
BREAKFAST	Full gourmet breakfast is served in the dining room, guestrooms, or outside and includes fresh-ground coffee, fresh fruit, homemade pastries, and favorites such as grilled French toast stuffed with strawberries and cream cheese. Dinner is also available.
AMENITIES	In-room whirlpool tubs and saunas, cable TV/VCR, phone, refrigerator, coffee-maker, microwave, air conditioning and heat, ceiling fan, robes, flowers, chocolates, hiking, fishing, birding, stargazing.
RESTRICTIONS	No smoking, no pets, children over eight are welcome. Allie is the resident Lab, Duncan is the Russian blue dog, and Tweety is the canary.
MEMBER	Professional Association of Innkeepers International, Texas Hotel & Motel Association

LONESOME DOVE RIVER INN AT CLIFFSIDE

600 River Road, Wimberley, TX 78676   512-847-6466
WEBSITE www.yeeha.net/kim/index.html   800-690-3683

OLD OAKS RANCH BED & BREAKFAST

601 County Road 221, Wimberley, TX 78676   512-847-9374
Susan & Bill Holt, Resident Owners   FAX 512-847-9374
EMAIL holtwcjr@aol.com

LOCATION	Go north on Highway 12 from Wimberley for 5.5 miles. Go right on County Road 221 and drive 0.75 mile. The inn is on the left.
OPEN	All year
DESCRIPTION	Three cottages built of cedar and stone under huge live oaks, with antiques and wood interiors.

NO. OF ROOMS	Three cottages with private bathrooms.
RATES	Year-round rates are $65-100. There is a two-night minimum stay on weekends and holidays.
CREDIT CARDS	Discover, MasterCard, Visa
BREAKFAST	Complimentary breakfast is served at the village café.
AMENITIES	TVs, air conditioning, peace and quiet on 20 acres, large cottage has full kitchen and satellite TV.
RESTRICTIONS	No smoking, no pets, children over 12 are welcome.

ONE HALLMARK PLACE

501 Sandy Point Road, Wimberley, TX 78676   512-847-9666

RANCHO CAMA BED & BREAKFAST

2595 Flite Acres Road, Wimberley, TX 78676   512-847-2596
Nell & Curtis Cadenhead, Innkeepers   800-594-4501
EMAIL ranchocama@aol.com   FAX 512-847-7135
WEBSITE www.come.to/ranchocama

LOCATION	From the town square, take the left fork at the Texaco station onto Hays County 173. Go 0.5 mile to the stop sign, turn left onto FM 3237, drive 0.25 mile, turn right onto Flite Acres Road, and continue for 2.2 miles.
OPEN	All year
DESCRIPTION	A 1975 Texas ranch-style host home and bunkhouse beneath a canopy of live oaks, with a 360-degree view of Texas Hill Country.
NO. OF ROOMS	One room with private bathrooms and two rooms share one bathroom. Try the guesthouse.
RATES	Year-round rates are $85 for a single or double with a private bathroom, $70-90 for a single or double with a shared bathroom, and $85 for the guesthouse. There is a two-night minimum stay. Please ask about a cancellation policy.
CREDIT CARDS	No
BREAKFAST	Full breakfast is served in the guestrooms or poolside on the deck and includes homemade favorites such as German apple pancakes with bacon, sausage log with seasonal fruit, fresh juice, coffee, and tea.

Rancho Cama Bed & Breakfast, Wimberley

AMENITIES	Fresh flowers, hot tub, swings, rockers on porches, air conditioning, ceiling fans, courtesy phones, electric organ, library.
RESTRICTIONS	No smoking, no pets, no children. The resident animals include 30 Nigerian dwarf goats, 50 miniature horses and donkeys, a mule, a dog named Cracker, and three cats. "They are adorable, love our guests (it's mutual), and visit guests on their porches."

RANCHO EL VALLE CHIQUITO

Wimberley, TX   512-847-5388
EMAIL *wimberly@kdi.com*   800-926-5028
WEBSITE *www.texasvacation.com/rancho.htm*

RED CORRAL RANCH

Wimberley, TX   800-926-5028
EMAIL *wimberly@kdi.com*   WEBSITE *www.redcorralranch.com*

SINGING CYPRESS GARDENS

Mill Race Lane, Wimberley, TX 78676
Robert Ireland &
Barbara Ireland-Derr, Resident Owners
EMAIL info@scgardens.com
WEBSITE www.scgardens.com

512-847-9344
FAX 512-847-9666

LOCATION	Within walking distance of the square in Wimberley.
OPEN	All year
DESCRIPTION	A 1981 three-story Tudor-style country inn with Victorian antiques and family heirlooms, on a heavily wooded setting on Cypress Creek with landscaped gardens, private decks, and ponds.
NO. OF ROOMS	Fourteen rooms with private bathrooms.
RATES	Year-round rates are $75-125. There is a two-night minimum on weekends and cancellation requires 72 hours' notice.
CREDIT CARDS	American Express, Discover, MasterCard, Visa
BREAKFAST	Continental breakfast is served. Catered meals are available.
AMENITIES	All units have air conditioning; cable TV; complimentary wine; meeting or banquet facilities; one handicapped accessible unit; a greenhouse with a 45-year-old orchid collection.
RESTRICTIONS	Pets are accepted in two units with a $50 deposit.
MEMBER	Texas Hotel & Motel Association

SOUTHWIND

Route 2, Box 15, Wimberley, TX 78676
Carrie Watson, Resident Owner
WEBSITE www.southwindbedandbreak.com

512-847-5277

WIDE HORIZON

781 Sunset Drive, Wimberley, TX 78676
Sallie Arbogast, Resident Owner

512-847-3782
FAX 512-847-2598

WINNSBORO

THE HUBBELL HOUSE

307 West Elm, Winnsboro, TX 75494   903-342-5629
WEBSITE *www.bluebonnet.net/hubhouse*   800-227-0639

LaVIE EN ROSE

208 West Myrtle, Winnsboro, TX 75494   903-342-9123

OAKLEA MANSION

407 South Main, Winnsboro, TX 75494   903-342-6051
                                                FAX 903-342-5157

THE OLDE VICTORIAN BED & BREAKFAST

504 East Cedar Street, Winnsboro, TX 75494   903-342-3090
WEBSITE *www.oldevictorian.com/*   877-262-3839

WOODVILLE

Between Beaumont and Lufkin on Highway 69, Woodville features the Heritage Village, the Tyler County Fair, and Dogwood and Fall Festivals. It offers easy access to the Alabama-Coushatta Indian Reservation, Big Thicket National Preserve, several lakes, and two state parks.

ANTIQUE ROSE BED & BREAKFAST

612 Nellius Street, Woodville, TX 75979   409-283-8926
Jerry & Denice Morrison, Innkeepers   800-386-8926

LOCATION   At the intersection of Highways 69 and 190, drive 0.2 mile west of
                    the Tyler County Courthouse. Go north on Nellius for 4 blocks.

Antique Rose Bed & Breakfast, Woodville

OPEN	All year
DESCRIPTION	An 1862 two-story southern federal–style plantation home with Victorian decor, four fireplaces, heart-o-pine flooring, cypress siding, three porches, and a gazebo. The B&B is landscaped with a water garden and antique roses.
NO. OF ROOMS	Three rooms with private bathrooms. Denice recommends the Ashley Room.
RATES	Year-round rate is $85. There is no minimum stay.
CREDIT CARDS	No
BREAKFAST	Full breakfast is served in the dining room and includes a variety of juices, fresh fruit bowls, frittatas, quiches, apple French toast, homemade cinnamon rolls, a variety of muffins, and lemon curd coffeecake.
AMENITIES	Air conditioning, ceiling fans, coffee-maker, cast-iron clawfoot tubs, fresh-baked breads, lemonade and other cool drinks on arrival, facilities for weddings and receptions.
RESTRICTIONS	No smoking, no pets, children over 13 are welcome.
REVIEWED	*Specialties of the House, Recommended Country Inns—The Southwest, Country Roads of Texas, Texas Bed & Breakfast*

YOAKUM

OUR GUEST HOUSE BED & BREAKFAST

406 East Hugo, Yoakum, TX 77995　　　　　　　　512-293-3482

INDEX